HOMESCHOOLING
The Early Years

LINDA DOBSON

HOMESCHOOLING
The Early Years

YOUR COMPLETE GUIDE TO
SUCCESSFULLY HOMESCHOOLING
THE 3- TO 8-YEAR-OLD CHILD

 THREE RIVERS PRESS • NEW YORK

Published by Three Rivers Press, New York, New York.
Member of the Crown Publishing Group, a division of Random House, Inc.
www.crownpublishing.com

THREE RIVERS PRESS and the Tugboat design are registered trademarks of Random House, Inc.

Originally published by Prima Publishing, Roseville, California, in 1999.

Front cover photos © EyeWire (photos on left) and © Vcg/FPG International (far right photo).

Printed in the United States of America

Library of Congress Cataloging-in-Publication Data

Dobson, Linda.
   Homeschooling: the early years : your complete guide to successfully homeschooling the 3- to 8-year-old child / Linda Dobson.
       p.   cm.
   Includes bibliographical references and index.
   1. Home schooling Handbooks, manuals, etc. 2. Early childhood education Handbooks, manuals, etc. I. Title.
LC40.D65 1999
371.04'2—dc21   99-32262
                                                                                                          CIP

ISBN 0-7615-2028-7

10 9 8 7 6

First Edition

To all *Early Years* contributors

· · ·

*This one's for you—
and the children who are
helping you get so smart*

CONTENTS

Acknowledgments • ix

Introduction: The Homeschool Learning Journey • xi

PART ONE Preparing for Your Family's Learning Journey • 1

1. The Homeschool Learning Journey and Today's Family • 2

2. Ready for Success: Learning Assets of the Early Years Child • 20

3. The Joy of Learning with the Early Years Child • 38

4. Getting *You* Ready for Homeschooling • 64

PART TWO A World of Curriculum Choice Instills A Lifelong Love of Learning • 89

5. Learning to Read, Reading to Learn • 90

6. Writing: Dear Grandma • 116

7. Arithmetic: 12 Cookies ÷ 3 Siblings = 4 Cookies for Me! • 136

8. Beyond the 3 R's: Covering the Rest • 160

9. Tailoring Homeschooling to Your Family's Unique Needs • 184

PART THREE Keeping the Learning Journey Fun and Successful · 205

10. Resources for Your Learning Journey · 206

11. The Learning Journey Merges onto the Information Superhighway · 224

12. Homeschoolers' Top Three Destinations · 244

13. Accommodating Younger Learners · 264

14. Keeping House (and Sanity!) As You Homeschool · 278

15. Part-Time Homeschooling: Complementing Private and Public Schooling · 294

16. Enjoying the Road Less Traveled · 308

Index · 323

ACKNOWLEDGMENTS

$\mathcal{M}$ANY THANKS to everyone at Prima Publishing for again providing me an opportunity to encourage new families to consider a rewarding homeschooling lifestyle. Ben, thanks for your vision.

A huge hug and loving thanks to my son, Adam, who has matured by recognizing Mom's limitations while on a writing deadline. Thank you for expanding your culinary horizons and once more rising to the occasion.

A similar hug is reserved for this book's contributors, scores of homeschooling moms and a dad, who despite busy schedules and the care, feeding, and learning with early years children, chose to steal the time necessary—oftentimes in the wee hours of the morning—to complete a time-consuming questionnaire. The depth of sharing was heartwarming, and it is presented as a helping hand to the hundreds of parents of early years children considering homeschooling each day. I am honored to have been trusted to present their accumulated wisdom.

Several respondents shared their experiences in spite of incredible personal challenges. Special thanks to the courageous mom who had just been told, the week before Christmas, she has cancer; to the mom whose father passed away as she received the questionnaire; to the mom who had just given birth to yet another little homeschooler only three weeks earlier; and to the brave mom who provided *additional* information, even though suffering chronic hand pain that frequently disables her from typing. My thoughts and best wishes for healing are still with you all.

INTRODUCTION: THE HOMESCHOOL LEARNING JOURNEY

CROSSING THE THRESHOLD of the twenty-first century, family freedom in education is capturing imaginations by the hundreds of thousands. It's called homeschooling, and it has been around long enough—and is growing fast enough—to stir up society's notions about the way we go about educating our children, indeed, about the very nature of learning itself.

Imagine for a moment that your family starts off every morning with that Friday afternoon feeling of freedom. Imagine that instead of being an act dictated by a schedule imposed on your family by others, learning now weaves smoothly from one day to the next, seamlessly joining the rhythm of family life. Liberated from its bonds to schooling—and guided by those who love the participants—imagine learning becoming an extended excursion into a great wide world of knowledge with stops at points of interest along the way.

This is a journey. . . .

And this book reveals to you all the adventure and rewards available when your family embarks on its own homeschool learning journey with an early years child.

You'll discover how to bypass the "middle man" of schooling, an increasingly obsolete notion in this Age of Information, and jump straight into your own extended excursion in education. You'll discover it's not as daunting or difficult a task as you've been led to believe. In fact, this journey is *best* accomplished from the comfort, warmth, and security of home, guided by your child's first and most important teacher—you.

WHO WILL GUIDE YOU?

AH, BUT YOU are fortunate to begin your journey now. Hundreds of thousands of parents have initiated journeys before you. They cheerfully report their findings when asked—so I asked!

Eighty-three hearty souls completed part or all of a formidable, four-part questionnaire. You'll soon learn more about homeschooling as these travelers share details of personal journeys with children aged three to eight and reveal their findings to you. All information sharing and gathering was accomplished via e-mail in response to a notice in the American Homeschool Association online newsletter. Recipients are a fascinating mix of travelers who own or have access to a computer and use it to receive up-to-date information about homeschooling nationally on a regular basis.

These folks hail from across the United States—from California to Maine (and from England, Canada, and New Zealand, too); families include from one to fourteen children; some travelers started homeschooling just this year, while others continue journeys that began more than a decade ago. They all call it homeschooling, but just wait until you read how differently they go about their excursions.

At the same time, they hold something very important in common. Each family exercises homeschooling's inherent freedom to create a journey that is not just different, but best for the unique needs of its children. After all, how exciting is a journey to a place you don't really want to go?

HOMESCHOOLING SUCCESS

HOMESCHOOLING IS NOT just an exciting idea of freedom in education, it's a successful one, too. In 1995 the Riverside Publishing Company released the Iowa Basic Achievement Test scores of 16,000 home-educated students. This is one of several standardized tests commonly administered in schools. Children taught at home averaged in the 77th percentile, 27 percent above what the testing company deems average ability.

University of Florida College of Education doctoral student Larry Shyers used the Piers-Harris Self Concept Scale and compared scores of traditionally schooled children and those who learn at home. In this test, the homeschoolers again came out on top. It's not much, but research like this may come in handy someday when discussing your journey with the in-laws.

While good test scores, both academic and social, provide important indications of homeschooling's success, they are only a small part of a bigger picture. More abundant and meaningful is the empirical evidence you can only get from those experiencing homeschooling. It's from these sources you'll find that a homeschool learning journey doesn't just involve your child's head. While they may have initially turned to homeschooling for its superior academic results, these travelers have unearthed a treasure far greater than they imagined—the equally positive effects the homeschool learning journey has on a child's heart as well.

> Imagine for a moment that your family starts off each and every morning with that Friday afternoon feeling of freedom.

Once you start learning where you live—and living where you learn—the artificial lines between the two grow less defined and, for the very fortunate, fade away. When living and learning blend, both are transformed, and the whole becomes greater than the sum of its parts. This living/learning blend can never occur in an institution. It's available only from home, the most love-filled environment accessible to any of us. Living and learning together, homeschooling families nurture the whole child, head and heart, in a comfortable, warm, and secure setting.

WHAT'S INSIDE?

OK, YOU'RE INTRIGUED, but where do you begin?

Each family exercises homeschooling's inherent freedom to create a journey that is not just different, but best for the unique needs of its own children. After all, how exciting is a journey to a place you don't really want to go?

Part One helps prepare you for your family's learning journey, beginning with the amazing homeschool continuum. The continuum is a unique tool to first help you to understand the endless variety of options available to your family through homeschooling. You'll move on to discover how many learning assets your child possesses, then to the joy of learning with the early years child who is more than ready for the journey. By the time you review your beginner's checklist in the chapter devoted to your preparation, you'll be ready, too.

Part Two exhibits the many options available in a world of curriculum. We'll visit reading, writing, math, then all the other subjects rolled into one (and discover why they are!). Our travelers share kid-tested, mother-approved approaches to the 3 R's, and these chapters are chockfull of indispensable money and time saving tips, as well.

In case you're thinking that only "ideal" families (whatever they are!) homeschool, here you'll find how families overcome personal and family challenges and shatter this misconception by tailoring homeschooling to fit their unique situations.

With Part Three you'll hit the road running, discovering how homeschoolers keep the learning journey fun and successful. First, you'll look around your home with the eye of a learning traveler, see how many learning resources you already have on hand, and learn about others that seasoned travelers recommend. There's even an "emergency starter kit" for those situations when homeschooling can't wait and you want to start *today!*

Next, let the learning journey carry you onto the Information Superhighway. Homeschoolers are putting today's technology and online resources to work. Good old television and videotape round out the ranks of homeschoolers' technology resources as we move on to homeschoolers' top three destinations: your community, libraries, and support groups.

You'll see you can journey to the far ends of the earth—or into your own backyard—and find lessons waiting for you. The great wide world around you is yours to visit, enjoy, and learn from . . . use as much or as little as suits your needs and pocketbook.

If you're the parent of a three- to eight-year-old child, you may also have a baby, toddler, or preschooler at home as well. These little travelers haven't been forgotten; homeschooling accommodates them, too. You'll not only learn inclusion and diversion tactics, you'll see how the smallest travelers may ultimately be the luckiest as parents observe the effects of birth order in a homeschooling household.

No matter the ages of our children, we all have an important and ongoing task in common—keeping house. How do homeschoolers do it? Are the children helping? Homeschoolers with both neat and not-so-neat houses share their thoughts on this—and on making time for themselves and their spouses.

Next, if you like what you've read about homeschooling but feel you can't turn it into a full-time journey, there's always homeschooling as a complement to traditional schooling. That's a wonderful quality of homeschooling; it can bend into a million different shapes to fit your lifestyle, and even if pursuing it only part time, you can use any of the same ideas and resources as those who do it full time. (But be forewarned: everybody in this book who used homeschooling as a supplement enjoyed the excursion so much they started full time!)

The last chapter contains what just may be the most important information of all—how to enjoy this road less traveled once you're on it. Even the most perfectly designed trip sometimes doesn't proceed according to plan, but homeschoolers have learned to look at challenges as learning experiences. They've also learned as much if not more than their children about life

> Those days of learning at home with children aged three to eight were laced with high energy and innocent wonder.

> Once you start learning where you live—and living where you learn—the artificial lines between the two grow less defined and, for the very fortunate, fade away.

and learning, and offer these lessons as parting gifts while they wish your family bon voyage.

You'll find Simple Starting Points and Resources listings for most chapters. Simple Starting Points contain practical suggestions for implementing the ideas you've read about, and the Resources help you keep on learning. Both sections provide quick and easy access for repeated referral. They're useful for parents of all three- to eight-year-olds, homeschooling or not, as all children will blossom through attention in the comfortable, warm, and secure environment of home.

A FINAL NOTE

I now have two homeschooled children out in the world and a "baby" eagerly anticipating receipt of his driver's license in just a few months. Reading the stories generously shared by homeschoolers with early years children opened a floodgate of memories. Those days of learning at home with children aged three to eight were laced with high energy and innocent wonder. Long walks picking blueberries, spending the entire Wednesday before preparing our Thanksgiving feast, bundling up and driving down to the potato fields late at night for the best view of an eclipse; life's simple pleasures I feel blessed to have shared with three of the most wonderful people in the world.

I know the memories I'll cherish for the rest of my life wouldn't exist if not for homeschooling. "Two roads diverged in a wood, and I—I took the one less traveled by," wrote Robert Frost, "And that has made all the difference."

May *your* journey make all the difference, too.

Part One

PREPARING FOR YOUR FAMILY'S LEARNING JOURNEY

THE HOMESCHOOL LEARNING JOURNEY AND TODAY'S FAMILY

In This Chapter

✦ Where are they going?

✦ The amazing homeschool continuum

✦ It doesn't matter where you begin, just begin!

✦ Simple starting points

✦ Resources

*J*Homeschooling. The word conjures up many different images in the minds of those who contemplate it.

Some see siblings gathered around the kitchen table as their mother reviews a list of vocabulary words prior to a test. Others envision the families they bump into at the grocery store, the nature center, or the skating rink during the day. Still others recall the teen down the street, an autodidact, accepting responsibility for his own education and tasting what the world has to offer. A growing number think of the family participating in the new charter school or alternative education program offering homeschoolers a variety of classes and a loaded computer for home use.

All these images are correct. Homeschooling is all of the above.

Homeschooling has permeated mainstream consciousness as an acceptable educational alternative. However, there's a lingering misconception that it's a *new* educational approach, a product of the last two decades, when more and more parents grew uneasy, for myriad reasons, with the idea of sending their children to public school. If you place tax-supported public schools on the timeline of humanity's learning history, though, the idea of public schools emerges as the recent educational idea, an experiment begun a mere 150 years ago.

Homeschooling is not new. It *is,* however, enjoying a remarkable renaissance, embraced by families in numbers unthinkable just twenty-five years ago. But it was about twenty-five years ago when Dr. Raymond Moore, former U.S. Department of Education programs officer, with his wife Dorothy, began sharing their research revealing the negative effects of too-early schooling with those who would listen, eventually including readers of *Reader's Digest.*

> Homeschooling has permeated mainstream consciousness as an acceptable educational alternative.

The year 1977 saw the creation of *Growing Without Schooling (GWS)* magazine, the result of former schoolteacher John Holt's belief that, despite his and others' best efforts at reform, the problems of the modern school system were a part of the system itself. *GWS* became a forum for the exchange of ideas, information and support, and soon many who thought they were alone in their desire to homeschool felt connected across the miles.

In the 1980s many private religious schools lost their tax-exempt status. This helped bolster homeschooling numbers as a large number of Christian-schoolers turned to homeschooling rather than put their children in public schools. Supported by already well-established networks, this segment of the homeschooling population bloomed.

More information-packed magazines, like the internationally distributed *Home Education Magazine* (1985), followed. Support groups sprang up in big cities and rural towns. Individual families engaged in legal battles. Homeschoolers in many states pitched in untold volunteer hours to create state organizations that helped knock down remaining legal barriers, resulting in the legalization of teaching your own children in all fifty states, which we enjoy today. In 1990, *Good Housekeeping* published my article titled "Why I Teach My Children at Home," one of the early instances of mainstream media interest, which grew into an October 1998 *Newsweek* cover story.

Figuring out how many families are actually homeschooling today remains an interesting but inaccurate guessing game. Current estimates range between a conservative 1 million and a recently heard 3 million. The true number probably lies somewhere within this range. More revealing and more important than anybody's guess at the actual number is the observable growth of support groups across the nation, and the ever-swelling variety of families turning to homeschooling.

> Homeschoolers in many states pitched in untold volunteer hours to create state organizations that helped knock down remaining legal barriers, resulting in the legalization of teaching your own children in all fifty states, which we enjoy today.

WHERE ARE THEY GOING?

THAT DEPENDS ON whom you ask. At the most basic level, homeschooling is the act of your family's taking full responsibility for the education of your own children. Acceptance of this responsibility lets your family step off the public school learning path, which in turn frees you from the accoutrements the public school learning path includes.

Some of these accoutrements are obvious: one-size-fits-all curriculum, mandatory programs having less to do with academics and much more to do with attitude adjustment, high student-to-teacher ratio, and negative peer influence and pressure.

Some accoutrements are less obvious: a time schedule ill-suited to your family's needs or your child's inner-sleep timetable, diseases easily spread through a classroom, high costs of the latest fashion trends, and lack of time for exposure to normal socialization available in the larger community.

Once off the public school learning path, your family creates its own educational path, going wherever you want to go. Admittedly, this thought can be overwhelming. The public school learning path is clear and well worn with use. Your family has yet to determine its direction or mark out the route you intend to travel. A homeschool learning journey looms over the horizon as a never-before-attempted experiment with unknown results.

Yes, each individual family's journey *is* an experiment, but it's one quickly modified if you see it becoming too easy or too hard, or if it just plain isn't working.

Just as no two families furnish homes in the same way or eat the same dinner at the same time or adopt the same pets, so no two homeschooling families head to the same learning place in the same way. If two families next door to each other purchase the same curriculum and use it with children of the same age, they'll still experience homeschooling differently.

HOW WE DID IT

You could call our approach pretty loose, but my son likes a little structure at times; "getting him started" is usually what I call it. I don't instruct but I provide materials, take him to the library several times a week, read to him a lot, and provide opportunities for him to be with others who share his interests.

—KARLA

One family starts at 8 A.M. right after breakfast, the other at 9:30 after a leisurely breakfast and household chores. One family does science experiments in the kitchen, the other joins with fellow homeschoolers at the home of a support group member. One family ends the day by going to the playground, the other by volunteering at the Humane Society. One family sticks to the curriculum provider's timetable, the other follows along for three months then tosses the whole thing in the trash.

The very nature of the freedom inherent in accepting educational responsibility through homeschooling creates an infinite variety of ways your family may go about its learning day. Indeed, the act can be so fluid as to dramatically change direction within the same household from one day—or one hour—to the next. It can be so fluid as to transcend a mere means of acquiring an education and lead your family straight to a satisfying new lifestyle.

Homeschoolers blaze unexplored trails every day. That's why they're going different places depending on whom you ask. You'll soon see that while this can make it challenging to find a place to start your journey, complete responsibility's freedom is a strong asset.

THE AMAZING HOMESCHOOL CONTINUUM

THE QUESTIONNAIRE respondents thought about eight homeschooling variables (See the Introduction for more information about the questionnaire.):

+ Motivation
+ Financial expenditures
+ Approach
+ Assessment
+ Use of technology
+ Physical space in home

✦ Parental involvement

✦ Outside assistance

Respondents imagined each variable as a long line, with the left side as structured and the right side as unstructured. Then they divided their lines by marks 1 to 100, #1 being the far left of the line and #100 being the point most to the right.

They first indicated, by numbers, where they are on the homeschool continuum with regard to each variable today. They next tackled the list remembering where they were on the continuum when they started homeschooling. Voilà, a unique way to show how different families, all sharing the umbrella term *homeschooler,* put homeschooling's freedom to work.

Meet the Respondents

Sixty-five homeschooling moms and one homeschooling dad provided us with information about the eight variables. We received one response each from England, Canada, and New Zealand, and the remainder from twenty-eight families in the United States. The residency of two respondents is unknown.

Respondents measured the length of time they've been homeschooling in two ways, a common phenomenon among homeschoolers. Some start with the date their child would have been required to attend school or with the date the child left a different educational method. Others say that homeschooling begins when a child is born and consider they started homeschooling then. The length of time homeschooling is included as the respondents self-described it:

One Year	11	Nine Years	3
Two Years	9	Ten Years	4
Three Years	8	Twelve Years	3
Four Years	4	Thirteen Years	3
Five Years	8	Fourteen Years	1
Six Years	3	Nineteen Years	1
Seven Years	5	Unknown	1
Eight Years	2		

How many children do the respondents have?

One Child	6	Five Children	3
Two Children	30	Six Children	4
Three Children	15	Nine Children	1
Four Children	6	Unknown	1

Finally, the ages of the travelers' children:

All children under eight years old	34
Some children under eight years old and some over eight years old	26
All children over eight years old	5
Unknown	1

Six respondents (9 percent) felt they hadn't moved at all on the continuum. Five have homeschooled less than three years; one for six years. The vast majority (60, or 91 percent) not only recognized they moved along the continuum, but most often said they changed tactics in all eight variables.

Motivation

0   100

Public school problems   *Principle*

No Answer—one

What motivates these families toward a homeschool learning journey?

Thirty-four parents (just over 50 percent) say their original motivation hasn't changed, and almost half of them began at 100 points, indicating a very strong philosophical, religious or political matter of principle set them on the path.

As they continued to homeschool, twenty-eight travelers (42 percent) slid closer to motivation by principle, and four (6 percent) said they moved closer to motivation by public school problems.

For all variables, we'll consider a change of 30 points or more in either direction "significant change." This was the case in motivation for twelve families (18 percent) homeschooling for anywhere from one to ten years—ten toward reasons of principle, two toward reasons of public school problems.

Financial Expenditures

0   100

Spend over $1,500 per year   *Spend nothing*

No Answer—two

When it comes to spending money on homeschooling, travelers were almost evenly split among three basic possibilities; twenty-four (36 percent) haven't changed the amount they spend since they started, twenty (30 percent) spend more, and twenty-one (32 percent) spend less.

Thirteen (19 percent) parents changed spending significantly, almost evenly split between those now spending more and those now spending less. All but one of these thirteen have homeschooled for five years or more, and most are now homeschooling middle school– and high school–aged children and/or four or more children.

Ten began homeschooling with very little money. One remained at the 99-point level, but the others have increased spending, with just two of those reporting significant increases.

Two families set off on the homeschooling journey spending nearly $1,500. One still spends the same amount four years later, and the other moved to the 30-point level during the first year of homeschooling.

Four respondents currently spending very little money have moved significantly in this direction since they began homeschooling five or more years ago.

Approach

0   100

Structured   *Unstructured*

No Answer—none

A different story emerged as respondents revealed changes in their homeschooling approach when they considered how structured or unstructured it is. Of all the topics addressed, approach saw the greatest overall continuum movement, and the greatest movement to the right, or toward less structure.

Sixteen (24 percent) haven't changed their approach since they started homeschooling, including four who started at the highest unstructured point. Eleven (17 percent) moved toward more structure, thirty-nine (59 percent) toward less structure.

Ten families (15 percent) began at the unstructured extreme and nine (14 percent) at the structured extreme, "extreme" being a convenient term for numbers 1–10 and 90–100. Seven of the nine starting at the structured extreme were among twenty-seven (41 percent) who experienced significant change toward unstructured. Five families (8 percent) moved significantly toward more structure.

Assessment

0	100
Regular testing	*Don't worry about it*

No Answer—one

Homeschoolers' assessment of their family's learning journey, measured by the amount of testing they administer, saw the third-greatest amount of change toward the right in twenty-nine (44 percent) of respondents' homes. Twenty of these twenty-nine moved significantly toward less testing.

Nine (14 percent) other families moved left, six of them significantly toward regular testing. Twenty-seven (41 percent) remain where they started.

Seventeen (26 percent) homeschoolers started at the nontesting extreme and all but one remain there. Nine families (14 percent) started at the regular testing extreme. One remains there while seven reported significant change toward less testing.

Technology Used

0	100

None   *We do all our learning on the computer*

No Answer—two

Computers are getting a workout in homeschoolers' homes. The topic of technology saw the second-greatest movement toward the right with thirty-five (53 percent) heading toward greater computer use, fifteen of these increasing use significantly. Eight families (12 percent) use computers less now than when they started.

Twenty-one respondents report their computer use remains at starting levels. Within this group, two families remain at 0–1, nine families at 20–49, and ten families at 50 and above.

There were sixteen (24 percent) families at the "no use" extreme when they began homeschooling. Seven (11 percent) increased their use significantly while four (6 percent) remain with low use.

Overall, fifteen (23 percent) increased use significantly and five (8 percent) decreased use significantly.

HOW WE DID IT

I have always known that I would homeschool. I discovered this concept after I graduated from high school and was fascinated. I guess that's because I figured I should have been homeschooled.

So I read all that I could find on the subject, which though it wasn't very much, it was definitely enough to convince me of its worth. When I married my husband I told him I was going to homeschool our children, so if he disagreed now was the time to speak up! I have always had his full support.

—PAULINE

Physical Space

0   100

Schoolroom in home   *No special accommodations at all*

No Answer—none

From a schoolroom in the home to nothing (well, all right, you're allowed a few bookshelves!) as physical accommodations for homeschooling, thirty-one (47 percent) respondents use the same physical setup they started with.

Twenty-one (32 percent) moved away from a schoolroom in the home, thirteen of them significantly. We find fourteen (21 percent) moved toward more accommodations in their physical space, eight of these significantly.

It's on the topic of physical space we find the highest number of homeschoolers, twenty-nine (44 percent), starting off at the extreme right, that is, with little to no special accommodations. Two of these moved much closer to a schoolroom at home, but the majority remained close to no special accommodations.

Conversely, seven (11 percent) families began with a schoolroom at home. Two of these homeschoolers moved to the extreme right with one remaining at the starting point.

Parental Involvement

0   100

Mother   *Father*

No Answer—none

When noting who's guiding the learning journey, we find the least amount of movement on the continuum. Thirty-five (53 percent) families remain where they started. Four of these split the journey evenly between the parents, and the remaining thirty-one report numbers indicating that the mother is handling the bulk of the homeschooling.

Nine (14 percent) report sliding toward less father involvement but none of them significantly. The lack of any significant movement in this subcategory could be a result of many reporting low numbers (or numbers toward the left) in the first place. Twenty-two (33 percent) slid toward greater father involvement with five of these families reporting significant increases.

Outside Assistance

0   100
_____

No help from others   *All learning occurs with*
                                                   assistance from others

No Answer—six

Homeschoolers are generally free to use as much or as little outside assistance as they feel necessary. As you'll discover in chapter 12, this assistance takes many forms, from enrollment in alternative education programs to Grandpa helping with French lessons.

Twenty-nine (44 percent) families report no change in the amount of outside assistance they use, and all but one of these report numbers at 50 or below, with the majority well below 50.

Here we find twenty-six (39 percent) starting with very little assistance and six (9 percent) starting with a great deal. Overall, twenty (30 percent) slid toward more outside assistance, three significantly. Eleven (17 percent) slid toward less outside assistance, seven significantly.

Continuum Conclusions

No two sets of continuum responses were the same. No two families set off on their homeschooling journey for the same reasons with the same financial investment in the same way.

The continuum results *don't* reveal, nor were they intended to reveal, trends by which homeschoolers could be further labeled, as in "All homeschoolers (fill in the blank)" or "The majority of homeschoolers (fill in the blank)." To the contrary, the variety of numbers and the movement along each continuum clearly show there is *no* recognizable trend or label, and that any label that could apply to a family today might not apply tomorrow!

> There is no one magical "right way" to homeschool.

The continuum results *do* reveal *there is no one magical "right way" to homeschool.*

Those who possess homeschooling's freedom put it to good use and make adjustments when necessary. Remember, significant change represented a move on the continuum of at least thirty points, quite a change on a scale of 1 to 100. This occurred most often on the high end of the scale in approach (toward less structure), in assessment (toward less formal testing), and in use of technology (toward increased use).

On the low end of the scale and in considerably fewer instances, significant change is seen most often in physical space (toward less specific accommodations), in outside assistance (toward less outside help), and in financial expenditures (toward spending less money).

These results give us a snapshot of a *very* small number of homeschoolers who are moving, for the most part, toward a more complete integration of life and learning, using their computers more and money less. As they spent more time on their homeschooling journeys, they moved away from the school model of structured lessons, classroom environment, and tests.

We'll visit these variables again in chapter 4, where we'll put them to work helping you get started.

IT DOESN'T MATTER WHERE YOU BEGIN, JUST BEGIN!

THE ABILITY TO change direction when something isn't working is a major contributor to an individual family's homeschooling success. If you're aware of this from the start, it will help you through initial rough spots you might encounter. If you find your material or your approach isn't working with your child, it's not necessarily an indication that *homeschooling* isn't working. Sure, it's painful to watch dust gather on books you thought would be appreciated, but at least you are free to do so to benefit your child. The amazing homeschool continuum showed you that the overwhelming majority of our respondents changed one or many aspects of their homeschooling since they began, constantly fine-tuning the journey to fill their needs. This can be done at any point, in any family, with any child.

With the abundant amount of information available on homeschooling today you could spend months or even years thinking about and discussing just where you and your family should begin. Now that the amazing homeschool continuum has disclosed just how flexible homeschooling can be, you can see that exactly where you begin isn't all that crucial. The most important thing is that you begin!

Approach homeschooling now in whatever manner you feel most comfortable. Spend money and gather resources only to the extent that your budget isn't strained. Make changes in your home to the degree that space or desire allows. Call in as much or as little outside assistance as you wish. Involve your spouse to whatever point time and energy currently allow. Any of these aspects of homeschooling can be fine-tuned as you grow more comfortable with

HOW WE DID IT

My oldest, just under seven, is retaining a lot. As she grows I plan to periodically test her to make sure we're on target. Or, if I achieve my ultimate goal of unschooling . . . plan to just observe.

—KATE

your journey, as you gain experience, and as you get better and better at observing your child's interests and learning style.

It's the journey that counts. And like all other journeys, this one, too, starts with the first step.

SIMPLE STARTING POINTS

✦   *Start dreaming and planning today!*

Homeschooling can be anything you want and need it to be, flexible enough to fit your unique lifestyle and situation. Talk to your spouse about the idea. Start thinking about the activities you would like to enjoy with your child, the books you would like to read together. Be sure to ask your child for suggestions, too. Think about living according to your own schedule and not a school's.

✦   *Read as many books and magazines about homeschooling as you can.*

Your local library should have some on its shelves, and an interlibrary loan search will uncover even more.

✦   *Search the word homeschooling on the Internet.*

Visit a few of the sites that catch your fancy. Join an e-mail loop and ask a few questions. Enter a chat room where parents frequently exchange information and answer questions. Follow the links to still more sites to get a taste of the wide variety of perspectives on the topic.

✦   *Attend a local homeschool support group meeting.*

Meeting schedules are often posted on the library, skating rink, or community center bulletin board, in the community notices section of local newspapers, or announced as public service messages on radio and TV. Here you'll meet homeschoolers, hear their concerns and triumphs, and maybe even get to meet a few homeschooled children, homeschooling's best advertisements!

✦   *Stop waiting for the "perfect" circumstances—get started!*

Because it's so easy to change any aspect of homeschooling when necessary, you can get started with a minimum of worry or preparation. Once you're on the road, you'll constantly discover new information, resources, and friends to help you fine-tune your journey into the most rewarding and fun possible.

RESOURCES

Books

Colfax, David and Micki. *Hard Times in Paradise.* Warner Books, 1992.

Dobson, Linda. *The Art of Education: Reclaiming Your Family, Community and Self.* Holt Associates, 1997.

Guterson, David. *Family Matters: Why Homeschooling Makes Sense.* Harcourt Brace Jovanovich, 1992.

Hegener, Mark and Helen, eds. *The Homeschool Reader: Perspectives on Homeschooling.* Home Education Press, 1995.

Holt, John. *Teach Your Own: A Hopeful Path for Education.* Delacorte Press, 1989.

Moore, Raymond and Dorothy. *The Successful Homeschooling Family Handbook.* Thomas Nelson Publishers, 1994.

Periodicals

F.U.N. News: 1688 Belhaven Woods Court, Pasadena, MD 21122-3727; 888-FUN-7020; FUN@unschooling.org; www.FUN-Books.com; quarterly, $10/year or $16/two years, free sample on request.

Growing Without Schooling: 2380 Massachusetts Avenue, Suite 104, Cambridge, MA 02140; 617-864-3100; holtgws@aol.com;www .holtgws.com; bimonthly, $25/year.

Home Education Magazine: P.O. Box 1083, Tonasket, WA 98855; 509-486-1351; HEM@home-ed-magazine.com; www.home-ed-magazine.com; bimonthly, $24/year.

Homeschooling Today: P.O. Box 1608, Ft. Collins, CO 80522-1608; 904-475-3088; homeschooltoday.com; bimonthly, $19.99/year.

Web Sites

American Homeschool Association: http://www.home-ed-magazine.com/AHA/aha.html

Home Education Magazine: http://www.home-ed-magazine.com

Homeschooling for the Uneducated: http://www.angelfire.com/tx/2laurasplace/Page2.html

Home Schooling Daily: http://www.infinet.com/~baugust

A to Z Home'sCool: http://www.gomilpitas.com/homeschooling

Organizations

American Homeschool Association: P.O. Box 1083, Tonasket, WA 98855; 509-486-1351; e-mail AHA@home-ed-magazine.com

Alliance for Parental Involvement in Education (AllPIE): P.O. Box 59, East Chatham, NY 12060-0059; 518-392-6900; e-mail allpie@taconic.net

Moore Foundation: P.O. Box 1, Camas, WA 98607; 360-835-2736; e-mail moorefnd@pacifier.com

2

READY FOR SUCCESS:

LEARNING ASSETS OF THE

EARLY YEARS CHILD

In This Chapter

✦ Curious George has lots of company

✦ Imagine it

✦ Enthusiastic and eager

✦ Innocence sprinkled with a sense of wonder

✦ Pure love and joy

✦ Simple starting points

✦ Resources

O N T H E G O , morning 'til night, doing, doing, doing. As naturally as a mountain spring, the early years child bubbles with energy.
Unfortunately for little ones today, childhood energy is often considered a bad thing. Interestingly, it's most often considered a bad
thing in the context of school.

This is, to a degree, understandable. Get too many children exercising too much curiosity in a classroom, and it's easy to sympathize
with a teacher charged with relaying a day's worth of lessons. Get too
many children exercising too much enthusiasm in a classroom, and
the teacher perceives a room full of behavior problems.

So the rules of school are such that the natural flow of childhood
energy must be plugged so the school can do what it does in the way

that it's set up to do it. A recent TV commercial for some chip or another shows all the teachers in the teacher's lounge singing while enjoying their snack. With teachers otherwise occupied, the schoolchildren's energy is unleashed and they run wild through the halls, kicking globes and freeing lab animals. It's a perfect visual image of what happens when you mess with the natural order of things.

The early years are a child's information-gathering time, and he accomplishes this as a physical, sensory being. Lacking ability to reason in the abstract (the province of the adolescent child), the early years child collects data by physical means—moving, touching, tasting, seeing, hearing, and smelling. The greater the sensory involvement in an activity, the better the chance the information will stick. It might help to imagine the early years child as working at the "job" of collecting millions and millions of information files. The more files collected, the more experience there is to draw from, as slowly but surely the child begins to process the information, figure out relationships, and reach conclusions that sometimes amaze, sometimes amuse. More sorting and more precise filing occur as the child grows intellectually.

> Unfortunately for little ones today, childhood energy is too often considered a bad thing. Interestingly, it's most often considered a bad thing in the context of school.

Now, imagine for a moment somehow you, too, are magically transformed into a similar information sleuth. Everything inside you urges you to gather more and more. Which behavior traits would you want to have?

You probably didn't answer that you wanted the ability to sit still, bottle up questions, or resist conversation with others. Lethargy probably wasn't high on your list, either. Maybe you said curiosity, creativity, imagination, enthusiasm, resilience, a sense of wonder, joy of discovery, and/or a willingness to try new things. If so, you've just found the traits that are the natural fruit of childhood energy.

These are your early years child's learning as-sets. When questionnaire respondents were asked to consider the most important learning assets their children in this age group possess, not one—not *one*—mentioned a computer, a set of text-books, or a beautiful classroom. No one even mentioned a great teacher! They pointed instead to behavior traits befitting an information sleuth and associated with childhood energy.

> The early years are a child's information-gathering time, and he accomplishes this as a physical, sensory being.

Does it make sense to bottle up this energy, even if doing so serves the rules of school? Or does it seem more sensible to let this energy flow, and to nurture and encourage your child's learning assets so they may best serve his needs?

Homeschoolers paint a picture of children eager to learn when doing so in an environment that accommodates and appreciates their bubbling energy. Your child also possesses the behavior traits necessary to enjoy the learning journey, and you can help nurture them if you but know what to look for.

CURIOUS GEORGE HAS LOTS OF COMPANY

RITA BEGAN HOMESCHOOLING with two children (aged five and eight) in the Orlando, Florida, area. When she first mentioned homeschooling to her second-grade daughter, Rita remembers she exclaimed, "Then I can ask all the questions I want!"

Respondents mentioned their children's curiosity three times more often than any other learning asset. Homeschooling parents of early years children field more questions in one day than Dear Abby juggles in a year. It always helps to look at your child's ques-tions as perfectly natural. Next you can appreciate them as an open window on the mind. The early years child asks questions about

> Curiosity creates interest, interest increases attention to the task at hand, and attention gives rise to learning.

what interests her at any given moment. This provides you with clues as to what books, activities, and field trips will hold her interest because they promise answers to important questions.

"Children homeschooling in the early years can follow their trains of thought and imaginations for an incredibly long way," says Michaela from California, who started homeschooling when "things were going badly" in her four-year-old daughter's preschool. "Contrary to popular belief, young children have quite long attention spans. When they're interested in a project just try to distract them—and shame on you if you do!"

Michaela has observed that curiosity creates interest, interest increases attention to the task at hand, and attention gives rise to learning.

Your curious child's questions also present you with an opportunity to observe and assess learning. They reveal what information is

HOW WE DID IT

The children were used to seeing toys related to movies in the stores. They expected we would be able to find stuffed animals, rag dolls, or action figures of every book we read. It came as a great shock to them that there weren't dolls of the characters of classic children's literature or of the historical figures they found fascinating.

They decided it would be a great project to make toys. We bought lots of felt and some fiberfill and I helped by making a simple gingerbread person shape on newspaper, which they used as a pattern. I showed them some simple sewing stitches.

being gathered and worked with at any particular moment. A question might let you know your child was listening to and comprehending the radio news report even as she seemed oblivious to it while painting at the kitchen table. Another question will show you she's digesting the background information gathered from your reading of a Laura Ingalls Wilder novel when you are asked why the family had to make their clothes and didn't just run to a department store to buy them.

"I try to catch my children and watch them solving their own problems with reading or fitting things inside each other," says Kate, a "relaxed" homeschooler from Charleston, South Carolina. "They are glorious to observe and even better if they are totally unaware that I'm observing them."

Kate's remark points to yet another benefit of a child's curiosity. Concentrated attention to the task at hand, created by curiosity, provides opportunity for lots of practice in problem solving. As a home educator, I have to admit I chuckle each time I see yet another new workbook that creates fake problem-solving opportunities for

Marla's first "felt friend" was Alexander the Great, and Jacob's was Julius Caesar. They drew marker faces on the felt and fashioned clothing for them. This has grown to be a continuing hobby and they've made felt friends of characters from Greek mythology, the American Civil War, and the musical *Cats*, among others. As the children have grown, the dolls have become more elaborate, more detailed, and more their own. They now create their own patterns and work at it independently.

—ANGIE

children. As Kate has discovered, a child living where she learns finds real-life problems to tackle each day. The joy Kate describes as an observer is merely one of many sweet side effects of sharing the learning journey with a child.

IMAGINE IT

SHE HAS ONLY to don a tiara and the early years child *is* Cinderella. As her brother closes the freshly cut door in the side of a refrigerator box, his voice moves down an octave to announce his brand new store not only *is,* but it's now open for business.

Imagination transports a child to the ends of the earth and brings him home safely again, which makes it a powerful learning asset. When a family homeschools, the children can benefit by having lots of time for unstructured play, the province of imagination.

Jacqueline has learned at her Austin, Texas, home with eight-year-old Tom since 1995, when she and her husband decided not to send the boy to school—although, she explains, "We really didn't do anything differently after the decision." Tom saw several home-school Christmas play productions and decided to write his own.

"He began by writing dialogue for each character on a separate piece of paper. Then I explained to him that it works better if all the dialogue for all actors is on the same page so the actors know what will be said before their lines so they know when to speak," says Jacqueline. "He's planned costumes and scenery. It's a one-act play with about eight lines and a song."

Through imagination, the early years child designs something new from what has been learned. When imagination breathes life into knowledge, the child can put that knowledge to the test. Like a scientist, she creates a hypothesis, investigates, analyzes, then does it again—and usually again. While safe and happy in the province of imagination, in an environment where there is no ridicule for doing so, the child is fine-tuning learning, all the while making adjustments based on the results of investigations.

"With a wooden train set we were amazed by what our daughter's play delved into by mixing in her other toys," says Michaela. "Lincoln Logs became Willy Wonka's chocolate factory (we had just read the book). Cuisenaire rods became a maze for Polly Pockets, and the magnet ends of the trains allowed us to explore magnetism using paper clips and other objects."

Michaela continues, "Building the track layout was an exercise in map reading as we followed the diagrams in the booklet, and problem-solving skills helped her connect the tracks and make them do fancy things.

"Polly Pockets gave musical performances on a stage of Cuisenaire rods. Rods were packed into the train for delivery around the track.

"I was astonished by how much math, history, literature, culture, physics, and who-knows-what-all was covered in just a week of play," Michaela concludes.

Sometimes, imagination works so well it rises *above* the occasion. Rhonda is the mother of four children aged four to thirteen who learn at home in Orem, Utah. Her son Michael taught himself to read at the fourth-grade level before kindergarten, and at four years of age took a test for giftedness.

"The tester sat there with a stopwatch and showed Michael a maze," Rhonda explains. "There was a girl on the outside of the maze and her dog on the inside. The goal? To get the line from the girl to the dog in as little time as possible.

"Michael was in rapture. He loved the thought of helping this girl find her dog. He started weaving an elaborate story about the girl and her dog and the great friendship they had. He took the girl through some real adventures in her search for her dog.

"The tester sat there with her stopwatch, frowning. Finally she turned it off and just sat back, watching Michael. He went on and on, in the most creative, imaginative way.

"Needless to say," says Rhonda, "he failed that section of the gift-edness test."

Imagination also provides young children with an early, gentle introduction to social roles. By "playing" Mom or the eye doctor or an astronaut heading for the moon, the children enter their pretend world wearing new and different hats, and they can try on many different perspectives in twenty-four hours. They learn empathy at the same time they add to their ever-increasing abilities to relate positively and understandingly to others.

The Play's the Thing

By now you've noticed that imagination and play dance together in a healthy expression of a child's inner world. Many who study young children, David Elkind and Thomas Armstrong among them, express concern that the busy schedules of today's families don't allow children enough opportunity to dwell in the province of imagination and play, thus denying them connection to and understanding of who they are. We notice the modern child "grows up" much too quickly, and this could well be the result of denying children the ingredient essential for imaginative play—*time*.

> Imagination and play dance together in a healthy expression of a child's inner world.

Rhonda has learned that "even on days when something exciting isn't going on, there are the luxuries of time and whims to follow, and probably the most important aspect of our homeschooling . . . *playing*."

With schooling so firmly established in our culture and in our personal experience as *the* method for learning, it's often hard to grasp and accept the idea that, for the early years child, play—unadulterated by adult "good intentions"—is a powerful learning method. Who knows, it may even be recognized someday as a superior method for learning because it lets the child exercise natural learning assets.

"We had a wonderful spy week when we learned everything in the context of being spies," says Rhonda. "We watched 007 movies and I bought trench coats, hats, and sunglasses for the children from the secondhand store. They made up spy stories and designed their own hideaways. They still remember this as one of their favorite playtimes."

Creativity—Imagination's Kissin' Cousin

Creativity is imagination's kissin' cousin. Its expression is most often recognized in the arts: drawing, painting, poetry, sculpture, dance, architecture, or 3-D computer graphics. If the resources homeschoolers say they value are any indication, homeschooling children are blessed with lots of time and materials for creative projects. (See chapter 10 for more.)

Creativity is also a quality that can be brought to bear on the thinking process itself, expanding the process to bring ideas together in new and unique combinations. If we can bend our own thinking

HOW WE DID IT

Cooking with my toddlers gave me patience. I see them counting as we scoop ingredients into the pan. They learn about portions and sizes as they try to make uniform cookies or meatballs. They read the American Girls cookbooks and want to try new foods. It's shown me they are more capable than I give them credit for. I wasn't allowed to cook until I was nine years old. Watching my five-year-old make sandwiches at lunch shows me I need to let go and allow them to do more and help more.

—KERRY

processes far enough to give play its rightful due, we could even call creativity the play of the mind.

One day, as Tanya and her five-year-old daughter Ev drove through their suburban California neighborhood, Ev asked, "What's two times three?"

Tanya answered, "Six."

"That's right." Ev continued. "What's three times two?"

Again Tanya answered, "Six."

"Right, it's the same. Well, it's not exactly the same," said Ev.

"What do you mean, 'not exactly'?" asked Tanya, perplexed.

Ev replied, "Well, it's kind of like a palindrome, but not exactly."

Tanya could only think, "Wow. She's right!"

Here's yet another five-year-old's mind-play, shared by Maureen, who homeschools with two early years children in British Columbia, Canada. When Gary (five years old) began learning addition with carrying two two-digit numbers, he caught the concept so quickly Maureen urged him to do some problems for Daddy.

"Almost immediately my husband commented that Gary was writing down the answer beginning with the number in the tens column first, *then* filling in the number in the ones column," Maureen explains.

Gary piped up. "The number you carry will always be a one, so it's easy to just add one to the two numbers already there, and write that down first."

Maureen and her husband looked at each other. "For the first time in our thirty-something lives we realized he was right—the number you carry from the ones column will always only be a one!"

ENTHUSIASTIC AND EAGER

WHEN I WENT to school I felt it was a chore to learn well. With this attitude it's easy to understand why I missed being enthusiastic or eager about the experience.

Homeschooled children, on the other hand, when free to use all childhood energy available to them, generally display a refreshing enthusiasm and eagerness about learning. Learning isn't a chore, they've discovered, it's a by-product of engaging in activity with a fresh, eager, hungry mind.

Enthusiasm for learning is also where self-motivation originates, a behavior trait welcomed by all parents. A child's self-motivation is satisfying when it means he picks up his socks without being told, but in the greater context of living and learning, it's a source of humility for homeschooling parents who realize many times, their role as teacher hangs by a thread.

> If we can bend our own thinking processes far enough to give play its rightful due, we could call creativity the play of the mind.

Holly's son Pete (aged five) is the older of two children. They've homeschooled in a small university town in Indiana since Pete's birth. "Again and again I see Pete dive heartily with both feet into an endeavor he's excited about: typing, illustrating a story we created, numbering the pages of his spy notebook, demonstrating his experiment on electrical circuits at our homeschool group's science fair. When he really wants to learn or do something, you can't stop him!"

The same phenomenon reaches beyond academic subjects. "Casey started to learn to ride his bike. I tried to help with the usual cajoling," Rhonda remembers. "He was very standoffish and wouldn't let us change the training wheels even though they stuck on our gravel.

"Then one day he took off the training wheels himself, finding the right wrench and everything. He put the bike away and didn't touch it for a month."

Rhonda continues, "We were heading to the park to meet friends one day and he wanted to take the bike. 'But Casey,' I said, 'you haven't touched it since forever and the training wheels are off.' We ended up taking it.

"Casey wanted the bike out of the car. He hopped on it and took off down the road. I couldn't believe it. I almost fell over except I was cheering too hard. Wish I had a picture of that face!

"This taught me a lesson I remind myself of constantly," Rhonda confides. "Leave him alone! He spends time observing and processing, and at his own pace will just do it."

INNOCENCE SPRINKLED WITH A SENSE OF WONDER

THE EARLY YEARS child's lack of experience is at once the reason for innocence and the creator of a sense of wonder. The most joyous moments of my family's homeschooling years were those when the children's eyes grew wide and beaming smiles spread across their faces as discoveries were met with an innocent sense of wonder. What a privilege to witness both the large and small indications of their awakenings! But you'll have to be alert: These moments often come when you least expect them.

Marla didn't know what to expect when the older of her two young sons called her into the bathroom of their Fredericksburg, Virginia, home one evening. They had just spent some time working on patterns in math. "From the toilet he excitedly told me the wallpaper was in a specific pattern and he pointed it out to me," Marla says. "See, every moment is open for learning and discovery!"

Gail homeschools in New Hampshire with four-year-old twins and a three-year-old. In the midst of days filled with innocence and wonder, Gail remembers when all three of her children were on the deck—they were "splatter painting with leaves when one of the twins stuck a brush covered with blue paint into the yellow paint and made green. They were all so excited. We'd gone over this before and made color wheels, but to happen magically on its own, that's what made an impression."

With a family currently in the third year of homeschooling in a rural area of Washington, Bernadette recalls reading the story of the first Thanksgiving to her then six-year-old daughter. "I took the opportunity to tell her that Governor Bradford is the ancestor of a relative of ours."

She was amazed. "You mean this is a *true* story?" she exclaimed.

"To share these moments of wonder is why we homeschool. It's fun," says Bernadette.

PURE LOVE AND JOY

LOVE AND JOY are the purest manifestations of energy, childhood or otherwise. Maybe it's the presence of innocence that makes childhood joy seem that much more special, that much more unconditional and spontaneous. Whatever the reason, many homeschooling parents understand what a precious gift joy is in their children's lives, and they do what they can to preserve it.

"Our children are full of joy for life and learning," says Laura, mother of two early years children. She knows too many of us lose that joy as we grow and notes, "All of us public school graduates have to learn joy all over again."

Laura is optimistic about the children growing up in her Canton, Michigan, home. "I don't ever want my children to be embarrassed out of their joy. Where might we be now if we all somehow managed to hang on to that joy from our childhoods? I hope my children will find out."

> Many homeschooling parents understand what a precious gift joy brings into their children's lives, and they do what they can to preserve it.

Kahlil Gibran has written, "Work is love made visible." I had to wait until my children became my "work" before I fully comprehended what Gibran meant by this. I daresay there are many adults today accomplishing work as a means to a financial end who may never understand it.

But what happens when a child, liberated from a school schedule and school lessons, sets out on the learning journey and puts this thought into practice right from the start?

Juliet, whose oldest child has homeschooled, gone to public school, and come back again, is raising two young sons and a baby girl on an air force base in California. One of her sons wants to be a naturalist and establish a wildlife preserve when he grows up.

"Because we're homeschooling he had a chance to read and read and read about the northern elephant seals and other wildlife of the Año Nuevo State Park in California before we went to visit," Juliet explains. "Because we're homeschooling he hasn't learned to 'sit down' at the very time he's eager and interested. As we walked across the dunes on the beach to see the seals with our tour, he was right up at the front, holding hands and conversing eagerly with the naturalist.

"On the way back," Juliet says, "he pretended to be the leader and recounted what he'd learned about the vegetation as we re-crossed the grassy areas and fields of wild willow."

From her Moreno Valley, California, home, six-year-old Alison and her family, which includes a baby sister, have had lots of opportunities to visit Sea World. Alison now loves dolphins and would like to be a trainer someday. "Whether or not she becomes one," says Celia, her mother, "this love sparked a desire to learn things she might not have had much interest in otherwise.

"After learning dolphins are mammals she wanted to study all mammals. When she realized dolphin trainers have to be good swimmers she threw herself wholeheartedly into her swim lessons. When she realized the dolphin diet consists primarily of fish, she was willing to try it at dinnertime.

"It amazes me that an interest in one thing is an energy, a momentum that carries children on to learn so many new things. Her life seems very much like this. Her world started out so narrow, but for every new dream she reaches for she accomplishes much more along the way."

While homeschoolers don't have a corner on the market of childhood energy and the learning assets that flow from it, their loose schedules and oftentimes more relaxed approach to education seem to consistently provide increased opportunity to exercise these assets. Such are the benefits of childhood energy when allowed to freely flow.

SIMPLE STARTING POINTS

THE FOLLOWING Starting Points are presented courtesy of New Mexico Family Educators; *The Connection,* Volume 8, Issue 10 (Dec 98–Jan 99); P.O. Box 92276, Albuquerque, NM 87199-2276.

- ✦   Put a smile on your face, in your eyes, and in your voice. Practice this, even if it seems awkward at first.
- ✦   Develop the habit of making eye contact and showing physical affection in small ways throughout the day. *You* already know you love your family; this way *they* know it, too.
- ✦   Develop the habit of looking for the positive things your child does. Give sincere verbal acknowledgment, but remember not to spoil it by "gushing" over everything!
- ✦   Focus on your child's expected future success and not on past failures. This is especially important for a child coming out of public school.
- ✦   Be eager yourself. Motivation is often contagious.
- ✦   By observing your child's abilities, plan activities for your child that are not too hard nor too easy. Too easy is boring; too hard is discouraging.
- ✦   Choose a specific short-term goal. "Inch by inch, life's a cinch, yard by yard, it's hard." The younger the child, the shorter the goal.

- ✦ Allow your child freedom. Let him choose some activities and projects for himself, then allow him to follow through with them.
- ✦ Provide a variety of materials and methods of presentation to stave off boredom.

RESOURCES

Books

Armstrong, Ph.D., Thomas. *Awakening Your Child's Natural Genius: Enhancing Curiosity, Creativity, and Learning Ability.* Jeremy P. Tarcher, Inc., 1991.

Baldwin, Rahima. *You Are Your Child's First Teacher.* Celestial Arts, 1989.

Diamond, Ph.D., Marian, and Janet Hopson. *Magic Trees of the Mind: How to Nurture Your Child's Intelligence, Creativity, and Healthy Emotions.* Dutton, 1998.

Elkind, David. *The Hurried Child: Growing Up Too Fast Too Soon.* Perseus Press, 1989.

————. *Miseducation: Preschoolers at Risk.* Knopf, 1988.

Healy, Ph.D., Jane M. *Your Child's Growing Mind: A Guide to Learning and Brain Development from Birth to Adolescence.* Main Street Books, 1994.

Luvmour, Josette and Sambhava. *Natural Learning Rhythms.* Celestial Arts, 1993.

Moore, Raymond S. and Dorothy N. *Better Late Than Early: A New Approach to Your Child's Education.* Reader's Digest Press, 1982.

Pearce, Joseph Chilton. *Magical Child.* Dutton, 1974.

Wallace, Nancy. *Child's Work: Taking Children's Choices Seriously.* Holt Associates, 1990.

Periodicals

Journal of Family Life: 72 Phillip Street, Albany, NY 12202; 518-432-1578.

Liedloff Continuum Network Newsletter: P.O. Box 1634, Sausalito, CA 94966.

Mothering Magazine: P.O. Box 1650, Santa Fe, NM 87504; 505-984-8116.

Staying Home: 812 Magnolia, Extension #5, Johnson City, TN 37604.

Welcome Home: Mothers at Home: 8310-A Old Courthouse Road, Vienna, VA 22182.

3

THE JOY OF LEARNING
WITH THE
EARLY YEARS CHILD

In This Chapter

✦ Pathway to knowledge

✦ Pathway to social opportunity

✦ Pathway to strong families

✦ Pathway to safety

✦ Pathway to health

✦ Pathway from school to home

✦ Simple starting points

✦ Resources

I REMEMBER the first time I received praise for homeschooling my young children, a rarity back in the early days of homeschooling. "How wonderful you'll sacrifice so much to do this," the praiser gushed. "I would *never* have the patience to stay home all day with my kids. You're so brave!"

Her words set off my thinking about homeschooling in a direction it had never been before. Sacrifice? This didn't feel like sacrifice. Patience? I've been working on it, but even to this day it's not my strong suit. Brave? I'd sent my first child to public school kindergarten—now *that*, I thought, was brave. Bottom line? The woman took a cursory look at what we were doing and got it all backwards!

> I'd sent my first child to public school kinder- garten—now *that*, I thought, was brave.

Darby, a Texan with two girls, two and four years old, sees homeschooling more clearly. "The mere fact that I get to be the one who is there to hear almost every amazing thing that comes out of my daughters' mouths (this happens on a sometimes hourly basis) is so incredible to me."

This joyful perspective should punch holes in thoughts you're harboring about sacrifice, super-human patience, or bravery as prerequisites for a homeschooling parent. With misconceptions out of the way, it's smooth sailing to-ward understanding the many benefits homeschooling can present your family—together.

PATHWAY TO KNOWLEDGE

THERE'S NO better place than home to guarantee your child will learn to read, write, do arithmetic, *and* be joyfully exposed to enough literature and science and geography and history so she grows to love and value learning for the rest of her life.

An Educational Approach That Fits Your Child's Learning Style

We all know all human beings don't learn best in the same way. This idea is now so accepted dozens of different interpretations exist of how to go about deciding just what learning style your child has, too many to share in limited space. You might find a little research inter-esting, so a few references are included in the Resources section to get you started.

Tuning In to How Your Child Learns

In chapter 1, I pointed out that it's more important to get started homeschooling than it is to suffer migraines figuring out how, where, when, and with what. It's always possible to adjust once your family grows more comfortable with homeschooling. Likewise, you don't need to know your child's specific learning style to begin your learning journey.

"Something happened early in our experience which clearly showed how we should to go about homeschooling." Joni, raising two children in San Antonio, Texas, tells how a backyard event revealed the clues she needed to proceed.

"Rose Anne was playing with three friends. They started digging and came across some snails. Each chose one snail and brought it to the patio to show me. I helped them have a snail race and keep track of who won. They wanted to inspect their snails and, of course, they curled up and wouldn't come out. I got one of our children's encyclopedias and the older children looked up *snail* as the younger two sounded out how to spell *snail*. After reading about the snails and looking at pictures, they decided to draw them."

Joni continues, "Released for drawing, the snails started moving again so the children observed. This went on most of the afternoon. They didn't notice they learned anything new . . . graphing the races, research, spelling, reading, science, and interactive play. Oh, and don't forget art."

When it comes to figuring out a child's learning style, negative experiences can be learning opportunities, too. "I gave my bad speller a test and he got 100 percent correct," Gretchen remembers about one of two sons who attended school until 1994 in Tucson, Arizona. "The very next day he wrote a paragraph using several of those words and misspelled them. That's when I realized spelling lessons weren't fitting his learning style. I forgot about spelling, throwing away the expensive spelling programs we'd tried.

"Several years later, after reading good literature and using the computer spell-checker,"

> When it comes to figuring out a child's learning style, negative experiences can be learning opportunities, too.

Gretchen says, "his spelling spontaneously improved without me having done anything. That paragraph with the misspelled words was the 'aha! moment' that relaxed our home education style and re-focused our educational efforts."

Trusting and Observing

Many homeschoolers find once they start homeschooling they need only trust the child will gravitate toward the style that's right for her, and observe the clues the child provides. This holds true no matter where the family falls on the approach continuum, from highly structured to totally unstructured and everywhere in between. The family moves and experiments until the education fits the child instead of forcing the child into a one-size-fits-all education.

Watch for clues regarding basic preferences first.

+ Does your child seem to learn more easily when she sees, hears, touches, or has a combination of all three?
+ Does your child like you or siblings present while working on a project, or does she prefer to work alone?
+ Does your child follow directions better if you tell her— or if you show her how to do something?
+ Does your child enjoy noise and activity while learning, or does she prefer quiet?
+ When preparing to read or listen to a story, does your child sit, lie down, or not really settle down at all?

Just these few simple observations reveal an important treasure trove of information. These observations show you:

+ What types of learning materials will likely be most effec-tive
+ The optimum learning environment
+ The best way to "teach"—and guide, inspire, and mentor—your child

Remember, too, your child may learn in a different manner than you do. "Each child brings a different viewpoint to learning. I don't teach them both the same way," says Maureen, who calls her homeschooling approach structured and child-centered. "My first son needs to *do* to learn. That wasn't easy as I learn best from workbooks. I was often at odds with him until I realized we're just wired differently."

Using Clues to Figure Out "When"

Along with guiding you in the "how" of your child's learning style, trusting and observing can help you figure out the "when," too. Marlene started homeschooling with nine children more than ten years ago. In their rural Oklahoma home, Marlene notes, "One of the greatest benefits of homeschooling is the ability to teach each child on the level he's ready for. Sometimes it's hard to be patient, but it's important not to force late bloomers."

Marlene and I aren't alone in having increased our personal patience quotas while homeschooling. "I remember feeling frustrated when a child simply couldn't grasp something," remembers Janelle, a registered nurse and another mother with a decade of homeschooling experience. "Over the years I've learned (and it took awhile) to just leave such a moment and come back to it a week, a month, or a year later."

As with any endeavor, practice makes perfect. The more often you trust and observe, the more accurate your observations become.

Shoring Up Weaknesses

You may notice topics and activities from which your child shies away. These are the topics and activities providing the least pleasure—and probably the most difficulty. Once you observe what they are, you can figure out improved ways to address them.

Adjustment to shore up weaknesses may mean using a book that takes a different approach to the subject—or not using a book at all.

> The more chances you get to trust and observe, the more accurate your observations become.

Conversely, you may think those hands-on manipulatives look great, only to discover your child is happier with a workbook and pencil. It may mean replacing a whole language approach to teaching reading with a phonics approach—or vice versa—or blending them together.

Sometimes a different "teacher" automatically provides a different approach. You might ask a spouse, an older sibling, or a neighbor to spend a few weeks helping your child over a hump you can't quite manage together. A homeschooling friend could be addressing the same topic with her family, and all the children would enjoy learning together. A support group may offer a class. A local college student might tutor your child for a short period of time, especially if lessons end just in time for a homemade supper.

Adjusting for weaknesses may mean learning to wait for your child's interest or ability to grow. This is most difficult when family and friends *know* children in school are addressing a particular skill. But having patience with learning children has been known to deliver unexpected rewards.

When Rhonda's family began homeschooling, she didn't worry about her then third grader's lack of desire to write. "When he was eleven, I started a Young Astronauts Club and I asked him to be editor of its newsletter. I paid him a candy bar for every issue he did, and his writing took a dramatic upward leap," says Rhonda.

"At eleven and a half, he got a job with the twice-weekly county newspaper. He wrote a humor column about life as a kid, and conducted celebrity interviews (Larry King, Miss America, a Nobel Prize–winner among them). At thirteen, he was hired as a columnist by our daily newspaper. His writing has been delivered to more than 120,000 households.

"The moral of the story," Rhonda concludes, "is don't worry if your child isn't writing by the time he's eight. Kids really do blossom at different ages."

Building on Strengths

A child with time and encouragement to follow her interests will drift *toward* those activities that provide the most pleasure (just as an adult will). Early years children aren't usually shy about asking to hear a book again (for the fourteenth time in a week), or use the paints again, or watch the video of science experiments yet again. These actions could all be early indicators of strengths.

With the time and freedom homeschooling provides, you have the opportunity to experiment with these early indicators and test your hunches by offering more on the topic—books, videos, classes, TV programs, blank paper, and anything else you can find. Just as a hungry child will eat until satisfied, so too will a hungry mind devour all made available to it. If the mind gets satisfied, hunger (interest) wanes. If not, hunger continues.

> A hungry mind will always find opportunity for more food, thus pursuing interests and potential strengths in more depth during other times of the day.

Again, this works regardless of the amount of structure incorporated in a family's homeschooling approach. Even if a family uses three, four, or five hours each day toward completing a formal curriculum's requirements, a hungry mind always finds opportunity for more food, thus pursuing interests and potential strengths in more depth during other times of the day.

You may find your hunch was wrong, and what you thought was a strength was merely a passing interest. Simply continue observing. You haven't lost anything; your family has been learning all along, and you're free to test a different hunch.

You may be thinking, "Teachers attend college for years to figure out this stuff. This sounds too . . . simple."

A teacher deals with twenty or more children at the same time. She can't observe and get to know any individual child as well as you know yours. Even if she notes a child's particular strengths or weaknesses, she's on the school curriculum's path and mustn't stray. Your intimate knowledge of your child, coupled with homeschooling's flexibility, does make learning comparatively simple.

There is a major difference between the group approach to learning necessary for a classroom situation and the individualized approach available at home. "I can customize a learning plan with my son's input so he always feels like he's on the edge of his chair, eager to learn the answers to his own questions," says Leslie, who homeschools in Seattle, Washington, about her seven-year-old son.

Because Maureen's older son has symptoms of borderline Attention Deficit Hyperactivity Disorder (ADHD), Maureen had to do a little more hunch testing than Leslie. "I thought he was just a boy who couldn't sit still and needed to be moving all the time," she recalls.

HOW WE DID IT

I found while my children were in school they picked up habits that refuted our family values—name calling, celebrity envy, rudeness, disrespect—and we continually worked to restore our way of life. Since homeschooling, life is easier in that respect. A child learns what the family lives. If we thank each other for what is done for us, the child learns to do so also. If we are respectful in our manner of speaking with each other, the child learns this is the way one speaks to another.

Last week in the supermarket I got into a line with a new cashier who made several mistakes, causing a delay. As I was thinking, "Why do I always get into the slow line?" the cashier apologized to the elderly woman she was waiting on. The woman graciously told her it was a small matter and that anyone could make a mistake.

When her purchases were finally totaled, the lady had trouble counting out her money to pay and she dropped several bills on the counter. The cashier carefully picked them up for her, waited patiently while the woman counted out her

"I would try to read to him and he would wander around the room. I asked him to sit and within seconds he'd be up again. Then I tried this: I read a couple of paragraphs to him while he wandered around the room, and asked some questions about it. He answered every one, almost word for word what I had read.

"Next I asked him to sit down while I read a little more. He sat. I read. I asked questions about that piece and he couldn't answer one. I learned just as much as I need quiet to learn something; my son needs movement and stimulation. He concentrates best when music plays or he can move.

"I try to work with this, allowing him to walk around the table while I read, or using the stairs when we do a quiz; he starts at the bottom and moves up one step for each correct answer."

dollars, and then picked the correct coins from the handful the elderly woman held out to her.

Then the cashier told her, "I'm going to stand here and wait while you get that money back into your wallet and get your purse zipped up."

The children were with me and on the way home we talked about the patience, respect, kindness, and concern we had just witnessed. I talked about my impatient feelings and how I realized I'd been wrong.

Homeschooling is full of moments like this. We don't use any special materials. We take it from life experiences, from things we read, from people we meet, and situations we encounter. When my son gets up to give his seat to an older man who has entered the waiting room where we sit, when my daughter suggests giving some of the vegetables we've grown to a neighbor, we see the fruits of our efforts.

—ANGIE

A little observation, an adjustment, and a weakness is bolstered.

In Vienna, Virginia, Shannon saw early signs of artistic strength in her daughter, Robin, and was determined to build on it. "We've always had art supplies around but Robin's mind generates so many ideas and she consumes such large quantities of art supplies, I started buying in bulk.

"When she was about three years old I gave her my kitchen table for her artwork and we started eating in the dining room," says Shannon. "Half of our kitchen is Robin's art studio. We do a minimal amount of 'book-work,' so Robin has many hours during most days for her art. If she's very involved working on a hot project we forgo bookwork that day."

A little observation, an adjustment, and a strength is supported.

The information you gain about your child's learning style or strengths and weaknesses is valuable to others who may also teach your child. Your observations save them time and energy figuring out how to best meet your child's needs, and make their time with your child more productive from the start.

PATHWAY TO SOCIAL OPPORTUNITY

HOMESCHOOLED CHILDREN socialize in the real world. The image of sheltered children raised as delicate orchids unable to cope with a climate change outside the home is a convenient myth for critics.

"I've started a group that for me is a homeschool support group, although I am the only homeschooler in it," explains Karla from Mountain Home Air Force Base in Idaho. The group is a preschool co-op that meets twice a week.

"I'm the only one who sees these three hours a week as an extension of what we already do at home," says Karla of the activities for her three-year-old son Jacob. "For us it's an opportunity to justify the big messes we like to make."

How does the group work? "We pay for our child's own supplies and put money into a pot for consumable materials like paper and paints. We collected donations for things like scissors, staplers, and other supplies.

"Jacob also loves attending a homeschool group every week in the summer and a couple of times each month in the school season. He enjoys the mix of ages with all the children."

While Karla works to create social opportunity for Jacob, Tanya's work creates social opportunity for Ev. "I work three to five hours each week in a musical theater class and I take Ev with me. She sees the older children rehearsing, singing, getting costumes, and creating sets," says Tanya of her job as an aide in the middle school where she worked before Ev's birth. "The children love her and watch her, but she also sees some of the negative things. The students think she's lucky to be homeschooling and tell her this."

> The image of sheltered children raised as delicate orchids unable to cope with a change of climate outside the home is a convenient myth for critics.

Most of the survey respondents who turned to homeschooling because of problems with public schools pointed to concerns about the escalating *negative* socialization on America's school playgrounds and in her classrooms.

A former homeschooling mom in Hawaii, now volunteering at her son's school, states, "On the first day of first grade, a girl slapped him on the face and the teacher said, 'We'll have to work on that.' The girl wasn't punished and my son was upset there was no consequence for her behavior. It was agonizing to think that I had made the 'wrong' decision by choosing public school.

"For the next six weeks I witnessed hitting, pushing, or shoving whenever I was at school. We had a conference with the teacher, the principal, and a school board member all within the first three weeks of school. (And this is considered one of the better schools in the area!) The principal informed us they were having a much higher rate of hitting than usual, and that they started having 'practice' recesses so the children would understand how they were supposed to behave."

The socialization offered this child at school could be considered "arbitrary" in contrast to the "guided" socialization available through homeschooling. Arbitrary socialization occurs by gathering children according to age and placing them under group control. Children are left to fend for themselves amid attitudes and influences often detrimental.

Homeschooling's guided socialization lets parents and child freely choose with whom the child will socialize. In this manner, the child establishes a solid ethical foundation prior to association with those whose values may be quite contrary to his own. This foundation originates in strong families.

PATHWAY TO STRONG FAMILIES

FAMILIES ARE THE building blocks of society. With families increasingly spending time apart, we're building more prisons, hiring more police, and watching personal liberty for all disappear.

Erin, a Seattle, Washington, mother of two, explains, "I want our life to be family-centered, not school-centered. I love being home with my children and having the freedom homeschooling gives. Being together with your children every day is so basic."

Homeschooling builds and strengthens family bonds, and the family dynamic changes. When enough families are closer—and thereby stronger—the societal dynamic will change, too.

Parent-Child Relationships

The act of physically nourishing a baby creates a memorable bond for child and parent. Some homeschoolers find nourishing the mind continues that bonding process. "Nursing my son allowed me to get to know him better as a baby, and homeschooling does that now," says Karla. "I can tell what he's thinking. I can anticipate his interests and steer him to further exploration. It helps me to be prepared."

Our culture recognizes and encourages the positive effects of such bonding for emotional health when children are very small, but sets aside this commonsense thinking when the children reach the still-tender ages of three, four, or five. Homeschoolers find it more logical and healthier to continue what they've been doing all along.

> When enough families are closer—and thereby stronger—the societal dynamic will change, too.

An autonomous homeschooler, Priscilla started her journey with the birth of her first child in 1992. She now learns with two children in an urban area of East Sussex, England. "It's all the events I don't miss that are so precious," Priscilla explains, "like the way my four-year-old will suddenly pipe up on a crowded bus and say, 'I love you, Mummy.'"

"My son (seven years old) is generally very loving toward me, but the other day he melted my heart when he verbalized how he thinks of me," says Leslie, a Seattle, Washington, homeschooler with two children. "I made three perfect waffles in a row and asked, 'Does that make me a perfect mom?'

"Without hesitation he responded, 'You're already a perfect mom!'"

If you're thinking only moms have all the fun, think again.

In Brenda's Idaho home, the pleasures of bedtime story hour belong to Dad. "He's been reading aloud an hour each evening since the girls were born," Brenda says. "I honestly don't know who enjoys it more."

For Hope's young family, one daughter's dance lessons had unintended bonding consequences.

"Our younger daughter will start lessons next year, too. It sparked an interest in music and dance for the whole family. My husband bought us a keyboard and I'm learning to play, something I've wanted to do since I was a little girl!"

Sibling Relationships

If my children are any indication, homeschooling is not a miracle cure for sibling squabbles. Sorry.

That said, brothers and sisters who spend time together as homeschooling siblings do form special bonds, especially when freedom from a school calendar means big brother or sister is there from the very beginning.

When Lenore knew she was expecting, she found it easy to weave information about childbirth into her then eight-year-old daughter's daily lessons. Daughter was right there with Mom in their northern Virginia home to help Lenore with labor and delivery. "During the weeks and months that followed, our daughter played a large role in welcoming our baby into our family," Lenore remembers. "Perhaps she would have felt so involved if she'd been in school, but I doubt it. I think homeschooling made a world of difference."

As the children grow, so do the bonds. Rita counts among her favorite moments those when her eight-year-old daughter teaches her five-year-old son: "Whether it's explaining something to him I've explained to her, or her reading to him, or exploring and creating together. They're not only learning schoolwork but love for each other."

Sibling relationships take on new meaning in Melanie's rural Idaho home, where she juggles the needs of five children between nineteen months and six-and-a-half years of age. "Being such a large group so close in age they're learning respect and compassion just by interacting with each other." Melanie adds, "In other words, they're learning not to hit—finally."

> If my children are any indication, homeschooling is not a miracle cure for sibling squabbles. Sorry.

Extended Family Relationships

"Homeschooling lets us keep relationships which will be long term for our daughter," explains Michaela. "Our daughter's cousins are the closest she has to siblings and they're her best friends. Although the cousins will eventually go to school, our daughter's homeschooling will allow us the flexibility and time to keep getting together with them, unless their schedules become hopelessly hectic!

"She will also continue spending time with her grandparents, aunts, and uncles, which is very important—here in the San Francisco Bay Area it's too easy to get caught up with so many activities that familial relationships go by the wayside."

> Grandparents read with the children, tell stories of their past, teach hobbies, and take field trips near and far.

San Francisco isn't the only area where familial relationships go by the wayside. Hectic schedules tear family members' attention in a dozen different directions and complicate relationships even within the immediate family, sometimes to the point where dinner together becomes a rare treat.

Like Michaela, other homeschoolers live close to extended family, and flexible schedules provide equally important bonding with family members. Grandparents enrich their homeschooling grandchildren's learning experiences in many ways. They read with the children, tell stories of their past, teach hobbies, and take field trips near and far.

Close relationships with grandparents also contribute to the children's sense of well-being. Laura recently began homeschooling with her young daughter and son in Michigan. "With the children home all the time family becomes the central focus in their lives. They gain confidence through the security of knowing that Mom and Dad, Grandma and Grandpa are always there for them. Security is critical at this age," Laura explains, "and the children will be more self-confident because they've been secure."

Sometimes grandparents enter hospitals, hospices, or nursing homes, often adding more stress for time-strapped families. In these instances, homeschooling can become a mobile endeavor.

Marie also lives in Michigan, where she started homeschooling four children ten years ago. When her father-in-law entered hospice care and a nephew needed therapy-center care after an automobile accident, Marie found herself making frequent two-hour round-trip drives. She packed the children—and their books and projects—into the car, making time to visit loved ones, using audiotapes to make even the long driving hours fruitful. "My children learned more about caring and empathy from these experiences," adds Marie, "than they ever could have learned at home."

Allowing her time to nurture relationships with grandparents, aunts, uncles—and more, Melanie considers homeschooling "co-parenting at its best." Along with her own children she homeschools two stepdaughters. "If I wasn't doing this they wouldn't even go to the same school; they would be strangers to each other," Melanie says. "It also connects us in different ways; my spouse, his ex, and I all work together better because of homeschooling."

Living Family Values

The early years are a crucial time for character development. This is the age when fertile soil receives the seeds of honesty, respect, responsibility, courage, and self-reliance, and timely planting ensures the seeds grow right along with the child. Can homeschooling really make a difference in this important aspect of raising children even at a time when family values appear a distant memory of a bygone era?

While not a panacea for any of society's ills, homeschooling gives a family plenty of shared time. In their own ways, homeschooling parents use this time for four key means to instill family values:

- ✦ Service as an example for the child
- ✦ Frequent and honest conversation

✦   Shared life experiences, including reading, as lessons
✦   Real-life opportunity to put values into practice

In this context, it's easy and natural to share religious teachings. "We share our values with our daughters through Bible study, reading books with strong positive values, following a Christian curriculum and setting a good example," says Hope. "We tie in Bible verses and stories to whatever our family has just experienced."

In a small, rural Pennsylvania town, Monique uses example, Sunday school, and the Bible to teach values to five children from eight months to fifteen years old. "We recognize their values in everyday things they do," she explains, "like when they take their own money and purchase a small toy to donate to Toys for Tots, or when they're willing to share their special candy or toy without being told."

> No matter the approach to homeschooling, family values are alive and well in these homes, transmitted to the children through homeschooling's gift of time together.

Values are easily incorporated into the homeschool experience without religious teachings, as well. Erica is a seven-year homeschool veteran with two children in rural Washington state. "We read stories with morals that teach 'do unto others as you would have done unto you.' There isn't a day that goes by that a moral issue isn't addressed or at least discussed," she says.

Louise in California witnessed the fruits of conversations resulting from reading meaningful books and using life opportunities for learning values. "Parents have always told me how much their children appreciate our son for his peaceful way of being," Louise explains.

Maria sees real life as the best teaching material, but adds, "Sometimes I *make* opportunity, such as cooking a meal to take to a shut-in or a new mother. When my youngest (eight years old) thinks immediately of doing something for someone in need, whether it's making a card or wrapping up something to share, it lets me see she's learning 'living for others.'"

No matter the approach to homeschooling, family values are alive and well in these homes, transmitted to the children through homeschooling's gift of time together.

PATHWAY TO SAFETY

FOR DARBY, living in one of Texas's large urban areas, crime statistics on her city were an eye-opener. "Our city ranks third highest in violent crime, and much of this is perpetrated by young offenders,"

HOW WE DID IT

My son (seven years old) knows it's always best to tell the truth and if he does something wrong he should come and tell me. I could tell these lessons had sunk in when he came to me, not long ago, and told me he had accidentally broken a toy of a neighbor child but that he didn't mean to. The child brought the toy to our door and told me my son had broken it.

My son and I, together, figured out a way to fix the toy by gluing it back together. We even taped the corners of the toy's box, which were torn before we got it, and returned it to its owner stronger and in better shape than before it had been broken.

I felt this was a good lesson—in honesty (my son told me about it before the neighbor boy did), in taking responsibility for our actions (fixing what he broke), and in going the extra mile (fixing the box of the toy, even though it wasn't our fault that the box corners had split).

—LESLIE

she says. Not surprisingly, Darby lists safety among the top three benefits of homeschooling.

Rachel lives in another large Texas city, but had no idea how unsafe her eight-year-old son felt until her family decided to homeschool. It still brings tears when she remembers her son Roy saying, shortly after they started homeschooling, "Mommy, I feel safe here."

"I hadn't realized how horrible public school was for him until then," says Rachel. "Now, most of the tension that had been plaguing our family has disappeared. It was like being given my son all over again. This is very precious and I never want to lose him again."

PATHWAY TO HEALTH

HOMESCHOOLING AS A pathway to health is a benefit frequently overlooked. A February 1999 article in *Colorado Parent* recently raised its importance several notches. "According to the American Academy of Pediatrics (AAP)," states the article, "there are very few illnesses that mandate exclusion from participation in school. There is no evidence that the incidence of acute common respiratory diseases such as the common cold, croup, bronchitis, or pneumonia can be reduced by exclusion, thus exclusion is not recommended for these diseases."

This so-called expert advice explains why a nearby school recently shut down entirely when the flu claimed a majority of students and teachers as victims. I remember keeping my children home from activities when they had communicable diseases for two reasons; to get the rest they needed to recuperate, and so they didn't needlessly spread the disease.

Sleep Deprivation, Sick Buildings, and Stress

The homeschool pathway to health covers more territory than the common flu. "With homeschooling, children don't remain chronically sleep-deprived," says Valerie, a Texan homeschooling for nineteen years. "This is a problem today and perhaps one of the reasons for the rash of childhood depression, as well as the perceived rise in Attention Deficit Disorder."

Valerie also considers the implications of sick building syndrome. "It's affected many who attended school buildings built when it was chic not to have windows to distract children from their tasks."

Pediatricians report more symptoms of stress in early years children, and it's no wonder. Between the rush toward earlier formal schooling and enough extracurricular activities to require a date book, many early years children are subject to the same stress any overextended adult might feel.

"At age three Amy started suffering stress attacks in response to social circumstances which were overwhelming her," reports Michaela. "At co-op preschool she didn't want me to put her down, she refused to participate in circle times (too loud), and she gagged so much it seemed she would throw up.

"When she finally *did* throw up (at a Thanksgiving dinner) I realized we had to change our lifestyle. I pulled Amy out of preschool and cut down outside activities to those that were only low-stress. The local homeschool group had park days and this worked well for us. We could come and go whenever we wanted. Sometimes we stayed an hour, sometimes all afternoon, hours after everyone else left.

"After two months the gagging stopped altogether. Amy was happy and self-confident again with other children and adults, even in crowded situations." Michaela concludes, "Homeschool works for us because we maintain the quieter pace she needs."

Long-Term Care Made Easier

An early years child requiring long-term health care presents yet another challenge to busy families. Schools have schedules, and a child absent for an extended period of time must somehow fit into them. But when the individual child becomes the central point of education as he does in homeschooling, the schedule works around him and his important health needs.

At seven years of age Jane's son, Karl, was diagnosed with cystic fibrosis, a high-maintenance disease requiring daily treatments and therapy. Challenging enough, but "once a year or so Karl usually needs to be admitted to the hospital for IV medications, which are then continued at home," Jane explains. "The flexibility of home-schooling makes this so much easier, and I think he would have been ill more frequently if he'd been in school and exposed to so much more. I believe he's stayed healthier because we homeschool."

Time for Healthy Readiness

We wouldn't dream of pushing an introverted friend into addressing a large gathering unprepared. Yet in a rush to "ready" a child for learning, some adults force the equivalent on an unprepared young child. In the drive for academic head starts, the young child's emotional well-being often gets lost or ignored. Some children of three, four, or five easily handle an expanded social environment. But for others at this tender age, the security of the known is preferable to the insecurity of the unknown. Once again, homeschooling's gift of time comes into play.

"Our son (four years old) still needs me near him," says Laura. "When I am there he's a very outgoing child. If I leave, he becomes hysterical until I return.

"This doesn't feel like something he'll 'just get over.' He'll *grow* out of it when he's convinced himself I'm a permanent feature he doesn't have to worry about. I wonder how many kindergartners are permanently harmed by this insecurity when they're forced to deal with it too soon."

Homeschooling's benefit of time for healthy readiness extends to the emotional impact of rushed learning experiences. Maureen

> Homeschooling's benefit of time for healthy readiness extends to the emotional impact of rushed learning experiences.

could tell her son wasn't yet ready to start reading in second grade. "He probably would have been put in the 'slow' group at school and been scarred for life. This happened to my husband," she says, "and he still feels it was one of the worst things that ever happened to him."

PATHWAY FROM SCHOOL TO HOME

ANECDOTAL EVIDENCE SUGGESTS that families who take the path from school to home have different initial challenges from those faced by those families who plan a homeschooling journey before their children reach school age.

Missing Friends

No matter how short the school experience, children grow accustomed to the assumption they should be around many other children, some of whom become friends. When Angie's children first came home from school she was afraid they'd miss their friends, and she was right. "I tried to provide good experiences in homeschooling which would be fun and interesting, especially in exploring areas of personal interest," Angie recalls. "I helped them connect with other homeschooled children for more social contact with people their own age and made opportunities to keep in touch with people from school. I sympathized, acknowledging that everything, homeschooling included, has pluses and minuses." Angie's children made a smooth transition from school to home because she acknowledged and filled a gap that was important to them.

> If you bring *school* home along with the child, you may find you create needless road hazards along the way.

Homeschooling Baptism by Fire

Bringing a child home from school, especially under emergency circumstances, can leave you feeling as unprepared for your new job as if you just walked into the local hospital and volunteered to perform brain surgery.

It happened to Shannon in 1991. "Not to worry" is her sound advice. "I just had to figure out what we were going to do as we went along. It caused a touch of jitters from time to time," she admits, "but we'd been in public school and saw the poor job they were doing. I merely figured, 'how could I do any worse?'"

Even if you're confident you can do a better job than the schools, when you bring your child home remember you can accomplish the job differently than the schools do. If you bring *school* home along with the child, you may find you create needless road hazards along the way.

After her son began hating school in first grade because he didn't get the knack of reading, Monique attended many school consultations that "did absolutely nothing." She decided to homeschool and began by teaching reading "from square one."

"We were so nervous we more or less made it school at home," says Monique. "We really didn't know there was a better way. It's taken us five years to get out of that mentality. I wish we could go back and change our first years of homeschooling," she adds wistfully. "It was an adjustment; I would definitely lighten up."

> The homeschool learning journey can lead your family to many pathways with life-altering implications.

Your early years child already possesses the most important assets needed to learn. Nurturing them at home can lead your family to pathways with life-altering implications, reintroducing the joy of learning, broadening social opportunities, strengthening family relationships, and benefiting your child's safety and health. One question remains: Are *you* ready?

Let's find out.

SIMPLE STARTING POINTS

✦   *Spend as much time as you can observing your child at work and play.*

Notice favored methods of play or learning, then consider what fun activities you can do together to take advantage of those methods. Talk about the topics he's interested in to uncover additional clues.

✦   *Give your child opportunities to make decisions and choices regarding activities.*

He'll be drawn to those that produce the most pleasure giving you clues to potential strengths. Note also those he's not particularly fond of, and think about ways to adjust your approach.

✦   *Look for ways to include extended family or close friends in your homeschooling.*

Inclusion allows your child precious time with the special people in his life. Additionally, you're likely to develop support for your homeschooling efforts from those who mean the most to you, too.

✦   *Watch for or create opportunities for you and your child to practice family values.*

The early years child can help you bake cookies, make a card, paint a picture, or pick wildflowers and deliver them to someone in need.

✦   *If you're taking a child out of school, be sensitive to his needs as he adjusts.*

If desired, keep in touch with a few good friends. Make the transition to a different educational approach slowly. Plan some fun activities that weren't possible while he was in school.

RESOURCES

Books

Bennett, William J. *The Children's Book of Virtues.* Simon & Schuster, 1995.

Canfield, Jack, and others. *Chicken Soup for the Kid's Soul: 101 Stories of Courage, Hope and Laughter.* Health Communications Audio, 1998.

Eakman, B. K. *Cloning of the American Mind: Eradicating Morality Through Education.* Huntington House, 1998. Highly recommended reading.

Faber, Adele, and Elaine Mazlish. *How to Talk So Kids Will Listen and Listen So Kids Will Talk.* Avon Books, 1991.

Gardner, Howard. *Frames of Mind: The Theory of Multiple Intelligences.* Basic Books, 1993.

Healy, Jane M., Ph.D. *Endangered Minds: Why Our Children Don't Think and What We Can Do About It.* Touchstone Books, 1991.

Jenkins, Peggy, Ph.D. *The Joyful Child.* Harbinger House, Inc., 1989.

Markova, Dawna. *How Your Child is Smart: A Life Changing Approach to Learning.* Conari Press, 1992.

Miller, Jamie C. *10-Minute Life Lessons for Kids: 52 Fun and Simple Games and Activities to Teach Your Child Trust, Honesty, Love and Other Important Values.* HarperPerennial Library, 1998.

Riding, R. J., and Stephen Rayner. *Cognitive Styles and Learning Strategies: Understanding Style Differences in Learning and Behaviour.* David Fulton Publications, 1998.

Tobias, Cynthia Ulrich. *The Way They Learn.* Focus on the Family Publications, 1996.

4

GETTING *YOU* READY

FOR HOMESCHOOLING

In This Chapter

✦ Are you already homeschooling?

✦ Fear, doubt, and other internal stumbling blocks

✦ More help overcoming fear and doubt

✦ Life as your child's primary role model

✦ Legal issues: nothing you can't handle

✦ A beginner's checklist

✦ Simple starting points

✦ Resources

*T*HE EARLY YEARS are a period of constant learning, stretching, and discovering. Children are born to put their learning assets to work, and these assets serve them well if they remain intact. Families use homeschooling freedom to simply continue nurturing these assets into the years when children are typically sent to school.

ARE YOU ALREADY HOMESCHOOLING?

YOUNG CHILDREN LEARN. That's just what they do, and they're very good at it. (One early years researcher once called them "big, mean, learning machines.") This is why they learn so much, so quickly, long before they go to school. If a very basic definition of homeschooling is the act of a family taking responsibility for the education of its own children, aren't you already homeschooling to a degree? If so, you now need only decide who will continue guiding your "learning machine" on the journey she's already been on.

Marie explains, "After homeschooling my two older children for a while I realized although I didn't know about homeschooling, I was automatically supplementing their education at home.

"Any good parent does this," she continues. "This is why I tell people considering homeschooling since they're helping their children so much at home, 'You're already homeschooling part time!' This often startles parents, giving them just enough courage to bring their children home."

Spend a week or so simply observing your early years child as a "learning machine." Note how much time you're already devoting to helping him learn what he wants to know, but note also what he appears to be learning on his own. You, too, may be as startled as Louise when she realized what her little learning machine was up to.

> In homes across the country, families use homeschooling freedom to simply continue nurturing innate assets into the years when children are typically sent to school.

"While attending first grade my son was home from school sick. It was a stressful school year and he seemed to need time to just be alone with his thoughts, so I wasn't surprised to see him lying in front of the TV for long periods," Louise says. "It felt sad, though, to see him staring at a high school physics class in which a teacher was droning on; sad because I thought it showed how much the little guy needed to vegetate.

"A few days later my husband and I decided we would home-school. One evening I noticed my husband looking worried while our son waved his hands around telling him at length about how atoms work.

"My husband approached me later, still looking worried, and said, 'Are you sure we really want to take him out of that school? I mean, do you realize the kind of education he's getting there? They're already learning about atomic structure in the first grade! You should have heard—'

"I burst out laughing," says Louise. "It was right out of that physics class he watched. He had taken in every word because of personal interest in it—he had begun homeschooling himself!"

FEAR, DOUBT, AND OTHER INTERNAL STUMBLING BLOCKS

IF YOU AGREE you're already homeschooling, you might be wondering why that knot in your stomach reappears every time you consider not sending a school-aged child to school, gulp, at all.

It's a rare homeschooling parent who doesn't find *something* to worry about. Most of us struggle with our unique blends of fear, doubt, and other internal stumbling blocks while making this important decision. Our questionnaire respondents shared some of the feelings they experienced early in their homeschooling journeys.

Fears About Your Children—and Their ABC's

Many parents begin by questioning their ability to be with their children all day.

"Starting out, my biggest concern was how to *like* being with my children all day," shares longtime homeschooler Brenda. "Our first daughter and I locked horns frequently. Now I couldn't see being without them. I like and get breaks but they are wonderful people and good friends."

In her second year of homeschooling an eight-year-old daughter in Springfield, Missouri, Mona agrees. "I feared homeschooling would ruin our relationship. But because we're home together all

> Most of us struggle with our unique blends of fear, doubt, and other internal stumbling blocks while making the important decision to homeschool.

day, we don't have much choice other than to keep working on it!"

Understanding the importance of their children's education, other homeschoolers expressed insecurity about whether or not they could provide a good one.

Six children learn in Jillian's rural Minnesota home. She figured she'd try homeschooling for the first child, adding, "I was afraid I wouldn't know what to teach him and that he'd somehow get behind, that the education I'd provide would be detrimental." The family decided to take homeschooling year by year; that was twelve years ago.

Shawna, another mother of six in Illinois, feared her children would pick up her own math phobia. "I overcame it by playing with the children using our math manipulatives and books," she explains. "They love being with me and I love watching their faces light up with the joy of counting and learning. I could have missed that!"

After three years Jacqueline admits, "Although I've always been comfortable with my ability, I don't know that I have yet overcome my fears. I still wonder if I'm doing it 'right', but very seldom do I ever wonder if I'm doing the 'right' thing."

Take strength from knowing you're doing the right thing. It can eliminate many hazards.

Fears About Socialization for Everybody

Only a few respondents worried about children's socialization during homeschooling—perhaps an indication that the stereotype of a child chained to a kitchen chair is fading. Still, Anita, whose three children are five years old and under, finds she hangs on to concerns about the "S" word. "Then the rational me comes in and says, 'So what?'" she explains. "I get over it. This is why support friends are wonderful. We can talk about everything."

Erin thought homeschooling made her "different," and she feared the implications. Homeschooling a boy and a girl in Seattle, Washington, she went through a trial-and-error process of finding a comfort zone.

"I feared being isolated from the mainstream," shares Erin. "Along with that was a fear of being so 'different' when I didn't have other homeschooling friends. I overcame these fears by putting my daughter into public school half-day kindergarten. There I learned that just because I was around other very nice parents it didn't keep me from being lonesome! I figured better lonesome following my convictions than trying to fit into a school.

"Funny thing is," Erin concludes, "since I took my daughter out of school in 1994, loneliness—my worst fear—has not been a problem."

MORE HELP OVERCOMING FEAR AND DOUBT

PAULA OF NEW JERSEY, homeschooling her two children "forever," reports she made her decision to homeschool years before she even conceived. Here's an excellent way to hold fear at bay!

"I decided to do this back in 1977, seven years before I had a child," explains Paula. "By the time my older child was two I was used to the idea."

Darby, who describes her homeschooling as child-led, knew there were lots of resources available to get help, if necessary.

And with an equally practical attitude, Sarah of rural Wisconsin, mother of six homeschoolers, figured, "How hard could it be to teach a kid to read and count?"

If your stomach knot still hasn't gone away, take heart. Knowledge overcomes fear, and reading

> Knowledge overcomes fear, and reading just a few of the many fine books and magazines about homeschooling is a very good starting place.

just a few of the many fine books and magazines about homeschooling is a very good starting place.

Kate, homeschooling for three years, says, "My son was only eighteen months old but I knew I had 'miles to go before I slept.' After many years of reading I realized that I really do know my children better than anyone else, and as long as I can find the resources, I am the best person to educate them."

Another way to gain knowledge is to speak with homeschoolers in your neighborhood. Find them at advertised support group meetings, gathered at the neighborhood park or roller-skating rink, or browsing the library during school hours.

Sometimes, volunteering to help other new homeschoolers wipes away doubts.

"One of the best things I've done over the years is offer support to others," explains Corinne. "When I'm feeling low about homeschooling there's nothing more revitalizing than a visit from someone who is just taking her bullied/underextended/depressed/lonely child out of school. It reminds me why I'm homeschooling."

Perhaps the best way to overcome fears and doubts, though, is to take a step back, look at the big picture, and contemplate what your children are *already* learning.

"I didn't know how much I doubted myself until I got my daughter's achievement test scores back and saw that she was at or above grade level in every subject," says Anita. "I read the results with tears of joy and said to my husband, 'I'm not ruining her!' That gave me the confidence to know I was teaching more than I realized. I've since relaxed a lot in my approach and feel comfortable with my style."

LIFE AS YOUR CHILD'S PRIMARY ROLE MODEL

ONE OF THE first lessons homeschooling parents learn is little eyes watch everything they do every day—the good, the bad, and the ugly. Life as your child's primary role model may take some adjusting, but it's an adjustment you'll be happy you made.

Choosing Role Models

The question of *who* fills your child's time may be just as important as the activity that fills it. New Zealand researchers reported children as young as six months can learn new behaviors simply by observing other people's actions for as little as thirty seconds, according to a January 1999 *Los Angeles Times* article. If six-month-olds can learn new behaviors by observing for thirty seconds, imagine what a kindergartner picks up while all day observing a score of age-mates!

> The question of *who* fills your child's time may be just as important as the activity that fills it.

Homeschoolers are choosing themselves as their children's role models, coupled with whatever help they deem necessary carefully chosen from their community.

Easing In to Role Modeling

Those homeschoolers who think role modeling is easy consider homeschooling a natural extension of being a good parent.

"I always accepted responsibility for my children," says Gretchen, whose two children are now eleven and fourteen. "I love to learn and welcome modeling this characteristic. I have high expectations," she continues, "and know that few situations can model behavior and love of learning as well as I can."

"Homeschooling or not we are still the first role models our children have, and probably the most influential," explains Jillian. "I hope they pick up some of what I feel are good qualities that my husband and I have, but I also want them to know we're human and make mistakes, too."

Other homeschoolers stress the importance of just being yourself. "I'm doing what I need to for my business and family, trying to improve myself as a person, mother, citizen, businessperson, and wife," explains Patty, mother of three girls in Colorado. "I don't try to pretend to be better than I am for the children's sake. I want them to know me as I am and see we all have strengths and weaknesses and should always strive to be better."

In East Sussex, England, Priscilla keeps a stiff upper lip. "My children get to see life and me, warts and all. They may grow up to be grumpy old trouts, but I live in hope!"

Stretching into Role Modeling

Homeschoolers who feel life as a well-observed role model is difficult echoed a common refrain: I have my faults but I'm working on them! As with so many other aspects of the homeschooling journey, it's not just the children who learn and grow.

> Ninety-seven percent of respondents said they'd had no legal trouble, with one commenting "I couldn't believe how easy it was!"

Laura worries about losing her temper only to find the children mimicking her. "I 'rant,' as my husband puts it. I loudly tell the children how angry I am and then go on about it for a few minutes. That's the hardest role model thing for me, and I'm working on it every day."

"My children keep me in line and help me 'check' myself, so that's a good thing," adds Jane, "even if oftentimes difficult."

Dee believes role modeling makes her a more conscientious parent. "I have to think about what my actions are teaching my children and if how I handle things is the way I want them to handle them. This makes for a stronger marriage because we want to teach our children this is the right way to raise a family."

At the end of the day, each homeschooling parent makes the best of role modeling in the way most appropriate to particular circumstances and personality. They know it's a big job . . . but who better to tackle it than one who loves the children?

LEGAL ISSUES: NOTHING YOU CAN'T HANDLE

QUESTIONNAIRE RESPONDENTS were asked if they had *any* legal problems when they started homeschooling. Of the eighty-three total, seven respondents didn't answer and five replied their children are still too young to have created legal issues. A Texas mom reports, "An uninformed school superintendent gave me false information when my oldest was kindergarten age but it was never a threat." After a move within the state, truant officers visited twice but, she says, "I knew the law," and these visits never threatened her family's homeschooling.

Another respondent had no problems when she started homeschooling, but now faces difficulty as part of an ugly divorce. In recent years a portion of the dwindling homeschool-related legal problems surfaced as one piece of the greater picture of personal and legal battles inherent in divorce.

Seventy-one respondents answered the question about legal problems. Sixty-nine (97 percent) said they'd had no trouble, with one commenting, "I couldn't believe how easy it was!"

Homeschool support organizations remain vigilant regarding potential changes to laws that could affect the current positive climate, and once you begin homeschooling it will be wonderful if we can count you among the vigilant! Right now, though, you have many other things to ponder, and no need to worry about the legality of homeschooling if you remember . . .

When in Rome . . . Know the Law of Your Land

Travelers find that any well-planned trip to unfamiliar territory includes a brief primer on the laws of the land. A joyful journey quickly becomes a nightmare if you end up in jail for driving on the wrong side of the road! You don't want to start your learning journey driving on the wrong side of the road, so it's best to know what's expected of you *before* you take your seat behind the wheel.

Laws and regulations governing homeschooling are created and enforced at the state level, making each state's rules a bit different from the next. Generally, though, homeschooling is governed under three basic categories:

- ✦ *Private school laws.* A homeschooling family is considered a private school and subject to the same laws as private schools; lowest regulation status.
- ✦ *Equivalency laws.* A homeschooling family is considered to be providing "equivalent" instruction outside of compulsory attendance laws; mid-level regulation status.
- ✦ *Homeschooling laws.* Homeschooling is specifically addressed apart from other education approaches; most variable and greatest regulation status.

COMMON CAUSES OF JITTERS AMONG POTENTIAL AND NEW HOMESCHOOLERS

- ✦ Doing it "right"
- ✦ Having enough patience
- ✦ Teaching reading
- ✦ Knowing what to teach or teaching everything the children need to know
- ✦ Picturing what will happen when friends and family are told
- ✦ Finding others for children to play with
- ✦ Liking to be with the children all day
- ✦ Finding enough time
- ✦ Dealing with school officials

No matter which type of law governs homeschooling in your state, it's important you read and understand it. This serves two purposes: You will know what you need to do to fulfill requirements; and you will know when an official is requesting something that transcends the bounds of the law and be able to defend your position.

There are several ways to access your state law.

✦ *Call your local library.* If they don't have it they can direct you to a branch or system that does.

✦ *Look it up on the Internet.* All states now maintain legislative Web sites. National and state support group Web sites provide state law information.

✦ *Contact your state or local homeschool support group.* Here you'll not only find your state's law but get information on the local homeschooling climate, too.

✦ Coping with potential legal problems

✦ Teaching children of different ages at the same time

✦ Having enough time for self

✦ Being organized enough

✦ Coping with a newborn in the home

✦ Answering children who want to go to school

✦ Dealing with people scrutinizing children's actions and behavior

✦ Wondering what happens if homeschooling just won't work

You don't need to be a lawyer to understand your state's law, and by contacting a support group you'll have lots of help keeping you on the right side of the road should you need it.

The Record-Keeping Hassle

Homeschooling laws bring homeschooling record requirements that are as variable as the laws themselves. Thanks to homeschooling's status as private schools in some states, record keeping merely means keeping an attendance sheet. ("Honey, are you here?" "Yes, Mommy." Mark the calendar. Done.)

At the other end of the record-keeping spectrum are states like New York with specific homeschool regulations. Requirements include submission of an Individual Home Instruction Program (intended curriculum) shortly after announcing intent to homeschool. Progress reports are required four times each year. An end-of-year assessment, approved by the school superintendent, is also required and may take the form of a written evaluation by a certified teacher (or sometimes the parent) or an approved standardized test. The standardized test is required in the fourth grade and every other year thereafter.

> Understanding beforehand what records are actually required can minimize the hassle they present.

Your record-keeping requirements could fall anywhere between these two extremes, and you'll know exactly what they are once you study your state's law.

Respondents required to keep records say they spend anywhere from five minutes to several hours daily or monthly to complete paperwork. Several use Homeschool Easy Records, a software program marketed specifically for the job. Others create computerized log sheets specific to their needs. Some parents employ my tried-and-true "backwards" method. We jot down notes *after* something is completed, changing the focus from a plan book to a record of accomplishment easily transferred to a required progress report.

Many homeschoolers keep records because they *want* to. In these homes you'll find memories tucked away in logbooks, parent and child journals, portfolios, scrapbooks, photos, postcards, and over-flowing boxes. They do so for a variety of reasons:

- ✦ To remember, as with a baby book
- ✦ To prove progress, in case homeschooling is ever questioned by authorities
- ✦ To provide records in case the child goes to or returns to public school
- ✦ To show the children as they grow

Understanding beforehand what records are actually required can minimize the hassle they present. You can then find the most ef-fective, comfortable method to satisfy the actual requirements. This will keep you from submitting any more than is required—some-thing to avoid, as it could establish a precedent other homeschoolers might then be requested, however illegally, to meet.

A BEGINNER'S CHECKLIST

YOU'RE ALREADY HOMESCHOOLING to some degree, you know fears are surmountable, you understand life as a role model leads to personal growth, and you're considering homeschooling at a time it enjoys its greatest legal acceptance. Time to get down to the nitty gritty.

In chapter 1, the homeschool continuum explained the variety available in homeschooling. The continuum addresses eight impor-tant factors parents consider during the course of homeschooling. Here the same eight factors turn into a "beginner's checklist" to help you figure out your own learning journey. Keep in mind there are so many variables it's impossible to address all of them here, so this is only a rough guide. Make choices as they help you create the happi-est, most successful journey for your children.

Motivation

Our motivation continuum moved from public school problems to philosophical, religious, political, or other matters of principle. You know what is motivating you to homeschool, and for the most part that's all that matters.

For your peace of mind, though, you might want to create a short answer to the question, "Why are you homeschooling?" You'll find your answer, created during a period of idealistic thinking, can inspire you on the less-than-perfect days we all experience. Lots of folks are going to ask you this question, probably sooner rather than later. Having considered your answer beforehand, you may be able to present it with enough confidence to sway your mother-in-law!

Financial Expenditures

At one end of the continuum families spend very little on home-schooling, replacing dollars with ingenuity. Textbooks are expensive, but the library is free. Lessons on videotape are expensive, but PBS and the History Channel are free. Tutors are expensive, but neighbors may exchange lessons in their specialty for baby-sitting services. Curriculum is expensive, but homeschooling families in your neighborhood constantly outgrow theirs and move to another level. (Find more money-saving ideas in chapters 5 through 8.)

Move a bit on the continuum and you find families spending $200 to $600 per child per year. With careful shopping, this amount could get you some combination of the used textbooks you might desire, a few computer programs, group-rate tickets to local theaters and museums, art supplies, a few field trips, and some fun games.

Prepared curriculum, private tutors, and independent study programs will push spending to the opposite end of the continuum with expenditures of more than $600 per year per child. And, of course, you'll probably still want to visit those theaters and museums and play those fun games, too.

How much money can you comfortably spend on homeschooling? *That's* the most you should spend, and not a penny more. Know your budget beforehand, and you'll make the wisest decisions about where your money should go. Even if money is no object for your family, think in terms of spending as little as possible. This way you may keep the focus of homeschooling on the learning instead of the tools for learning. Your children will remember that they—not the tools—create an education worth having.

Approach

The approach continuum runs from structured to unstructured. How will you bend homeschooling to make a comfortable fit for your family? Many families start with the only model of learning they know—the classroom design—with Mom as teacher, children as students, and sometimes Dad filling the role of principal. The family works through subject textbooks, possibly following a prepared curriculum throughout a school-length day. If using a prepared curriculum, the children's papers may be sent off to the provider for grading and use in transcript preparation. This structured approach is often referred to as "school at home" or traditional homeschooling.

> How much money can you comfortably spend on homeschooling? *That's the* most you should spend, and not a penny more.

As noted in chapter 1, many homeschooling parents move further away from the structured approach the longer they are involved in homeschooling. Maybe they've spent some time observing a child's learning style, and notice that he learns better if he does something instead of reading about it. Parents may recognize a rigid schedule doesn't fit their lifestyle now that a younger sibling is in the "curious twos" or a new baby keeps Mom awake with the owls. Perhaps the family becomes involved in several activities outside the home as the children grow, and begins to feel stressed following a tight schedule. Maybe the

> The *eclectic* approach means almost anything goes as long as it works.

paperwork produces symptoms of burnout as it creates one too many demands on someone juggling the needs of a growing family.

You could begin somewhere in the middle of the approach continuum. Here, families might combine a math textbook with reading good children's literature together while snuggled under a warm quilt. Add some kitchen science experiments, educational videos from the library, the local support group's weekly writing meeting—and you note your time is well distributed among the typical school subject areas. This is often called the *eclectic* approach, meaning most anything goes as long as it works.

Starting at the unstructured end of the curriculum you might be called a *child-led* homeschooler or an *unschooler*. Here, daily-life activity, combined with your child's curiosity, provide "teachable moments": arithmetic in the grocery store, science through baking, history while Grandpa recalls World War II, writing via thank-you notes for birthday presents.

And there are all the points between these three examples! Deciding where your family will be most comfortable on the ap-

WAYS TO OVERCOME THE JITTERS

✦   Take strength from knowing you are doing the right thing.

✦   Join a homeschool support group.

✦   Make the decision *before* your children reach school age.

✦   Read about homeschooling.

✦   Volunteer to help others.

✦   Look at the big picture and focus on what your children *are* learning.

proach continuum helps you see how much homeschooling will cost. If your desired starting place looks too expensive, adjust your approach. Preparation narrows down the type of resources you'll peruse, saving time and possibly costly mistakes.

Even if you do make a mistake, you've got plenty of wiggle room to change and bend and adjust until you find something that works better.

Assessment

How will you judge how well your children are doing? Here, the continuum ranges from regular testing, required in standardized test form in some states, all the way to "I don't worry about it."

Your decision regarding assessment will be guided to a great degree by your approach. Traditional homeschooling and/or a prepared curriculum lend themselves to regular testing, oftentimes weekly.

The eclectic homeschooler, using a math text, for example, may feel comfortable her child is "getting it" if chapter tests are completed. An annual standardized test may calm a parent, child, or relative—easing the jitters and providing a snapshot of a year's growth. The test could also point to potential problem areas, as well as gifted areas, and provide guidance for adjustments in homeschooling approach beneficial to the child.

> The majority of respondents don't use tests because their intimate knowledge of daily learning replaces the need for testing.

The "I don't worry about it" end of the continuum most often accompanies the unstructured approach. No standardized test has yet been created that is capable of measuring this type of approach, anyway, because it doesn't follow a prescribed curriculum or even a learning timetable. The unstructured approach is very individualized in comparison to a curriculum.

In addition to or in lieu of administering state-required or optional standardized tests, some homeschoolers use the Children's

Skill Test, administer weekly spelling tests, review a self-made goals list, provide individual review for each child, have the children keep journals subsequently read by the parent, prepare a weekly log, or create a portfolio.

The overwhelming response to method of assessment, however, was observation. Respondents alternatively called this awareness, "we live with them," conversation, listening, "getting their commentary on books, news, and TV," "watching and seeing what's learned," involvement, and "it's quite obvious." These answers came from both curriculum purchasers and non-purchasers alike.

The majority of respondents don't use tests because their intimate knowledge of daily learning activity replaces the need for testing. Let this information save you money and stress.

Technology

For several years major trend analysts have predicted that computers, especially Internet access, will feed the growth of homeschooling. Today information, the basic tool of education, is yours for the taking through Internet Web sites and computer software. But is a computer necessary for homeschooling?

The computer is a tool for the homeschooler, one among books, paper, finger paints, and Play-Doh. A computer is unquestionably a powerful learning tool, but it's no more necessary to your child than it was to Alexander Graham Bell, Thomas Edison, or Agatha Christie, all homeschoolers who managed to do okay without the Internet. (See chapter 11 for more on computers and their use in homeschooling.)

Physical Space

Where will homeschooling fit into your life—literally?

You may choose to create a classroom in your home, complete with chalkboard, American flag, desks, and maps. At the other end of the continuum, you'll find no special accommodations at all.

Some homeschoolers find if they can spare the space, a room devoted to the "stuff" of homeschooling helps keep inevitable messes centralized. A table for writing, reading, and projects is useful, as are organizational bins stacked or on shelves easily reached by the children.

Homeschoolers making no special physical accommodations at all just may not have the space. Sometimes they don't want to encourage their children to think learning is separate from daily life. In these cases Mom and Dad's bed is a perfect place for reading, the couch is used for writing in one's journal or watching educational TV shows or videos, and your standard kitchen table doubles nicely as space for cooking and art and science labs.

> Dads who work full time take over bedtime story hour, participate in weekend field trips, or help turn family vacations into learning experiences.

If you're trying to create space, don't overlook attics, porches, patios, backyards, and forts. Thomas Edison's mother found the basement the best place for his laboratory.

Parental Involvement

How will the joys and work of guiding your children's learning journey be split between you and your spouse?

Typically, the honors go to Mom, but personal circumstances can easily change this. Some families find if one of two jobs must go, it's best that Mom retains hers. Dad could find his job lends itself to working from home and easily make the transition. In some cases, illness or injury keeps the father home and, if not serious, allows him a greater role in homeschooling, particularly if the mother must then go to work.

The homeschool continuum showed that in one-third of the homes, dads' roles increased over time. These fathers saw how much fun learning with the children can be, and soon realized they could make time to participate, even if it meant changing the family's schedule to keep the children up a bit later at night. Dads who work full time take over bedtime story hour, participate in weekend field trips, or help turn family vacations into learning experiences. They share favorite subjects with the children in the evening, or become the "sounding board" who happily receives excited reports of the day's experiences.

Use homeschooling's flexibility to keep participation comfortable and realistic for everybody as you decide who will take responsibility for what on your journey, remembering it can always change with circumstances or desire.

Outside Assistance

You'll soon discover the programs locally available to your children. Typically, the greater the general population in your area the greater the number of opportunities. Uncovering programs in rural areas can be a challenge, so you may have to dig a little harder than your urban counterparts, or even consider starting your own activities, which will eventually draw others.

Most families find there's plenty of time available, regardless of homeschooling approach, to incorporate several outside activities into their schedules. Consider what you would like the outside-the-home activity to accomplish. Some possibilities:

+ Fill an academic gap.
+ Allow your child to pursue an interest in more depth.
+ Provide additional socialization opportunities.
+ Provide volunteer experience.
+ Increase opportunity for physical activity.

This should help you narrow down the possibilities. Considering how far your pocketbook will stretch might further narrow your choices. Some activities are far more expensive than others. Here are some possibilities, ranging from those generally found to be most expensive to least expensive:

- ✦ Private tutors
- ✦ Private lessons
- ✦ Classes outside the homeschool community
- ✦ Classes within the homeschool community
- ✦ Community activities, such as Scouts, 4-H, sports teams, and so on
- ✦ Homeschool activities, like choir, park days, group-rate theater tickets, and so on

One additional consideration is "best use of time." Take just a few activities per week, multiply per child, and you might find you feel more like a taxi driver than a homeschooling parent. While this can leave you with a greater appreciation for quiet days at home, it can also lead to stress and constant concern as to whether you're spending enough time on other pursuits.

If you find you've created a schedule only a parent with three clones could fulfill, it's hard to take activities away from your child. For these reasons, start slowly. This will give you time to learn more about your child's needs and interests, further helping you choose just the right type and amount of outside assistance needed.

Congratulations. Consider yourself "prepared" as you now enter "A World of Curriculum Choice."

> One additional consideration is "best use of time." Take just a few activities per week, multiply that per child, and you might find you feel more like a taxi driver than a homeschooling parent.

SIMPLE STARTING POINTS

- ✦ *Read at least a few books and magazines about homeschooling.*

The exciting homeschool learning journey starts with your decision to travel along with your child. Reading just some of the vast amount of literature available will show you a wide variety of approaches, resources, benefits and challenges, and more.

+   *Seek out homeschooling support groups and meet other homeschoolers.*

While reading can expose you to a much larger cross-section of the homeschooling world, there's nothing like meeting other homeschoolers who can become friends who understand and support your decision, share information on the local climate, and answer your specific questions.

+   *Attend homeschooling conferences.*

While still not available everywhere, these gatherings are worth seeking out to provide you with fountains of information, opportunities to ask questions, and a sense of camaraderie rarely equaled elsewhere.

+   *Volunteer to help others who want to know about homeschooling.*

This is a great way to boost your own information stores on homeschooling, get to meet new families, and reaffirm your decision to homeschool.

+   *Observe your child's progress.*

Doubt and fear can vanish when you recognize your child is skipping down the learning path and revealing previously unobserved skills, abilities, and ideas.

RESOURCES

Books

Colfax, David and Micki. *Homeschooling for Excellence.* Warner Books, 1988.

Dobson, Linda. *The Homeschooling Book of Answers: The 88 Most Important Questions Answered by Homeschooling's Most Respected Voices.* Prima Publishing, 1998.

Griffith, Mary. *The Homeschooling Handbook.* Prima Publishing, 1997.

Hood, Mary. *The Relaxed Home School: A Family Production.* Ambleside Educational Press, 1994.

Part Two

A WORLD OF CURRICULUM CHOICE INSTILLS A LIFELONG LOVE OF LEARNING

5

LEARNING TO READ,

READING TO LEARN

In This Chapter

✦ A brief primer on how we read

✦ Homeschoolers and reading

✦ What does the early years child learn about reading?

✦ So many roads to reading

✦ Simple starting points

✦ Resources

$\mathcal{N}$O OTHER SKILL opens the potential for independent learning as much as your child's ability to read.

As a parent involved in the process, it's a thrill: "The day he 'clicked' in his reading was a great day," says Danielle of her first of five readers in Kansas. "I wouldn't have wanted to miss it for anything. He was glowing."

It's heartwarming: "My favorite thing is having a warm five-year-old cuddled in my lap, hearing the glee in his voice as he sounds out a new word then continues reading a simple sentence," says Marcia, who learns at home with three early years sons in Monterey, California.

A FEW WORDS ABOUT CURRICULUM

✦　*Curriculum: 1. All the courses of study offered by an educational institution*

Choosing or creating your child's curriculum isn't a frightening proposition when you understand a curriculum is simply the course of your family's study laid out. Your local elementary school chose one curriculum. You may choose the same, similar, or a completely different curriculum. Four basic options are presented for your consideration, all of which may be implemented individually or combined any way you like.

✦　*Purchase complete curriculum*

Proponents of particular educational philosophies offer curriculum based on their methods, among them Montessori, Waldorf, Charlotte Mason, Core Knowledge, classical, and religious education.

"We're about to purchase curriculum for kindergarten for our oldest," says Veronica, homeschooling in a rural county seat of Tennessee. "We picked this curriculum because it's relaxed and includes many of the same books we would buy, anyway."

✦　*Purchase curriculum components from a variety of sources*

"We purchase math, English, and reading curriculum," explains Ariana, "and supplement with computer programs, lots of maps and library materials. We homeschool year-round five to six days a week for about two-and-a-half hours

And it's not as hard as you might imagine: "I was afraid I wouldn't be able to teach my five-year-old to read, so I read everything I could get my hands on about teaching reading, about phonics and the controversies associated with teaching reading, about how writing and each day. We take materials along while on vacations. We do lots of field trips and camping. Doing a little every day," she says, "keeps the children motivated. They don't like to miss a day and want to 'do school' on Sundays."

✦ *Create your own curriculum*

Joni uses online resources and information from other homeschoolers to set benchmarks for each homeschooling session. "I use library, Internet, reference books . . . whatever is available to outline how to accomplish each benchmark. Then we dig in!" says Joni.

Marlene outlines yet another approach. "I use various books and usually have a plan at the start of the year, but seldom do we finish everything as originally planned. If something isn't working we drop it and find something else. We don't stick to a traditional school calendar."

✦ *Use daily life as a curriculum*

Using the simplest of plans, Holly's family "wakes up, does, learns, sleeps. The learning year begins on January 1 and ends December 31."

As homeschooling opens the door on a world of curriculum choice, it provides your family with many ways to accomplish your educational goals. This chapter and the two that follow will show you how homeschoolers find success in the early learner's acquisition of the basic skills—reading, writing, and arithmetic. Chapter 8 covers the rest.

reading intertwine, and numerous scholarly opinions on what works and what doesn't. I tracked down references and heavily used the interlibrary loan department of my local library. Meanwhile," says Bobbi, an Illinois mother of three with six-year-old twins, "my daughter learned to read."

QUICK & EASY

LETTER SOUNDS

My daughter arranges her magnetic letters into words, even nonsense words, and I sound them out for her. She adds letters to the word and I add the sounds. She's picking up letter sounds on her own just by playing this way.

A BRIEF PRIMER ON HOW WE READ

TAKE ONE magnetic resonance imaging device (MRI), a few computers, and a team of scientists and doctors who know what to look for, and you can watch a brain read. Oxygen-rich blood rushes to working brain cells. Researchers can observe this process because oxygenated blood has unique magnetic properties perceived by the MRI.

As reported in a 1997 *Baltimore Sun* article by Kathy Lally and Debbie M. Price, researchers showed subjects imaginary words, asking them to signal whether or not they rhymed. They asked if two words belonged to the same category, and had participants identify single letters. The results revealed "one part of the brain, the extrastriate cortex, identifies letters. Another part, the inferior frontal gyrus, identifies the sounds associated with those letters. And a third section, the superior temporal gyrus, reaches for meaning."

After two decades of research that included these findings and cost untold millions of dollars provided by the National Institutes of Health (your tax dollars at work), researchers say it shows children best learn to read with a three-part plan.

1. Phonemic awareness, or in plain English, learning the individual sounds that constitute a language, for example, "buh" as the sound of "b."
2. Phonics, or the letter-sound relationships available in the language.
3. Exposure to meaning, in other words, what you'd be doing anyway—continued reading aloud and providing books to exercise your child's growing skills.

Looks like a happy marriage of phonics and whole language, the two sides engaged in the "Reading Wars," doesn't it? The war rages on in public schools, however, each side insisting it advocates the "right way," even as researchers lament their discarded findings.

HOMESCHOOLERS AND READING

PARENTS TEACHING young children to read don't have two decades to fool around finding the best way to help them. Charged with educational responsibility, they rise to the challenge by applying a mixture of common sense and instinct, a mixture that comes out looking much like the researchers' recommendations. In practice, the challenge isn't all that expensive or difficult, especially when those little "learning machines" start itching to make sense of the symbols—the written words—that surround them.

Three traits emerge as common in homes where children are getting ready to read:

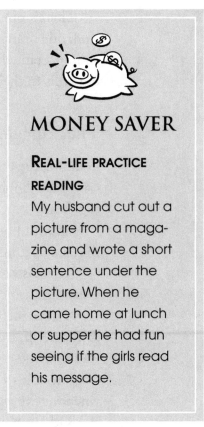

MONEY SAVER

REAL-LIFE PRACTICE READING
My husband cut out a picture from a magazine and wrote a short sentence under the picture. When he came home at lunch or supper he had fun seeing if the girls read his message.

+ Parents spend much time reading aloud a great variety of books.
+ The idea there is a perfect age or grade level at which to learn to read is often set aside in favor of waiting for the child's "readiness signal," usually between four and ten years of age.
+ Parents recognize that a successful approach for one child may not work with another, and experiment with different approaches as needed.

There's one more factor to consider as homeschoolers learn to read, one immeasurable by an MRI, one that may one day emerge as an important clue to homeschoolers' relative ease in passing on reading skills to their children.

The Snuggle Factor

Look for the common thread among responses to a memory jogger for homeschoolers: "Please share a favorite location for reading books together."

"We read books together either on my bed with a blanket or on the sofa in front of a fire," responded Kate.

Jane answered, "Mom and Dad's bed is the setting for reading every night since they've been babies."

"I have such precious memories of being able to snuggle under a comforter in front of the fireplace and read wonderful things to him way into the night—as late as we wanted," adds Louise. "And then we were able to get up in the morning and do more of the same until whenever we wanted."

Rather than the head, this phenomenon relates to the inner workings of the heart and emotions during reading. There's only one thing we can call it—*the Snuggle Factor.*

Your beginning reader is reaching into the unknown, a circumstance that causes uncertainty for most of us. The Snuggle Factor provides the early years learner with complete environmental comfort. Curled up next to her first and most important teacher, her biggest fan and most enthusiastic cheerleader, your child is surrounded by warmth, security, and love as she leaps into new territory. The Snuggle Factor frees her from any negative effects of uncertainty so all of her energy is employed in the task at hand. The Snuggle Factor effortlessly combines attention to head and heart, the whole child.

What of the Snuggle Factor in relation to you as parent teaching your child to read? That warmth, security, and love permeate your environment, too. Imagine how different an experience it is cuddled with your child under a blanket from standing in front of thirty children under the glare of fluorescent lights! With each story you share, with each step forward, no matter how small, connection grows.

When a Child Is Ready to Read

When asked how they knew their children were ready to learn to read, questionnaire respondents overwhelmingly described—in their own words—clear indications of phonemic awareness sprinkled liberally with an interest in the written word in the environment. Children who are ready for reading try to read store signs, street signs, cereal boxes, computers, and, of course, the books the families enjoy together each day. Readiness indicators appear at a wide variety of ages, with or without warning.

"Kerry had some foam letters for the bathtub and she could name them all at two years of age," Jane remembers about her now eleven-year-old daughter. "We read books constantly. She would ask what things were and my husband would tell her that the 'g' made a 'guh' sound and so on.

"One day, at four years old, she looked over my shoulder when I was reading my Bible and told me, 'Mom, that says Lord.'

"At that point," Jane explains, "we got out the easy readers and she just read, almost fluently. It blew us away. Our son Karl was almost as easy, but he was quite a bit older. He didn't have the passion for it that Kerry did."

Shannon, looking back at her experience with three children, remembers, "They enjoyed being read to and started trying to figure out how to do it themselves. When they started asking questions

MONEY SAVER

PRE-READING SKILLS
Something I learned early on was that if a child knows his shapes, it helps him learn his letters. So we made shapes out of sliced cheese. It was a favorite snack and I always asked how they wanted it: in squares, rectangles, or triangles; big or small; how many?

EARLY YEARS READING FAVORITES

READ-ALOUDS

A Wrinkle in Time

Caddie Woodlawn

Charlotte's Web

Chronicles of Narnia

The Drinking Gourd

From the Mixed-Up Files of Mrs. Basil E. Frankweiler

The Phantom Tollbooth

The Read-Aloud Handbook

The Secret Garden

Wizard of Oz

LEARNING TO READ

Bob Books

Chicka Chicka Boom Boom

Curious George Learns
    the Alphabet

Dr. Seuss' ABC: An Amazing Book

Hop on Pop

One Fish, Two Fish, Red Fish, Blue Fish

ON THE READING ROAD

American Girls series

Billy and Blaze series

Box Car Children series

Frog and Toad series

Hardy Boys series

In His Steps (children's version)

Little House Books series

Mad Libs

Miss Spider's Tea Party

Thunder Cave

Tin Tin series

SOFTWARE PROGRAMS FOR READING

Reader Rabbit series

Reading Blaster

Bailey's Book House

Livingbook series

like, 'What's that word?' I realized they were trying to figure out how to read," she explains. "So as I read aloud to them, I used my finger to point to the words. They followed along, watching the words above my finger. When they asked questions, I stopped and explained then returned to reading."

Sometimes children are neither ready nor interested according to the typical school schedule. While this brings in the psychologist cavalry and leads to disability labels in school, it's often just the naturally occurring difference of children's internal timetables. Liberated from the school's narrow timetable, your homeschooling child may follow her own.

MONEY SAVER

LEARNING LETTERS
We wrote letters on each other's back and guessed what they were.

Marie's two oldest children learned to read before the family started homeschooling. Her third child, a boy, was a toddler in their Michigan home when their homeschooling began. "I realized his learning style was much like his oldest sibling's who had so much trouble in public school," Marie recalls, "so I vowed I would take a 'hands off' approach—wait for readiness. We did play some phonics games and he listened to audiotapes of phonics sounds with books sporadically when he was in the mood. He learned to recognize signs, like McDonald's and Wal-Mart, and I read, read, read to him about everything.

"The child taught himself the basic math facts using a calculator and discarded workbooks, but didn't learn to read until he was one month shy of nine years old. Then he went from nonreader to reader in one day! Six weeks later he was reading one of his Dad's Louis L'Amour westerns, the newspaper, and everything else he picked up."

"Neither of my girls asked for significant help until age ten," says Paula of her child-led learners. "Reading is about the only area in which neither child proceeded far alone without a lot of drill offered in a structured format."

So Paula enlisted the aid of tutors, and noticed approximately one grade's progress in two months with one child. The other "started reading by choice at age twelve. Then she mostly read articles in the *Wall Street Journal* or *Business Week*."

QUICK & EASY

LEARNING LETTERS
We bought *two* sets of A Beka letter flash cards and played all sorts of games with them, spreading them out all over the living room, matching games, hide-and-seek games until my son knew the sounds they all make, which was at two to three years old.

Once ready, homeschooled children learn to read at age three—or thirteen. They learn to read in one hour—or over the course of three years. They use workbooks—or comic books. They begin with easy readers—or Louis L'Amour novels. Their preparation includes phonics or whole language or both or none—or their parents don't really know what they use because they're too busy reading and learning to worry about naming it.

WHAT DOES THE EARLY YEARS CHILD LEARN ABOUT READING?

LOCAL SCHOOL DISTRICTS may add their special touches, but early years curricula not only look much the same no matter the source, they review the same skills over and over throughout several years. Conversely, a majority of questionnaire respondents report their children became readers within three months to a year of attention to building reading skills *once they showed readiness*. Think about it: In homeschooling you know exactly what your child has learned. You note acquired skills and build from there. You have absolutely no need to repeat the same lessons year after year.

A typical early years phonics reading curriculum addresses the nuts and bolts of reading skills. These skills are laid out step by step in textbooks and workbook series available at many discount stores. If this approach fits your child's learning style, feel free to use it. If not, you have other options. Here's a brief look at curriculum items and what seasoned homeschoolers add to their frequent read-alouds (immersion in printed material) as learning aids both fun and effective. Keep in mind that writing skills go hand in hand with reading. We'll address these in the next chapter.

Letter Names and Sounds

Do you know the names of all the parts of your eyes? Or do you just *use* your eyes, with-out worrying about the terminology? Your child needs to know the *sounds* of letters to use them, not their names. Save yourself some time and use sounds as a starting point. She'll easily pick up letter names along the way, by asking, from ABC books, children's television, and learning the ABC song for fun.

Consonants and Consonant Blends

There's nothing magical about teaching consonant blends. Most simply combine their letter sounds. Watch for the few exceptions during reading sessions and use the opportunity to discuss them—constant exposure leads to retention. Here are the trickiest to watch for:

+ Consonants with more than one sound:
  c (cut, cell)
  d (dog, baked, educate)
  g (gum, giraffe)
  s (sit, has, sugar)
  qu (quest, lacquer)
  x (fox, exist, xylophone)
+ Combinations of consonants that create unexpected sounds:
  ch (Charlie, chenille, choir)
  gh (enough)

MONEY SAVER

WHAT BEGINS WITH "B"?
I write letters on Post-it notes and send the children off to stick the letters on things that begin with those letters or sounds.

ng (rang)
ph (pharmacy)
sh (show)
th (that, think)
wh (when)

✦ Combinations that create silent letters:
ck (rock)
gh (ghost, aghast)
gn (gnome)
kn (knick knack)
mb (comb)
rh (rhythm)
wr (wrinkle)

Here are some common homeschooling ways to learn consonants and consonant blends (Remember, these families also read, read, read!):

- ✦ Child asks, parent answers
- ✦ Sounding letters out, individually and together
- ✦ ABC Bingo
- ✦ Magnetic letter games
- ✦ Playing "What do you see that starts with 'buh'? Ends with 'guh'"?
- ✦ Computer phonics games
- ✦ Flash cards, making up games to play with them
- ✦ Alphabet song sung with letter sounds instead of letter names
- ✦ Tracing letters with colored pencils while saying the sound, individually and together
- ✦ Homemade picture stories
- ✦ Posters

Long and Short Vowel Sounds

Which comes first—long or short vowel sounds? Your choice. The nice thing about long vowel sounds is that they are just saying their names, an easy concept to grasp. On the other hand, more (and easier) words include short vowel sounds, leading to a larger reading vocabulary more quickly. If your child learns short vowel sounds first, teaching the long sounds goes along with the concept of adding silent "e" to the end of a word.

Again, the English language provides a few exceptions to the rules just so homeschooling parents can stay on their toes, watch for, and discuss them!

HOW WE DID IT

When we first started homeschooling my son was almost eight years old and knew how to read very basic things, like the *Little Bear* books. We got caught up in a lot of activity during our first month of homeschooling, and I hadn't spent time helping him with his reading so I started feeling anxious about it.

One day we had a long car ride ahead of us so I took along a few *Little Bear* and *Frog and Toad* books for him to read to me. I told him I had some books I'd like him to read aloud to me. He complained that he had planned on reading his Nintendo magazine.

After some fussing back and forth he asked if he couldn't just read aloud from his magazine instead. Thinking he was only looking at the pictures I got frustrated and smugly challenged him to do that.

He began to read a complicated passage with lots of long, multisyllable words—and he perfectly understood the instructions he was reading. I was astonished. He had pushed himself into real reading to get the information he wanted out of those magazines.

That was the beginning for me of a whole new way to look at homeschooling.

—LOUISE

✦ Vowel Sounds:
   a (cat, cape, want)
   e (hem, see—and silently changes other vowel sounds
   in a word)
   i (pin, ice)
   o (octopus, so, do)
   u (under, flute, put)
   y (happy, fly)

✦ Sounds of Vowel Pairs:
   ai, ay (pair, say)
   au, aw (laud, paw)
   ea (each, bread, steak)
   ee (feed)
   ei, ey (weight, they, ceiling, donkey)
   eu, ew (feud, new)
   ie (niece, tie)
   oa, oe (goat, hoe—changes in "shoe")
   oi, oy (oil, toy)
   oo (boo, book)
   ou, ow (shout, how)
   ue, ui (glue, suit, guide)

HOW WE DID IT

The thing that truly gave Joe mastery over his reading was reading to his little brother. Every night they would crawl into bed together. Joe was eight, Jim was almost four. And Joe would read him ten books every night, easy books. It gave Joe a chance to master reading. And, in the meantime, he taught Jim how to read! It was pretty amazing.

—RENEE

Here are some common homeschooling ways to learn vowel sounds:

+ Child asks, parent answers
+ *Teach Your Child to Read in 100 Easy Lessons*
+ Computer games
+ Applying sound vocabulary to written words
+ Dr. Seuss!
+ Rhyming books and games
+ Letting child read what she knows, helping her sound out other words, talk about how to tell when to make which sound

QUICK & EASY

INCORRECT GRAMMAR FUND

If someone used incorrect grammar and got caught she paid a nickel into the fund, which we used for family fun. As the children grew, it evolved to where if the person who caught you could correct you, then he got the nickel.

Lowercase and Uppercase Letters

Again you hit the question, Which comes first? Lots of ABC books focus on uppercase letters; they're easier for a child to write, and knowledge of them allows keyboard use. The Ball-Stick-Bird reading series uses all capital letters. If uppercase letters have captured your child's attention, or if these are the first letters she's picked up from the environment and she remains content to be read to, you might want to continue on this path.

However, books and magazines—even early readers—use lowercase letters. If you know your child is rarin' to read independently, she may feel she's on a slow boat to nowhere if you start with uppercase letters. In this case, common sense dictates lowercase letters as your starting point.

Here are some common homeschooling ways to learn lowercase and uppercase letters:

- ✦ Child asks, parent answers
- ✦ Alphabet books, puzzles, charts, flash cards
  (*Dr. Seuss' ABC: An Amazing Book,* a definite favorite)
- ✦ Computer games
- ✦ Magnetic letters
- ✦ Tracing with finger
- ✦ Computer keyboard (uppercase)
- ✦ Sponge letters
- ✦ Alphabet coloring books
- ✦ Notes, scavenger hunts, secret messages

Sight Words

Some English words are used so frequently, yet take so many illogical spelling twists and turns, they're best learned by sight. These are some of the first words, along with your child's name and other words personally important to her, that begin to turn your reader into a speller. Relax; there are only eighteen of them:

✦ the	✦ could	✦ said
✦ of	✦ would	✦ some
✦ was	✦ should	✦ come
✦ from	✦ one	✦ there
✦ any	✦ two	✦ other
✦ many	✦ says	✦ people

Have fun with these. Choose one as "word of the day" and have your child shout it out when encountered in the day's stories. Put one word each on index cards—which is the shortest word? Longest? Which ones start with "s"? End in "e"? How many phrases can you create with the cards? Sentences? Let your child write the phrases and sentences. Have her make another set of cards—spread one set on the floor and let her place matching cards on top. Using both cards for half of the words, turn them upside down, and you've got a "concentration" game. Exposure through play will lead to recognition and spelling proficiency.

SO MANY ROADS TO READING

WHILE HOMESCHOOLERS pass on to their children the same basic reading skills as those included in a public school curriculum, the methods used are as individual as fingerprints. Take a look at just some of the "reading journeys" already traveled to help you map out your own route.

The Osmosis Method

For some homeschooled children, the ability to read simply appears, as Minnesota homeschooling mom Jillian discovered, "by reading and being read to, I guess."

In New Zealand, Corinne learns at home with four sons. "I didn't teach my first and my second son to read—it 'just happened' long after I had given up on it ever happening," says Corinne. The boys were nine-and-a-half and eight-and-a-half years old.

"He learned to read by reading," says Washington homeschooler Erica of her oldest child. "We would go over basic phonetic rules if he wanted to and I'd remind him of the rules as he read.

"We read out loud, he to me and I to him. It was so difficult for him to read out loud he came to dread it. He started picking up different things and reading silently on his own."

Erica's son likes cooking, "and I noticed he could easily follow written cooking directions, the first clue he could read," she says. "He finally said he wanted to read and bought some secondhand *Goosebumps* books (I think he liked the covers more than anything). There is no question in my mind he is reading and comprehending." Erica concludes this reading mission was accomplished

QUICK & EASY

PHONEMIC AWARENESS
Play with sponge
letters at bath time.
Say or sing the sounds
they make. Make
rhymes, use alliter-
ation. Get wet—
have fun.

when her son was about eight or nine and reading fluently.

The Building-Block Method

With phonemic awareness as the first building block, a child can begin to puzzle out books. With a reading sibling or parent by her side pointing out important clues and answering questions, the learner assimilates the building blocks necessary to reach reading proficiency.

Jacqueline remembers her only child began asking about letter sounds, capital letters, and punctuation at about four-and-a-half years of age. Then, as he tried to read to his parents, "he would sound out a word, following the 'rules' he knew.

"If there were new rules that applied or if a case was an exception, we talked him through it," says Jacqueline of the very irregular English language. "We always praised him for following the rules as he knew them and said, 'That's just how you would think it would be, but English is weird, and this word is . . .'"

This Texas-based homeschooler acquired the building blocks necessary to become a reader at seven years old.

The Reading Wars Reconciled

Carly of western Kentucky used a modified phonics approach with her three children, who learned to read at age four, six, and five, respectively. "We've used grammar texts but we depend primarily on learning from context in recreational reading and conversation," she explains.

Pauline uses some phonics—"but also whole language; Darla seems to need both to truly grasp these concepts." She reports this first of two children, at five-and-a-half years old, "is on the verge" of independent reading.

Traditional Method

Things look different still in Kathy's Denver home where "well planned" is the homeschooling style for her six- and seven-year-olds.

First, the children wrote rows of uppercase, then lowercase letters until they could recognize the letters out of order. Then, with the Bible, McGuffey readers, *Comprehensive Curriculum,* and age-appropriate workbooks, Kathy's family learned one lesson each day. There's lots of reading together, too, and the older child reads for thirty minutes before bedtime. Crediting consistency, Kathy reports that her children began reading at five and six years of age.

At suppertime in a suburban area of British Columbia, Canada, you'll find Maureen's two children (ages five and a half and eight) practicing skills in story order. When Dad gets home, the children tell him what happened in the book they read that day.

A "structured, child-centered" homeschooler and an early reader herself, Maureen was concerned when her second grader wasn't reading independently. "We used *Learning Language Arts Through Literature*—blue book primarily, and *Hooked on Phonics* a little bit." It was her husband, "who didn't read anything he didn't have to until university," who suggested not pressuring their son.

"I made sure he had access to lots of books," Maureen says. "The first two chapter books he eventually read were short chapter books

QUICK & EASY

GROUP READING
Use reading-level appropriate books and apply variety. One day you can read aloud then suddenly stop, clueing your child it's her turn; then she does the same. You may read aloud asking your child to chime in every time she knows the word. You may read one page, your child the next. She can watch for the "sight word of the day."

> You can read aloud books above her skill level, increasing her vocabulary as she uses context clues and conversation to understand new words.

I'd read to him before. He said he chose them because he figured he would remember the story well enough to figure out any hard words."

Marcia, another traditionalist, is happy with her family's slow, gentle, diligent approach.

"We read five stories from *The Beginner's Bible* every day," she explains, "with one child on my lap and the other two beside me. I point under each word while reading, randomly pausing at words for the children to read them, which keeps their eyes following the text.

"For phonics," Marcia continues, "we work through the Noah Webster blue-backed speller, doing pages 1 through 4 day one, pages 2 through 5 day two, pages 3 through 6 day three, and so on, so it works out that each page has four days devoted to it." For reading enjoyment, Marcia's beginning reader chooses Bob Books.

Continue reading aloud even as your child develops reading skills. You'll both continue receiving the benefits of the Snuggle Factor. You can read aloud books above her skill level, increasing her vocabulary as she uses context clues and conversation to understand new words. She'll strengthen comprehension skills by hearing more complicated stories, all the while being exposed to fine examples of proper English grammar. These skills will help as she also becomes a writer.

HOW WE DID IT

We all pile on the couch and snuggle under a blanket with a big pile of books next to us. The children will sit for over an hour at a time, and I usually have to throw them off when I go hoarse . . . and we get to do this almost daily!

—GAIL

SIMPLE STARTING POINTS

✦ *Read, read, read together!*

Reading together exposes your child to written language and builds interest in unraveling its mysteries. But reading time is also snuggle time; a time to gather close together under covers, alongside siblings and the family pet. This emotional warmth feeds a lifelong love of reading.

✦ *Build your child a personal library.*

Purchase as many books as you can, as favorite books are subject to *many* repeat performances.

Request highly regarded children's books as gifts from relatives and friends when birthdays and holidays roll around.

Hit those yard sales and library book sales where treasures can be purchased for dimes and quarters.

✦ *Visit your library often.*

Both of you should select a wide variety of books from which your child may choose throughout the loan period. For the youngest readers, bright, colorful illustrations grab attention. Simple rhyming books increase phonemic awareness. Easy books provide the beginning reader with satisfaction and success early and often.

✦ *Let your child see you read.*

Talk about why you're reading: to learn more about this new computer (finding facts); to know more about the earthquake (a way to get news); to discover how my friend is doing (personal communication); to see how this story ends (enjoyment).

✦ *Plant early seeds that reading is fun, then make it so through games!*

Lots of games are available for purchase, but you can also create your own. (See sidebars.)

✦ *Make sure your child has quiet time to practice her new skills.*

When you sit down for cookies and milk or at dinnertime, ask her what's happening in the new story or what interesting facts she's gleaning from a nonfiction book. This will give her a chance to share the book with you, and you can gauge comprehension or answer questions she may have.

RESOURCES

Books for Teaching Reading

Branstetter, Kacy, ed. *Comprehensive Curriculum of Basic Skills.* American Education Publishing, 1994.

Duffy, Cathy. *Christian Home Educators' Curriculum Manual 1997–1998—Elementary Grades.* Grove Publications.

Engleman, Siegfried, and others. *Teach Your Child to Read in 100 Easy Lessons.* Simon & Schuster, 1986.

Kaye, Peggy. *Games for Reading.* Pantheon Books, 1984.

McGuffey, William Holmes. *McGuffey's Eclectic Readers.* Van Nostrand Reinhold, 19889.

A Common Heritage: Noah Webster's Blue-Back Speller. This is out of print, but you may be able to find a copy. ASIN: 0208019081.

Modern Curriculum Press Practice Readers. Call 800-321-3106 for information.

Books About Reading

Chall, Jeanne S. *Learning to Read: The Great Debate.* Harcourt Brace Jovanovich, 1995.

Flesch, Rudolf. *Why Johnny Can't Read: And What You Can Do About It.* HarperCollins, 1986. A classic.

Williams, Jane. *How to Stock a Home Library Inexpensively.* Blustocking Press, 1995.

Periodicals

Book Links: Information on books by themes; 434 W. Downer Place, Aurora, IL 60506-9954; 800-545-2433, ext. 5715; http://www.ala.org/BookLinks; bimonthly; $24.95/year.

The Horn Book: 11 Beacon Street, Suite 1000, Boston, MA 02108; 800-325-1170; www.hbook.com; bimonthly; $36/year.

LUNO (Learning Unlimited Network of Oregon): 31960 S.E. Chin Street, Boring, OR 97009; 503-663-5153 (inquire about newsletter and Phonetic Fun booklets; sample newsletter for $1 plus stamp; indicate age level required).

Programs

Alpha-Phonics. 888-922-3000; www.alpha-phonics.com.

Ball-Stick-Bird Publications. Box 592, Stony Brook, NY 11790; 516-331-9164.

Children's Book of the Month Club. Camp Hill, PA 17012-9852.

Hooked on Phonics. 800-ABCDEFG (many more respondents disliked this program than liked it; expensive).

Learning Language Arts Through Literature. Common Sense Press; 352-475-5757 for a dealer in your area.

Scaredy Cat Reading System. 800-745-8212.

Sing, Spell, Read & Write. International Learning Systems, Inc., 1000 112th Circle N., St. Petersburg, FL 33716; 800-321-8322; www.singspell.com.

Curriculum Sources

A Beka. 800-874-2353, ext. 37.

American Education Corporation. 7506 North Broadway, Oklahoma City, OK 73226; 405-840-6031; http://www.amered.com.

AZ Home Academy. P.O. Box 13172, Tucson, AZ 85732; 888-235-1595; www.azhomeacademy.com.

Calvert School. 105 Tuscany Road, Baltimore, MD 21210; 410-243-6030; www.calvertschool.org.

Charlotte Mason Resource and Supply Company. http://www.charlotte-mason.com/.

Christian Liberty Academy. 800-348-0899.

Clonlara School. 1289 Jewett Street, Ann Arbor, MI 48104; 734-769-4515; http://www.clonlara.org.

Five in a Row. 14901 Pineview Drive, Grandview, MO 64030; 816-331-5769; http://www.fiveinarow.com.

Oak Meadow School. P.O. Box 740, Putney, VT 05346; 802-387-2021; www.oakmeadow.com.

Robinson Curriculum. 2251 Dick George Road, Cave Junction, OR 97523.

Unschoolers Network Curriculum. Level I (K–1); Level II (2–3); 2 Smith Street, Farmingdale, NJ 07727; 732-938-2473.

Waldorf Education & Curriculum Resource Guide. 9200 Fair Oaks Blvd., Fair Oaks, CA 95628; 916-961-8729; free introductory material.

Catalogs

Chinaberry Book Service. 2780 Via Orange Way, Suite B, Spring Valley, CA 91978.

Dorling Kindersley Family Learning. 7800 Southland Blvd., Suite 200, Orlando, FL 32809; 407-857-5463; www.dk.com.

EDC Publishing (U.S. source of Usborne books). P.O. Box 470663, Tulsa, OK 74147; 800-475-4522

Harper Trophy (children's paperbacks). 10 E. 53rd Street, New York, NY 10022; 800-242-7737.

Progeny Press. P.O. Box 223, Eau Claire, WI 54702-0223; http://www.mgprgeny.com/progeny (Christian perspective).

Stories on Cassette

Family Classics Library. Newport Publishers, 100 North Lake Avenue, #203, Pasadena, CA 91102; 800-579-5532.

Greathall Productions, Inc. P.O. Box 5061, Charlottesville, VA 22905; 800-477-6234.

Growler Tapes Audio Adventures. 800-GROWLER.

Jay O'Callahan. Box 1054, Marshfield, MA 02050; 800-626-5356.

Odds Bodkin Rivertree Publications. P.O. Box 410, Bradford, NH 03221.

Software

Bailey's Book House. Edmark Corp.; 800-691-2986.

Living Books. Broderbund; 800-521-6263.

Reader Blaster. Davidson & Associates; 800-545-7677.

Reader Rabbit. The Learning Company; 800-622-3390.

Web Sites

Aesop's Fables: www.pacificnet/~johnr/aesop

Amazon for Kids: www.Amazon.com/kids

Carol Hurst's Children's Literature Site: www.carolhurst.com

Grammar/Reading Packets: www.readybygrade3.com

Homeschool Teacher's Lounge—Teaching Ideas for Structured Home-schoolers: www.geocities.com/Athens/Oracle/4336

Kids' Reads: http://www.kidsreads.com (reading lists and reviews by ability, children's reading club)

Phonics Worksheets: www.schoolexpress.com/free/phonics/index.html

Reader's Digest Children Books. www.readersdigestkids.com

Seussville. www.randomhouse.com/seussville

6

WRITING:

DEAR GRANDMA

In This Chapter

+ Homeschoolers and writing

+ What does the early years child learn about writing?

+ Motivation to keep writing

+ Simple starting points

+ Resources

*H*EALTHY CHILDREN learning to break reading's mysterious code naturally want to create some code of their own, making reading and writing as inseparable as *Frog and Toad*. Reading breakthroughs solidify for your children the notion that words communicate ideas. What better way to start writing than by communicating their own ideas? With a little help from you ("Mrs. Mom, could you please come take dictation?"), the thrill of making ideas real and accessible to others helps inspire attention to writing's less glamorous, mechanical aspect. . . .

Maybe. Some children, perfectly content to absorb ideas from the world around them (remember, early years children are generally file *collectors*) aren't as eager to write during this time frame.

> The little "learning machines" who learn to walk by walking, speak by speaking, and read by reading also learn to write by writing.

QUICK & EASY

COMMUNICATE

Help your child develop the habit of snail mail or e-mail communication. Letters can go to siblings, parents, grandparents, pen pals, favorite food company, editor of a favorite magazine, favorite toy manufacturer, or whoever catches the child's interest.

The physical act of writing requires eye-hand-brain coordination some early years children haven't yet developed. For these children, writing practice is a laborious struggle, and they can make practice into a laborious struggle for everyone involved. Further, writing a word without visual aid requires a mental image, an abstraction, another skill that children have to grow into—at different rates in their own way.

You're developing your observation skills, however, so you'll be the first to know when it's time to help your budding Ernest Hemingway on to the writing road.

HOMESCHOOLERS AND WRITING

THE LITTLE "learning machines" who learn to walk by walking, speak by speaking, and read by reading also learn to write by writing. If using a purchased curriculum or traditional method, some families follow the step-by-step approach you remember from grade school. Textbooks and workbooks spend a lesson or three covering one writing or grammar skill, such as printing the letter "A" or using capital letters, followed by practice in application.

Other homeschoolers tend toward a more natural, "in context" approach. Frequent sessions of reading together, along with the child's original dictation or stories, present just as many opportunities as workbooks for lessons regarding writing. This approach frequently increases learner *interest*.

Increased interest moves the learner beyond the "what to do" to "Why did they add capital letters to *Sam* and *Minuteman,* Mom?" It's just as easy to find and discuss the "A"s or other capital letters in a passage from this, his favorite book, or his own story about pirates, as it is to find them in disjointed workbook sentences with no particular significance.

Coupling this approach with patient waiting for signs of readiness may lend greater efficiency to your lessons, again helping explain home-schoolers' relative ease in passing on skills that take years to acquire in public school settings. Rather than occupying separate lessons, subjects like reading, writing, vocabulary, and, let's say, history all fit within the same reading and subsequent discussion. The learning sticks better because it holds meaning. And if observation shows you that your child already understands that all proper nouns begin with capital letters, you don't need to repeat this lesson over and over. You move on.

When a Child Is Ready to Write

Letters and their sounds are the building blocks of both reading and writing, so your child's questions about "sounding them out" in either reading or writing lead to understanding their use in the other.

Give the pre-writing, early years child pencil, pen, crayon, marker, or paint brush, and you'll be treated to "play" writings, a sign the child understands "what" he's supposed to do—put marks on paper. Interest in "how" to do this to communicate appears at various ages, often starting with the very high-interest word known as one's name.

QUICK & EASY

We practiced writing on paper but also using nontraditional media, such as writing in powdered Jello mix spread in a baking pan—shake the pan to erase each letter. My son licked the Jello powder off his finger between letters, which he thought was really fun!

Generally, home-schooling parents see writing as an ongoing process built through exposure to the written word over an extended period of time, as the child's interests and abilities grow.

Jacqueline knew her son was ready to write when he began asking how to write his name as he pretended to write.

"Soon after my oldest child turned four," explains Doris, who has always homeschooled three children in Charlotte, North Carolina, "she began writing her name everywhere—I knew she was ready!"

Joni's five-year-old is "just now starting to work on writing as a subject versus doodling letters and pretending to do her writing lesson. Her interest in playing at writing is why we've started learning about real writing."

Interest expands to additional sounds and significant words. Melanie's six-and-a-half-year-old now "constantly asks how to do this. He tries to sound out words," she says, "and is starting to recognize writing patterns. I find putting his spoken stories to paper for him to illustrate has done a lot to further his interest."

Keep plenty of interesting writing materials where your child can easily get them. Make a letter chart and hang it where it is easily seen from a comfortable writing spot. Continue playing games with word cards, ABC Bingo, and the many other reading proficiency games, and interest will grow into skill.

Age of Interest Varies

Primarily information gatherers, some children in this age group aren't inclined to disperse information through writing. Indeed, some homeschooling parents report their children didn't move far beyond very basic writing skills until reaching ten, eleven, or twelve years of age, at which time something personally important compelled them to begin. At these ages, they polished and honed additional writing skills quickly.

Generally, homeschooling parents see writing as an ongoing process built through exposure to the written word over an extended period of time, as the child's interests and abilities allow.

WHAT DOES THE EARLY YEARS CHILD LEARN ABOUT WRITING?

AS WITH READING, schoolchildren across the country study a fairly standard writing curriculum that presents basic skills bit by bit and repeatedly. Inexpensive, consumable handwriting workbooks abound, and are great inspiration for self-directed practice at this stage. They can encourage more practice than a blank sheet of penmanship paper.

We'll cover the nuts and bolts of incorporating early writing skills into the homeschooling environment, where immersion in printed material occurs daily.

Printing and Cursive Handwriting

There's no getting around practice when learning to form both print and cursive letters. Tracing letters, followed by copying models, sets many homeschooling children on their printing way.

Sarah's children learned "mostly by watching other people write, asking questions, and copying letters off the list I put on the wall." She also remembers, "They had access to one of those cheap handwriting workbooks for good measure."

"We used some drill books our daughter hated," says Tanya. *"Teach Your Child to Read in 100 Easy Lessons* had some 'sound writing,'

MONEY SAVER

Practice printing with chalk on a sidewalk or driveway—alphabet hopscotch, anyone?

HOW WE DID IT

Our daughter writes very little, only lists and words of her choice with help from others. But she loves to read, so she will write someday. Our oldest rarely wrote anything until she was twelve or so. Now she writes beautifully, mostly e-mail, but she's also beginning to write creatively. Now that she has read so much she's developed her own opinions and has something to say. Writing is just an extension of speaking your mind. You have to have something to communicate first.

—PATTY

which was similar to lots of lowercase letter practice. I used manuscript paper and wrote something she copied."

Tanya adds, "Currently we're using *Draw Write Now,* which she likes a lot. She draws using a series of shapes, then copies three to five sentences that go with the picture. I also let her trace everything at the end with a 'grown-up' marker which gives her a second practice at the letters."

One of Erica's sons started printing by writing his name at four. "We worked in workbooks but he hated them," she says. "Various needs for writing caused him to use what he knew, like thank you cards, party announcements, or signs to sell things. I think he was writing before he could comfortably read. Everyday, useful, and important things to a child gave him opportunity to learn to print."

Following guidelines and using lots of practice, Doris focused on printing for three to four years before introducing cursive writing. "I didn't feel their motor skills were ready for cursive," she explains. "I wanted them to have manuscript under their belts first."

The Cursive Dinosaur?

The path to cursive writing skills runs parallel with that of printing. It's so similar, in fact, Sarah taught this skill by showing her children "the printed letter 'hiding' in the cursive letter, and how the curly parts are there just to connect one letter to the next."

While a major Christian curriculum company starts teaching cursive writing in kindergarten, many questionnaire respondents noted they save these lessons until the children are older and/or express interest; that is, if they have lessons at all.

When I decided the aggravation with my last child over cursive writing just wasn't worth it, I thought it an anomaly, but apparently my son was onto something. Gretchen's older child learned cursive in school "but it's largely forgotten." The younger, at eleven years old, doesn't use it, either.

QUICK & EASY

PRE-WRITING SKILLS
Start by drawing waves, loops, and swirls, big and little.

Blame the times—and the computer. "We haven't bothered about this at all," says Priscilla. "Most, if not all, of what we read is printing. So as long as they can write legibly, and even this begins to fade somewhat the more we use keyboards, I'm not bothered about 'joined-up' writing in the least."

Maureen's cursive plan for her two boys includes "showing them what it looks like and helping them read it." If they don't want to learn, "I don't think I'll spend time on it. In this day and age, cursive writing isn't as important as it used to be. Legible printing and keyboarding skills are essential."

Will keyboard lessons replace penmanship lessons? Only time will tell. This possible trend is presented so you can gauge "best use of time" regarding these skills, and consider the value of "cursive skirmishes" should they break out in your home, too.

Here are some common homeschooling ways to learn handwriting:

- ✦ Child asks, parent answers
- ✦ Tracing—sometimes with colored pencils or highlighter marker
- ✦ Copying parents' writing, books, packaging, and so on
- ✦ Computer programs
- ✦ Practice writing family names, thank you notes, signs to sell things, making lists, and so on
- ✦ Inexpensive handwriting workbooks and penmanship paper
- ✦ Keeping a journal
- ✦ Whiteboards, chalkboards, easels with big pencils and lined paper
- ✦ Letter chart hung on wall
- ✦ *Ready Writer*
- ✦ *You Can Teach Your Child Successfully*

Spelling and Grammar

There's an unproven theory that some folks are natural born spellers—and then there's the rest of us. Whether your child picks up spelling by osmosis, as some homeschooling parents report, or is one of those who'd rather put off learning the skill until needed and then catch up quickly, homeschooling lets you meet his needs.

> Like wine, children's spelling often improves with age.

Those books you loved to hate as a kid, the ones with age-appropriate spelling lists for weekly tests, are still around and thriving. Leslie put a twist on this idea when her son "read a new story from a Modern Curriculum Press Phonics Reader. We would write a list of words from the material." Leslie continues, "I selected words demonstrating the skill he was studying—blends, digraphs, long vowels, whatever. I let my son try to fig-ure out how each word was spelled by saying its individual sounds slowly, then I helped him with the variable parts. Between self-exploration and guided study he learned to spell each word correctly."

Shannon's family uses reading, writing, answering questions, and a spelling workbook, while Marlene employs a phonics approach, and Paula primarily asks questions and corrects mistakes.

Like wine, children's spelling often improves with age. Doris tried the memorization route without success. "My nine-year-old is now beginning to spell well based on her experience and reading."

When Corinne's oldest was an early years child he resisted in-struction and struggled with spelling. "He improved a lot doing a couple of correspondence classes," she says, "and knowing his work would be seen by strangers!"

Louise's son left school in first grade, and left the "useless" spelling approach behind. "Now, at age sixteen," says Louise, "he's a very good speller—and he's learned just from reading and observing the errors his word processor's spell checker catches. His spell checker rarely has to find errors anymore."

Approaches to grammar mirror those of spelling, with the notable addition of *Mad Libs,* those fun little books available everywhere which inspire children to learn basic grammar vocabulary through the funny stories they create themselves.

Modeling correct grammar, gently correcting children's oral grammatical mistakes, and rephras-ing incorrect usage and repeating it correctly go a long way in help-ing your early years child tune in to the grammatical nuances of English. "Speaking with proper grammar will make writing with proper grammar fairly simple," Sarah advises. "More thorough grammar training can be accomplished easily at an older age."

MONEY SAVER

SINGING PRACTICE
We make up silly songs to help us remember those things my daughter has a hard time putting into prac-tice otherwise.

Marie keeps a grammar book handy "as a resource when we have a question. I don't teach grammar as such. It comes up when we're writing or when the children read out loud to me during Bible reading time, or when we're reading a story together."

Computer games and the "find the mistakes" approach of *Daily Grams* offer a painless way for your budding grammarian to keep building his skills until one day, watch out. He just may gently correct *your* oral grammatical mistake!

Here are some common homeschooling ways to learn spelling and grammar:

Spelling

+ Child asks, parent answers
+ Computer games
+ Keeping a journal
+ Creative writing dictation
+ Playing games with word cards
+ Spelling lessons and lists
+ Writing notes
+ Spelling bees

Grammar

+ Child asks, parent answers
+ Computer games
+ Correcting children's writing
+ Learning a foreign language
+ Through daily conversation—parent listens, corrects mistakes
+ *Mad Libs*

Punctuation, Capital Letters and Contractions

Thanks yet again to lots of reading, aloud and independently, questionnaire respondents found little need for formal lessons in these writing basics. "Practice is what works," says Paula, and most agree with her.

Practice in punctuation and use of capital letters and contractions can occur via computer word processor, editing the children's writing, or using *Daily Grams* for correction opportunities. Learning happens quickly this way, most notably with contractions.

"My daughter figured these out from reading," explains Tanya. "One day we talked about them, wrote a whole bunch in the margin of the newspaper, and that was that."

Maureen couldn't wait to use "a neat idea for a concentration-type game to help learn contractions I'd found, but my son caught on so quickly, I never got to use it! Maybe with my second son?"

It's important to note that while this sounds easy—and it *is* easier than the typical school route—homeschooling parents succeed with these methods because reading with their early years children is a daily top priority. You too will observe progress on a minute-by-minute basis, and therefore continually correct, commend, and move forward. In this way, no time is wasted in building a strong foundation for your child's ability to communicate with the written word. Next you move toward encouraging application of the skills, building on the foundation.

Here are some common homeschooling ways to learn punctuation, capital letters, and contractions:

+ Child asks, parent answers
+ Writing
+ Computer games

MONEY SAVER

EDITING PRACTICE

My daughter dictates stories that I type into the computer. I put them in 18-point type so she can read them when we're done. After a paragraph or two, I'll read to her what she's dictated and she'll make changes or I'll prompt her with questions to help focus her writing.

> It's important to note while this sounds easy—and it *is* easier than the typical school route—homeschooling parents succeed with these methods because reading with their early years children is a daily top priority.

- ✦ Parent tells child—again and again as necessary, until writing reflects understanding
- ✦ Keeping a journal
- ✦ Creative writing dictation

MOTIVATION TO KEEP WRITING

FROM PRETEND WRITING to well-practiced printed letters, words, and then sentences, your early years child masters the rudiments of writing. If he is to apply his newfound skill, not to mention improve his penmanship, he needs reasons to keep on writing.

You can force things like "What I Did During Summer Vacation" out of him, but this doesn't appear to nurture creativity or help your

HOW WE DID IT

If they had a pen or pencil in their hand and wanted to know how to make something, we'd show them then. They're not currently writing every day but go in spurts. Every once in a while, they go on a writing binge. I think they've picked up punctuation and grammar as they've read. If they write letters to be sent off, I'll help if requested, otherwise we've kept it low key. Neither of them cares for the physical act of writing, so I let them use the computer and Mavis Beacon for typing skills. I had a book on italic writing, but my daughter wanted to 'write like Mom' so at her request I purchased a cursive workbook.

—JANE

child learn to enjoy writing. Real-life reasons to write, however, do nurture an appreciation for the act. The keys are to keep writing simple, fun, and meaningful for the early years child.

Computers and word-processing programs were a boon to adult writers, and there's no reason they shouldn't be so to a young writer as well. Help your child explore computer commands "copy, cut, and paste" with his own words. How does the sentence look in thirty different fonts? In 8-point type? 36-point?

Children's writing and publishing software can inspire even the most reluctant writer to create literal works of art. Computer programs offer starting ideas or fun facts upon which to base a story. Clip art, stamps, and paint tools let your child illustrate writing then send it all to print. If you have an auditory learner, look for one of the programs that will let him hear his story aloud.

Need more real-life reasons to write with a computer? Create a Web page (use programs such as Hot Dog or Netscape Composer); keep in touch with e-mail pals; use a newsletter template and create a family newspaper. Of course, your child will have to "write" a mailing list including recipients' addresses.

MONEY SAVER

EARLY CREATIVE WRITING
We used what we called a Project Book, a large art pad on which the children drew a picture. If they wanted to write a long story about it they would dictate it and I wrote it down.

Play word games that keep children thinking about letter sounds and relationships. Commercial games include Junior Scrabble, Balderdash, and Boggle. Early years children enjoy hidden word puzzles (you can make your own with many computer applications) and the perennial favorite, hangman. On your way to field trips or support group activities, use other cars' license plate letters to create slogans, book or song titles, or think of a word that includes all the letters.

Children this age also like lists. Why should you have all the fun making the grocery list? Your child can also write a list of what he wants to do today, the members of his soccer team, books he's read, favorite songs, names of the rocks in his rock collection, all the toys in his room. . . .

She can make greeting cards and comic strips, write poetry, and copy recipes for you from a magazine. She can send frequent "Dear Grandma" notes, give Grandpa directions on how to work his VCR, enter writing contests, and fill out entry forms for cereal company contests. After field trips or vacations, she can create a brochure about the places she visits or write a letter convincing a relative to visit.

Perhaps your child could appreciate penmanship as art. Italic handwriting is simpler to learn than cursive, easier to read, and, at least in the words of my daughter, "prettier." A child seven or eight years old who appreciates "prettier" might love a calligraphy set, available at most art supply or office supply stores. Materials may be purchased separately, but there are kits that contain the old-fashioned fountain pen with several different-sized nibs and a colorful assortment of ink cartridges (some including gold and silver—ooh!) or markers with calligraphy tips (which are easier for an early years child to deal with), practice paper, and instructions. A calligraphy set could lead to hours of hand-eye coordination practice.

For creative writing, "clustering" is fun as a group activity with early years children, provides brainstorming practice, and helps a child employ innate creativity. "Clustering" is a pre-writing exercise during which ideas flow without hindrance from the writer's "inner editor."

In the middle of a piece of paper, put a word or phrase you'd like to write about. Broad categories, like *cold,* for example, are best for

QUICK & EASY

POSTAL SERVICE

Our son didn't want to print, so I made a mailbox for him out of a cereal box. It had two slots: one said "To Matthew" and the other side said "To Dad." They wrote notes back and forth to each other. Dad tried to use words Matthew could read for himself.

beginners. For five minutes or so, everybody calls out what they think of when they think about *cold.* You, as dictation taker, "connect" these thoughts to the word *cold* with lines, or "spokes." Some spokes may have subspokes as each word encourages more words. For example, *cold* may first inspire *hurts,* leading to *bites* and *stings.* Every contribution gets recorded, as the "editor" is out to lunch.

This is a great device for generating short stories and poetry. When your five minutes are up, you'll have before you a dozen or more key ideas "connected" to cold. Now, instead of sitting down to write about cold with nothing more than that vague word in mind, your child has related words and phrases that can fill writing with rich imagery. Using the results of a first clustering experience with *cold,* here's what a six-year-old and an eight-year-old came up with, with very little help:

> Your child can also write a list of what he wants to do today, the members of his soccer team, books he's read, favorite songs, names of the rocks in his rock collection, all the toys in his room. . . .

A WINTER DAY

Cross-country skiing,
Ice skating in the park.
Cheeks blaze red and nose runs.
Frosty hands burn
As air bites skin.
Colder than ever now,
Snow still gently touching.
Snow pants crackle with each long step
Until I come in.
Slipping into slippers
I sip hot cocoa
Sitting by the fire.

If your child tends toward the auditory, turn on the family tape recorder or video camera and let him tell a story, then transcribe it for him later. Maybe it will become an illustrated book!

If your child tends toward the auditory, turn on the family tape recorder or video camera and let him tell a story, then transcribe it for him later. Maybe it will become an illustrated book!

Note that many of these activities aren't "writing" in the form required to turn in a school writing assignment. Rather, they provide opportunities to use and play with written words at a level that isn't intimidating to a young child.

Daily life and personal interests will inspire many more opportunities for your child to put pencil to paper. Now, doesn't this sound like a lot more fun than "What I Did During Summer Vacation"?

HOW WE DID IT

I let the children see that just because they're not writing yet doesn't mean they're nonwriters. Letting them come to writing in their own time has a big benefit. They're not paralyzed by spelling, grammar, and punctuation rules. This allows the creativity of writing to be foremost. This doesn't mean I consider such rules unimportant. The children know I'm quite picky regarding the rules. But they also know I expect them to learn these rules by reading and conversing. The day will come when Mom whips them through a painless but boring review of writing rules. But these are issues for older children to deal with.

—SARAH

SIMPLE STARTING POINTS

✦ *Keep reading aloud!*

As your child grows, expand your reading sources. Keep reading good children's literature, but read aloud and share advertisements, greeting cards, postcards, comic strips, newspapers, and magazines. This way your child sees how often and widely the written word is used in communication.

✦ *Give your child a beautiful diary or journal as the next present.*

Discuss the many uses for diaries and journals and let your child decide what special writings she'll record there. Respect privacy if requested. Be prepared to spell lots of words out loud for her!

✦ *Create a comfortable place to write.*

Any nook or cranny or corner of your child's bedroom will do. Size-appropriate desk and chair is a plus, but a comfy pillow and writing board will do. Make sure the area is well lit and has storage space for paper and pencils or pens (colored ink has been known to induce writing).

✦ *Value your child's writing.*

"Mommy, listen to this!" is a welcome sound when followed by your child's very own poem or story. The early years child's creations aren't very long, so stop what you're doing and contribute your full attention. A little encouragement goes a long way, and your poet will glow with pride when you ask if you can hang the creation on the refrigerator for all to see.

✦ *Learn about the authors whose work you're reading.*

Who wrote your child's favorite book? Find out what you can. What was life like for the authors of old classics? Digging for this information can take you off on many different journeys. What makes

MONEY SAVER

At first we used a chalkboard instead of paper so my daughter could write large.

writing good? Discuss examples of both good and bad writing, so your child begins to understand the difference and watches for instances in his own writing.

✦ *Be a good writing example.*

Grab the opportunity to take care of your own correspondence in front of your child. Whether you work on paper or in cyberspace, your child will get the idea he's learning something he'll use for the rest of his life.

RESOURCES

Books for Teaching Writing

Andreola, Karen. *Simply Grammar.* Charlotte Mason Research, 1993.

Phillips, Wanda C. *Daily Grams: Guided Review Aiding Master Skills for 4th and 5th Grades.* Isha Enterprises, 1987.

———. *Easy Grammar.* Ages four to eight; Level 1. Isha Enterprises, 1994.

Eagle's Wings Comprehensive Handbook of Phonics for Spelling, Reading, and Writing. Eagle's Wings Educational Materials, Duncan, OK 73533.

Stout, Kathryn. *The Natural Speller.* Call 302-998-3889 for information.

Periodicals Publishing Early Years Children's Writing

Boodle: Box 1049, Portland, IN 47371; 219-226-8141; quarterly $12/year; ages six through twelve.

Nifty Nibbles: Children Literary Magazine: 1525 2nd Street, Hull, IA 51239-7351; www.angelfire.com/ia/niftynibbles; bimonthly $16/year; grades K–12; Christian.

Stone Soup: Box 83, Santa Cruz, CA 95063; 800-447-4569; www
.stonesoup.com; 5 issues $26/year; ages up to thirteen.

The Writer's Slate, Box 664, Ottawa, KS 66067; 913-242-0407.
Beginnings for grades K–3.

Software

Creative Writer. Microsoft; http://www.microsoft.com/kids/creative
writer.

Davidson's Kid Works Deluxe. Davidson & Associates; 800-545-
7677.

School Font Collection. Mountain Lake Software; 800-669-6574.
Creates penmanship paper-type lines with print, cursive; "trace-
able" print, cursive, printing with arrows to show writing direction and more. "Arithmefonts" also available.

Spellbound. The Learning Company; 800-622-3390.

Storybook Weaver. MECC. The Learning Company; 800-622-3390.

Programs

Hablitzel, Marie, and others. *Draw Write Now.* Barker Creek Publications, 1994. A series of five books combining handwriting
and drawing for ages four through eight.

Italic Handwriting Series. Portland State University; 800-547-8887.

Modern Curriculum Press. Modern Curriculum Press; 800-321-3106.

Writing Strands. National Writing Institute; 800-688-5375.

Web Sites

Eeyore's Mad Libs: http://www.teleport.com/~rbpenn/pooh/adlib
.html

Mad Libs: http://www.amtexpo.com/babbooks/adlib.cgi

Wizard of Oz Mad Libs: http://www.fc.net/~pamcam/p_madlib.html

7

ARITHMETIC:

12 COOKIES ÷ 3 SIBLINGS =

4 COOKIES FOR ME!

In This Chapter

✦ Homeschoolers and arithmetic

✦ What does the early years child learn about arithmetic?

✦ Simple starting points

✦ Resources

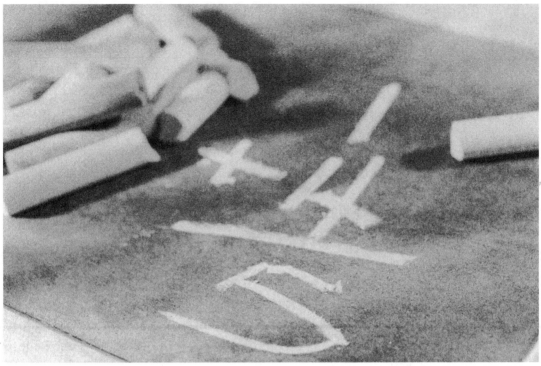

*L*ITTLE ELSE INSPIRES as much fear in the heart of potential homeschooling parents as the thought of teaching arithmetic. The best advice you'll get from homeschooling veterans regarding this subject? Relax!

The early years are not the time to create the next Einstein, but rather to lay a strong foundation regarding numbers, develop an understanding of math's many uses, and inspire enjoyment. If you harbor arithmetic phobia from your own school days, consider yourself a student alongside your child so you may relearn the subject for yourself. It's the most effective way to rid yourself of the phobia, which could silently and negatively influence your child if you let it hang around.

As a homeschooler, you've got a great advantage over the school approach to arithmetic. Free to participate in life's daily activity together, homeschooling families find themselves immersed in foundational arithmetic concepts at every turn. Learn to watch for and take advantage of them, and you'll be amazed by how effective natural, daily exposure can be.

HOMESCHOOLERS AND ARITHMETIC

IF YOU'RE FOLLOWING the trend established here—learning reading by reading, writing by writing—you've probably guessed I'd say homeschoolers learn arithmetic by doing arithmetic, and you're absolutely correct. Even families employing a structured curriculum and/or textbooks would find it impossible to ignore daily life opportunities for arithmetic appreciation and application. Think about it: They'd have to prohibit their children from baking, helping in the workshop, grocery shopping, looking at speed limit signs and maps, setting the table, using a clock, calendar, thermometer, scale, and money, and playing games!

> The early years are not the time to create the next Einstein, but rather to lay a strong foundation regarding numbers, develop an understanding of math's many uses, and inspire enjoyment.

The Early Years Child's Arithmetic Abilities

Remember, the early years child is a sensory being intent on collecting information, which is gradually "processed" and made part of in-depth understanding. Understanding this, you can see that arithmetic's abstractions (numbers and signs as symbols representing ideas) should be preceded by concrete understanding, following the natural order of your child's thinking development.

To make arithmetic concepts concrete families use manipulatives, the most convenient of which are fingers. Candy, popcorn, coins, spoons, and cereal bowls are also manipulatives, things your child can touch and manipulate to develop the concept of, for example, *three*. Early addition and subtraction—even multiplication and division—can be practiced simply by counting manipulatives. In fact, as Sarah says, "Any normal five-year-old will know that if her brother has five cookies and she only has three cookies, she'd better be getting two more cookies and quick!" The abstract 3 + 2 = 5 becomes very clear when cookies are at stake!

After lots of practice counting and touching and manipulating, your child will begin to understand arithmetic concepts at a higher level. She will be able to visualize *three* and manipulate it mentally, thanks to her practice. Slowly she leaves manipulatives behind as their use becomes cumbersome and slow compared to what she can do in her head. Don't put away your manipulatives just yet, though.

After lots of practice counting and touching and manipulating, your child will begin to understand arithmetic concepts at a higher level: She will be able to visualize *three* and manipulate it mentally, thanks to her practice.

EARLY YEARS FAVORITE MATH SOFTWARE

Mad Minute Math

Math Blaster

Math Journey

Math Rabbit

Millie's Math House

Moneytown

Operation Neptune

Richard Scarry Best Math

Treasure Math Storm

They'll come in handy again if you observe she's having trouble with a particular concept. Then you can use the manipulatives to show the concept in simpler form or demonstrate different manipulations that might make more sense to her.

Your child will eventually leap again, beyond visualization to the abstract thinking necessary for higher mathematics, but this doesn't typically occur until your child reaches ten to twelve years of age (and moves into the age group addressed in the next book in this series).

MONEY SAVER

SHAPES

We made different shapes out of masking tape on the carpet, like a big Twister game. Then I'd call out, "Everyone stand on a square, put your belly in a circle, walk around the edge of a rectangle, put your sister in a triangle." They loved it; probably some of the most fun we've had.

When a Child Is Ready to Do Arithmetic

Arithmetic is such an integral part of day-to-day life, your child began experimenting with it when, as a toddler, she sat in the bath pouring water from one cup to another, put the square plastic puzzle piece in the square hole, and nestled the smaller cup inside the larger.

"We've always done arithmetic," says Renee, "adding this, counting that, looking at different shapes." Indeed, arithmetic readiness signals were harder for questionnaire respondents to describe than for reading and writing, in large part because they appeared so early.

"He learned the rudiments as a baby through natural conversation about his toys," Leslie says. Tanya noted her daughter adding small sums and making a one-to-one connection with counting at three years of age. Holly's son started counting at the dinner table one night at the same age.

"I wasn't aware my daughter was ready or that we'd already been teaching her," explains Celia. "One day before we started homeschooling we were playing marbles. I had won, and she told me I had more marbles than she did. I saw the opportunity and taught her 'greater than, less than, and equal' on the spot."

Pauline believes her "very descriptive language approach" helped ready her children. "What I mean by this is instead of saying to the child, 'Oh, look at that pretty car,' I'd say, 'Oh, look at that bright royal blue Mustang with the lovely curve on the back of the convertible roof,'" Pauline explains. "Using descriptive words that are defined when you're asked is a very effective way of teaching children not only concepts, but a rich vocabulary."

"I had a first-grade math workbook someone had given me, and at five years old my son found it and wanted to do some of it," says Abby, Indianapolis, Indiana, homeschooler since 1985. "He worked away in it with interest until he mastered the concepts of addition and

QUICK & EASY

RECOGNIZING AND WRITING NUMBERS
I'd have the children look up the hymns in the hymnal, write phone numbers of friends on a list, and other real-life practice.

EARLY YEARS FAVORITE GAMES THAT TEACH MATH CONCEPTS

24

Candyland

Chess

Chutes and Ladders

Dominoes

Legos (patterns)

Monopoly

Playing Cards

Set

Tangrams

Uno

MONEY SAVER

100!

I designed a hundred chart on my computer. Each day my son colored in one number, then counted up to that number. One hundred days later he could count to 100.

If you listen carefully, you can almost hear the jingle of coins changing hands in homeschoolers' homes everywhere, especially in play "stores."

subtraction, as well as simple time-telling, money, and measurement. Then he put it aside and hasn't shown a lot of interest in math since, although he has retained the concepts. I know this because he can play any game involving math skills easily."

If your child's learning assets, like curiosity and wonder, are intact, she will ask questions. "This is how my children learn everything," says Laura. "My five-year-old knows addition and subtraction up to twenty. She's asking about short-cuts, as she calls them, so we're reading fiction books which discuss the ideas of multiplication and division. When she's comfortable with that I know her well enough to know she'll ask me to write out a page of problems for her.

"When she's interested she asks." Laura adds, "I just offer up lots of things for her ask about."

WHAT DOES THE EARLY YEARS CHILD LEARN ABOUT ARITHMETIC?

ELEMENTARY ARITHMETIC TEXTBOOKS vary in the skills they first present to children, influenced by everything from politics to promises of large orders by high-population states to political correctness—and sometimes by an understanding of early years children's ability. Examining a textbook can give you a good idea of the scope and sequence for a child of the same skill level as your own. This way you can choose to use it as a guide to *what* you will cover, figuring out your own *how*. If you choose to use a textbook as intended, check it before purchase to see if it honors your child's natural progression of ability. Many textbooks plunge children into abstract concepts far too soon, losing or confusing them or, worse, creating yet another generation of arithmetic phobics.

Shapes and Sizes, Patterns and Counting

Children usually acquire foundational knowledge of shapes and sizes, patterns, and counting during the preschool years from an environment that includes appropriate playthings and lots of conversation—or watching *Sesame Street*. Discuss shapes as you play with toys. Turn shapes into the theme of an "I Spy" game during your afternoon walk. Food comes in, or can be cut into, lots of shapes.

Preschool computer software makes learning shapes and sizes easy and fun. Reinforce the "lessons" throughout the day by using the vocabulary—bigger, smaller, more than, less than, thinner, wider, longer, shorter, shape names, number names, and ordinal numbers (first, second, and so on). Don't let the ease of these lessons belie their importance.

"*Ladybug Magazine* has activities in each issue. I think this magazine was very helpful teaching my daughter to count when she was little," says Michaela. "She loves *Anno's Math Games* books. She plays a lot with paper clips, strings, ribbons, beads, stringing things together in intricate ways. These are helping her learn patterns."

Angie, a New York homeschooler since 1995, counted aloud from the time her two children were babies while going upstairs or downstairs with them. "They picked it up," Angie says. "They

QUICK & EASY

RESTAURANT
ARITHMETIC

We play a game in restaurants where the white sugars are one, pinks five, and blue ten. Our daughter "buys" things from us and we make change. It messes up our table while we wait for food, but she's good about returning all the sugars when we're finished.

MONEY SAVER

TELLING TIME

We mounted a cardboard clock with moving hands to our refrigerator. Throughout each day I asked my son to match the hands on the cardboard clock to the hands on the real clock nearby. Then we talked about what time it was. After a while, he caught on and could tell time by himself.

enjoyed the patterns from early Saxon books so we began making up our own every day and then completed each other's patterns. We also bought a counting board with ten beads on each of ten wires which the children played with, counted with, and used while doing addition and subtraction problems from the time my youngest was about four years old."

Recognizing and Writing Numbers to 100

If you recall from the last chapter, handwriting takes eye-hand-brain coordination, which develops at different rates in different children. If you observe your child isn't ready for writing numbers, provide instead lots of fun practice in recognizing numbers. A great aid is a large "Hundred Chart," a square ten rows across by ten rows down. Each square contains one number; numbers one through ten running across the top horizontal row, eleven through twenty across the next horizontal row, and so on. You can purchase a hundred chart, or save money by making your own by hand or computer. If you keep the template on your computer, you can print out individual copies to be written on.

The chart can be used for your beginner's number recognition and counting, but don't stop there. This simple chart can help your child recognize number patterns (what happens when you add four to six? to sixteen? to twenty-six?), for addition and subtraction practice as she moves from hands-on manipulatives to visualization, for "skip-counting" (count by twos, fives, and so on) forward and backward, for skip-counting starting with a number other than one, and for number games you've yet to create based on what your child is learning at a given time.

You can create a number line to 100 for a fun alternative to the hundred chart. A strip of adding machine paper is just the right size for your line, and can be as long as your living room if you'd like!

"We had numbers one to ten posted around the house, in the playroom and kitchen," remembers Angie. "It didn't seem a big jump for either child to go above ten and to understand that one repeats a sequence in what they would come to know as the ones column for each of the tens. We counted aloud by tens together, often using dimes to illustrate."

Copying numbers written by hand or in workbooks, flash cards, and drills work well for some families at a variety of ages. Jillian's family "just decided it would be fun to see how high the children could count, or how high I could count."

The "osmosis method," so frequently cited by homeschooling parents, works with numbers, too. "They just seemed to recognize numbers from the time they could talk," explains Valerie. "Writing numbers took longer. We demonstrated the accepted techniques for 'drawing' 4, 5, and 8, but the other numerals weren't a problem. We had a couple of lessons in place values, talked in terms of money, and the leap to generalize was very quick."

Melanie's family took the artistic approach to writing numbers once her children had plenty of practice in recognition. "We used a fat pencil and typing paper with a single numeral filling the page. The children traced the numeral with the pencil, then with five different colors," Melanie says. "We call it 'rainbow tracing.'"

> Many textbooks plunge children into abstract concepts far too soon, losing or confusing them or, worse, creating yet another generation of arithmetic phobics.

Signs and Sequencing

You can help your child carry fascination with patterns generally to the number patterns of sequencing. Saxon math books consistently include fill-in-the-blank opportunities for this skill, but you can make up your own, too. (Example: 2, 4, __, 8, 10.) Here's another skill your child can develop before actually writing numbers, if necessary. If you use a textbook, she can just say the answers.

Erica notes, "Both of my boys know sequencing and ordering in their minds but may not be comfortable with the abstract symbols on a page. By talking, I can tell if they understand the concepts."

Talking is just how Sarah helped her children understand arithmetic's basic signs. "When we first look at math notation, I give real-life words to the signs:

=   "same as"
+   "and"
−   "take away"
x   "groups of"
÷   "divide by" (This is a real-life word because you have to divide up the cookies and muffins and marbles.)

"After the children really know what the signs mean," continues Sarah, "I start alternating the math word with the real-life word. For example, sometimes for '+' I will say 'and,' while other times I'll say 'plus.' Sequencing and ordering just seem to be common sense."

When Melanie's children aren't rainbow tracing, they work on signs and sequencing "in spiral notebooks the children take with them to church! I make up pages of 'what comes next' and 'fill in the blank' and 'which is bigger' types of problems for them to do to keep quiet," she explains. "I teach the < and > as ice cream cones—the big end holds more ice cream."

> If you observe your child isn't ready for writing numbers, provide instead lots of fun practice in recognizing numbers.

Single and Double Digit Addition and Subtraction with Regrouping

The concept of "ones" becoming a "ten" is often difficult for the pre–abstract thinking child, so once again lots of counting and manipulatives come in handy.

"We counted fingers. We counted objects. We practiced with a curriculum," says Sarah. "Regrouping works nicely with bundles of toothpicks or, if a child already has a good concept of money, with pennies, dimes, dollars, and ten-dollar bills."

Besides using curriculum, money, and fingers, homeschoolers report this concept clicks when repeatedly used during higher-grade-level computer games, card games, and hours of Monopoly and other games requiring the use of two or more dice in which the children add together the amount of their roll themselves.

Jacqueline's son recently conquered double digit addition, providing a snapshot of the "awakening" that frequently occurs in homeschooling.

"Tom sold popcorn during a Cub Scout fundraiser," she begins. "He needed to add up the money he collected, so he asked questions. I went through it with him, adding all the checks together, then the cash. I was a little frustrated," Jacqueline adds, "so I changed my approach. He then asked for more problems so I made up a few. He worked through those, but still didn't quite get it. He asked for more problems. I think he worked about ten before the light came on. That night he asked for nineteen problems; the next day about twenty more.

"He seems very comfortable with it now," concludes Jacqueline. "He's gotten up to hundreds and thousands inventing his own problems."

QUICK & EASY

FRACTIONS

From the time my son was about two years old I let him choose how many pieces he wanted his sandwich cut into. If he chose ten, he got ten pieces. As he ate the pieces we talked about how many tenths he'd eaten and how many were left. "You've eaten 3/10 and you have 7/10 left!"

Money, Time, and Other Measurements

Money—the root of early math concepts! With the built-in incentive money provides, early years children catch on to this concept quickly. If you listen carefully, you can almost hear the jingle of coins changing hands in homeschoolers' homes everywhere, especially in play "stores."

QUICK & EASY

FRACTIONS ON THE MOVE

We played this game in the car. One of us would instruct the other to roll the window down one-half, one-third, one-quarter, and the rest of the way. We took turns, and when it was my turn I sometimes did it wrong to see if he would "catch" me—and he did!

"You can't keep a child from wanting to know more about money!" exclaims Holly. "Pete gets an allowance and enjoys saving and spending his money. He helps when I'm running errands and loves to play store."

Doris's children learned about money from a workbook, "But as it's part of daily life," she explains, "much was discussed as we went through the day. At ages three, five, and seven, our children got allowances. They learned to distinguish between the different coins. When we went to the store they would use their money to purchase things, then they'd come home and play store."

Along with allowances, food shopping provides incentive in Angie's home. "The children help by going through our coupons and taking with us what we'll need that day. In return for their shopping help they each get part of the money we save using coupons and the household gets the remainder. This," says Angie, "has done wonders helping them figure out money."

Managing their own money, children learn another important life lesson quickly. "We like garage sales and flea markets," explains Valerie, "so the children learned early how to make change, calculate if they had enough money for more than one purchase, and bargain if need be. Both had the same reaction the first time they didn't get the expected change because of sales tax added to the listed price . . . they claimed false advertising!"

As noted earlier, a child comfortable handling money can transfer what he knows to the regrouping concept. Coins can also be used to help explain the "equal parts of a whole" present in lessons on fractions, right alongside measuring cups and spoons, cut-up

HOW WE DID IT

We've used a variety of things, switching around if something isn't working. If the children cook, measure, or do something hands-on I don't worry about getting out the math book. If they don't have a project going on that uses arithmetic in some way I do ask them to do a page in one of several workbooks or use a lesson out of a Saxon book or watch the next segment of *Math-U-See*. We don't do any of this religiously, any more than we do in any other subject.

Arithmetic is probably the one I've worried about most in the past, but here's something for thought. My child, who taught himself the addition and subtraction facts at four years old, is now twelve. He hates doing math pages; gets bored. So I got out the Saxon 5/4 test booklet and challenged him. "Okay, see if you can pass this test and you won't have to do this book." He hasn't made less than a 90 percent on any of them—and they were silly mistakes. If there's something he simply doesn't know, we turn to the lesson and learn it together. Once he gets through the tests we'll see how he does with the 6/5 book. Why do the whole book ad nauseam if you know the stuff already?

Where did he learn it? I don't know—real life, in many instances.

—MARIE

oranges and candy bars, and the tried-and-true pizza or apple pie, which you can purchase as games or make yourself.

Computing with fractions during the early years isn't necessary; your child will grow into that ability. Lessons and conversation now merely introduce the concept and build understanding of fractions as measurements, a task made easier with manipulatives. If your child seems to pick up fractions easily, you might want to move from 1/4, 1/3, 1/2, and so on to "What is 1/2 of 10 M&Ms?" and similar problems.

Time is another measurement early years children learn. Digital clocks may soon make the old-fashioned clock face obsolete, but until then learning to tell time can be fun.

You can buy colorful plastic or cardboard clocks as aids, or help your child make one. Or maybe, like Pauline's husband, Dad can help. "My daughter loves to call her father at the office during the day. Every time she does, she asks, 'When will you be home?'

"He tells her to look at the clock we have on the kitchen wall," Pauline says, "and he tells her when he will be home, explaining where the clock hands will be. It only took her a couple of weeks of this activity to tell time."

Receiving watches when they were between six and seven years old encouraged Doris's children to tell time. For equally practical reasons, Holly's son needs to know how much longer he can play his computer game.

Other measurements in the early years child's arsenal involve length, weight, and temperature. A ruler, especially one marked only with inches instead of all the fractions for ease of reading, or a tape measure—and a reason to measure—are all your child needs to learn measuring length. How big is her room? Will his dresser fit by the window if you move the furniture? How tall is she?

> Your child can track the temperature throughout a day, at noon every day for a week, a month, or longer. Which day was hottest? Was Monday or Tuesday cooler? By how many degrees?

How long is Rover? Can he help you measure material? Can she help out in the workshop measuring wood for cutting? Give him things to measure; he'll build the skill.

The same applies for using scales. If you can find a kitchen or postal scale at the next garage sale, your child can weigh small items, make comparisons and graph results. Point out the difference between a scale that measures ounces and the bathroom scale that measures pounds.

Large thermometers to measure indoor and outdoor air temperature are all the tools you need for real-life lessons in reading temperature. Here's another opportunity to collect data for graphing. Your child can track the temperature throughout a day, at noon every day for a week, a month, or longer. Which day was hottest? Was Monday or Tuesday cooler? By how many degrees?

MONEY SAVER

GRAPHS
We used a placemat with a grid on it to graph M&Ms to see which colors were the most or least frequent. We also used animal crackers to graph which animals we had the most or least of.

Communicating Measurements: Graphs and Tables

Simple graphs and tables are a perfect follow-up to the information-gathering process of measuring. Not only do they show there's a reason to collect information and a way to clearly communicate it to others, the act of creating graphs and tables builds ability to read and understand them, too.

Your child can make pie, line, and bar graphs by hand or with computer programs. Alysia's four-year-old, homeschooling since 1997 in Lawrence, Kansas, "enjoys graphing everyday things, like family eye color and the number of different shapes in our living room," she says. "She likes putting the data in the computer and seeing what the graph will look like."

Keep your eye out for graphs and tables appearing in newspaper and magazine articles. You can use these for discussion and as models on which your child can base her own. Help her make a pie, line, *and* bar graph for the same information, and discuss which one works best and why.

Gather an assortment of real-life tables; bus and train schedules are good, and so is your paper's TV schedule. You and your child can have fun making up word problems for each other based on the schedules.

Math textbooks typically provide graphs to practice with as part of the curriculum, too.

Single Digit Multiplication and Division

Multiplication and division are just counting shortcuts, and a child who tackles them understanding this concept at the starting gate is ahead of the game. Approaching multiplication and division this way, you're in for some repetitive counting practice with your manipulatives at the start. (How many are in nine groups of ten poker chips? Let's count and find out. How many groups of four peanuts can we make with twenty peanuts? Let's count and find out, and so on.)

> There's no law stating multiplication facts must be learned in order, and you may find the 2, 3, 5, and 10 times tables are easiest for beginners.

There's no law stating multiplication facts must be learned in order, and you may find the 2, 3, 5, and 10 times tables are easiest for beginners. To help cement the counting shortcut concept, use your hundred chart for skip-counting, noting how the answers coincide with the answers on that overwhelming-looking times table.

A "Multiplication March" may work for your kinesthetic learner. To a rhythm, march through the house, count with each step, then clap on multiples of two or three or whatever multiplication group you're studying.

Many math computer games drill children in arithmetic facts, in a fun way, of course. You may find, as some homeschoolers do, these games lead to memorization of the facts seemingly effortlessly.

Word Problems

Word problems help keep abstract number concepts rooted in reality for your child. This works so well, Sarah says, "Sometimes my children have to put their math facts into word problems so they can figure them out."

Without realizing it, much of your conversation about arithmetic comes out as word problems that can be understood even at early ages. "You had two mittens. You lost one and now there's only one left!"

Textbooks will supply you with abundant word problems, or you can use their problems as your clue to what skill they're providing practice in, and make up your own problems that relate directly to your child's life and interests yet practice the same skill.

Word problems can be worked out on paper, but let your child do just as many mentally, too. Keep the manipulatives and hundreds chart handy. Not only can they help your child if she gets stuck, she can use them to figure out word problems she writes for you to solve, very good practice for all budding mathematicians.

Here are some common homeschooling ways to learn early years arithmetic concepts:

MONEY SAVER

BUDDING BUSINESSMAN

Gil would make up businesses and use a lot of math in the process. For one, "The Three Cats Bookstore," he made order forms, checks, and receipts and I would be customers for whom he would fill and mail orders. All the children made stores with their friends, using play money and a toy cash register to help run them.

HOW WE DID IT

We approach all this arithmetic in real-life situations. We take time to figure things out. We include our children in financial issues. I ask my daughter what time it is when I need to know even though she doesn't know how to tell time. By asking her enough she is learning.

We use a calendar. We buy things. We save for things. Both my daughters have their own tape measures and like to measure things. For now this is our approach. When it's time for higher math I imagine this will need to be studied since it's not used every day the way basic arithmetic is.

—WENDY

- ✦ Child asks, parent answers
- ✦ Hundreds chart, number line, abacus
- ✦ Drawing
- ✦ Computer programs
- ✦ Food
- ✦ Puzzles, books, videos, and educational TV
- ✦ Playing games
- ✦ Blocks, Legos
- ✦ Cuisenaire rods and other manipulatives
- ✦ Using real money, clocks, silverware, socks, plates, and so on
- ✦ Using real rulers, tape measures, thermometers, measuring cups and spoons
- ✦ Music theory
- ✦ Playing store

SIMPLE STARTING POINTS

✦ *Do you have a positive mental attitude about arithmetic?*

If not, now's the time to develop one! Consider yourself fortunate in getting an opportunity to learn arithmetic all over again, with your child as a co-learner a lovely bonus. As you make arithmetic understandable and, yes, even fun for your child, you'll share the joy of learning—which can erase negative attitudes you may harbor.

✦ *Arithmetic is everywhere for everyone—seize opportunities for your toddler.*

As you learn to seize (or create) opportunities, even toddlers can get in on the arithmetic fun. Help her count the napkins as she gets the chance to set the table. Can she find a bigger spoon for you? How many pairs of her socks were in the laundry today? How many socks was that? Is the car moving faster or slower than it was a few minutes ago? Which is the tallest tomato plant in the garden? What shape is her cheese, her cookie, her bed, her game board? Who will get their soup first? Conversation about these things introduces beginning arithmetic concepts during the course of a day.

✦ *Arithmetic is everywhere for everyone— seize opportunities for your elementary- aged child.*

For a pleasant change from—or in lieu of— lists of arithmetic exercises, use the time throughout the day for real-life applications that relate the same concepts. At home, you can bake your way to understanding fractions, count shirts in the laundry, subtract as you eat grapes, and figure out how many hours until a music lesson. On the road to the lesson, there are license plates from which to mentally add numbers and plenty of

Without realizing it, much of your conversation about arithmetic comes out as word problems that can be understood even at early ages. "You had two mittens. You lost one and now there's only one left!"

time for estimating how long it will take to get to your destination and reading all the signs with numbers. And don't forget that nifty speedometer in the car. Opportunities exist in the grocery store, the yard, the garden, and the home workshop. Use them all.

✦   *Invent new games.*

Cover an abandoned game board firmly with blank paper, gather assorted game pieces, and your child can create the next Monopoly! A great thinking exercise, too, as your child will have to determine how a player wins, and set forth the game's rules. Arithmetic games don't necessarily have to be played on a board—can you create a card game? A game to be played in the car? In the yard?

✦   *Create colorful arithmetic fact posters.*

It's amazing how helpful simple visual exposure to these facts can be. Change the posters frequently so they don't become as familiar as the furniture. Too many arithmetic facts could get overwhelming, so you might want to concentrate on the facts your child is currently studying, or the ones you observe are the most difficult. Hang them where your child will see them frequently throughout the day.

✦   *Remember arithmetic while you're on field trips.*

There aren't any "arithmetic museums"—but there are lots of folks who daily use numbers in their work. Make a point of asking about this while visiting the post office, bank, architect's office, artist's studio, or science lab.

RESOURCES

Books

Anno, Mitsumasa, and others. *Anno's Mysterious Multiplying Jar.* Putnam Publishing Group, 1983.

Anno, Mitumasa, and others. *Anno's Math Games I, II and III.* Paper Star, 1997.

Bryant-Mole, Karen. *Charts & Graphs.* Usborne Math Series, EDC Publications, 1994. Look for other fun, inexpensive Usborne titles, too. Lots of homeschoolers are Usborne distributors.

Burns, Marilyn. *Collection of Math Lessons from Grade 1 Through 3.* Cuisenaire Co., 1993.

Glenn, Suki. *Patterns in Arithmetic: Activities to Develop Mathematical Thinking.* Patterns Press, 1994.

Help Your Child Learn Number Skills: EDC Publishing, P.O. Box 470663, Tulsa, OK 74147; 800-475-4522; http://www.edcpub.com.

Kidder, Harvey. *The Kid's Book of Chess.* Workman Publishing, 1990. Includes chess set.

Murphy, Stuart J. *The Best Vacation Ever.* HarperCollins Juvenile, 1997.

Slavin, Steve. *Math for Your 1st and 2nd Grader.* John Wiley & Sons, 1995.

Stanmark, Jean Kerr, and others. *Family Math.* University of California Press, 1986.

World Book. *World Book Clever Kids: Math Ages 5-7.* World Book, Inc., 1995.

Ziefart, Harriet. *A Dozen Dozens.* Viking Children's Books, 1998.

Programs

Christian Liberty Academy: 502 W. Euclid Avenue, Arlington Hts., IL 60004; 800-348-8899.

Cuisenaire Company of America: P.O. Box 5026, White Plains, NY 10602; 800-872-1100; http://www.cuisenaire-dsp.com.

Math-U-See: 888-854-MATH; http://www.mathusee.com.

Miquon Math Materials: 800-995-MATH.

Saxon Math: 1300 McGee, #100, Norman, OK 73072; 800-284-7019; http://www.saxonpub.com.

Catalogs

Audio Memory Publishing: 2060 Raymond Avenue, Signal Hill, CA 90806; (sellers of audiotapes *Multiplication Songs, Addition Songs,* and *Subtraction Songs;* oral "flash cards," possible help for auditory learner).

Delta Hands-on Math: P.O. Box 3000, Nashua, NH 03061; 800-442-5444; www.delta-ed.com.

Discovery Toys: 800-426-4777 for a consultant in your area.

Institute for Math Mania: P.O. Box 910, Montpelier, VT 05601; 800-NUMERAL.

Judy Instructo: 4424 West 78th Street, Bloomington, MN 55435; 800-526-9907.

Math Products Plus: P.O. Box 64, San Carlos, CA 94070; 415-593-2839.

Periodicals

Dynamath: Scholastic, Inc.; 800-SCHOLASTIC; www.scholastic.com; grades three through six; $9/yr.

Games Junior: Games Magazine; 800-827-1256; ages seven and up; biannual; $15/yr.

Wonderful Ideas: 800-92-IDEAS; grade three and up; five issues/yr.; $18.

Web Sites

A+ Math: http://www.aplusmath.com

Elementary Math: http://www.stmary.k12.la.us/elemmath.htm

Free Download of LOGO (programming language children can use): http://www.softronix.com (books and links also available)

Free Math Worksheets: http://www.schoolexpress.com/free/math/index.html

Homework Helpers: http://www.viewz.com/webguide/homewk.htm

Lauri Products: http://www.liveandlearn.com//auri/.

Math Forum: Ask Dr. Math: http://forum.swarthmore.edu/dr.math/drmath.elem.html/

Math Stories for Grades 1-5: http://www.mathstories.com

Math for Morons Like Us: http://library.advanced.org/20991/home.html

Reading and Math Support (bulletin board): http://www.vegsource.org/wwwboard/reading/wwwboard.html

8

BEYOND THE 3 R's:

COVERING THE REST

In This Chapter

+ Homeschoolers and other subjects

+ Scope and sequence of "other subjects"
in the early years

+ Resources

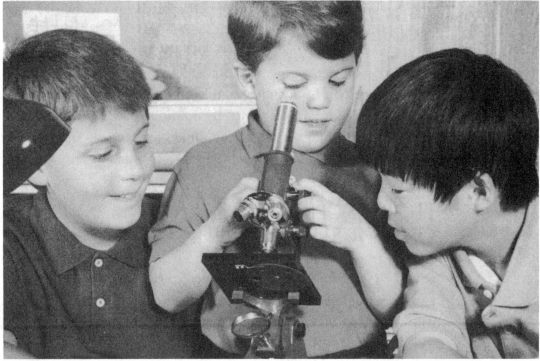

*Y*OUR EARLY YEARS child is learning to read, write, spell, and understand beginning arithmetic concepts. You've already discovered many ways beyond texts and workbooks to lead your child to these basic skills, but now the world of curriculum choice grows ever larger as you contemplate moving beyond the 3 R's to introduce other subjects. Typical early years curriculum requirements usually include science, social studies, U.S. and/or state history, health, art, music, and physical education.

The wide range of choices available to homeschoolers prompted numerous questionnaire respondents to note just how difficult it is for them to describe the teaching of "other subjects." In fact, I'm finding the same problem trying to compartmentalize their answers in any fashion resembling orderly!

As you discover the various ways in which homeschoolers address other subjects, remember there are no definitive lines separating one approach from another, and you are free to pick and choose ideas that fit your family's needs. By doing so, you'll create an indelible imprint of uniqueness on your child's learning, an imprint that is yet another reason for homeschooling's remarkable success.

HOMESCHOOLERS AND OTHER SUBJECTS

IF YOU AND your child are reading *Sam the Minuteman* together and he asks about the use of commas and the funny spelling of a word, are you still studying American history, or have you switched to language arts—or spelling? If he asks where England is and you pull out the world atlas, are you now studying world geography? If after reading he runs off to make a three-corner hat, are you still studying American history—or art? If you don't pick up an American history textbook today, have you really studied American history at all since you only read an easy-reader fictional story?

POPULAR EARLY YEARS UNIT STUDY TOPICS

- ✦ Ancient Egypt, Greece, and Rome
- ✦ Favorite Animals
- ✦ Bugs
- ✦ Dinosaurs
- ✦ King Arthur, Knights, Castles

- ✦ *Little House on the Prairie*
- ✦ Roller Coasters
- ✦ Space Shuttles
- ✦ Trains
- ✦ Weather

Can you see the difficulty in reviewing the learning taking place and trying to compartmentalize it by school subjects? The key to understanding how homeschoolers deal with other subjects is to once again remember the enormous amount of reading they engage in. Very few, if any, real books—fiction or nonfiction—remove either a subject or a skill from the greater context in which the story or information is presented.

As you engage in what is basically one-to-one tutelage of your child, you don't need to remove a subject from its greater context, either. You're free to include the greater context as you study, answer questions related to the context (if not the subject), and go off on context-related tangents if and as they occur.

Traditional Possibilities

The traditional approach, based on the school model, includes time to address each subject separately each day, often following a purchased curriculum or one prepared by a parent. This is the most structured among typical possibilities.

"We study all the subjects each day," explains Kathy, a Denver, Colorado, homeschooler since 1995 with two early years children. "I structure our day with the subjects which are the most difficult for them first (spelling, reading, piano) to the easiest subjects (comprehension, math) later in the day. Other subjects or electives are in between. Most electives, like crafts and cooking, are outside of the school time.

"We've never tried unit studies," Kathy adds, "and I don't like to get off track too much. We stick with the basics. I think you can give your child too many electives and push too hard. I try to keep the children in their grade levels with reading, writing, and arithmetic."

If you and your child are reading *Sam the Minuteman* together and he asks about the use of commas and the funny spelling of a word, are you still studying American history, or have you switched to language arts—or spelling?

Notice that within this traditional approach Kathy uses her intimate knowledge of her children's strengths and weaknesses to her children's advantage. She schedules the day so the children will study the subjects most difficult for them first, while they're at a high energy level from a good night's sleep.

> Use your intimate knowledge of your children's strengths and weaknesses to their advantage.

Other families create a daily schedule outlining what needs to be accomplished, then the children decide what they will do first and next. Some who create a weekly schedule leave to the children the possibility of completing the week's assignments in fewer days, giving them a day or two off.

There are other schedule decisions to be made—and often changed if you find they don't work as you expected. Your family may follow the September to June school year, decide to homeschool year-round, follow a six or eight weeks on, two weeks off pattern, or something entirely different. If you continue lessons through the summer, they could become more project-oriented or based on travel and field trips. All these schedules can be arranged to fulfill your state's minimum requirements for number of study days and hours.

Within this yearly schedule, what will your daily schedule look like? Books in the morning? Afternoon during baby's nap? Evening when both parents are home? Some book-work in the morning *and* evening? Just figure out what you think will work best and try it. A whole week will probably go by before you change it.

Unit Study Possibilities

Unit studies begin with a topic, often one a child has expressed interest in. From here, study of that one topic encompasses typical school subjects. Unit study can be woven into any curriculum from the structured to the unstructured. Let's use a fictional unit study on pirates as an example of how it could unfold.

Your child watches an old pirate movie—he's hooked. First, you go to the library and bookstore to find books you can read aloud, and others your child reads independently (reading, vocabulary). Can you find another pirate movie at the video store?

Your child writes or dictates, then illustrates, his own story and poem (spelling, penmanship, grammar, art). Verbal or written arithmetic practice during this period capitalizes on the pirate theme. (If the captain gives each of his sailors two pieces of eight, and he has ten sailors, how much gold has he passed out?) If the pirate ship needs fifteen barrels of flour before it sails but has only seven, how many more are needed? Have some fun!)

Notice you've covered basic reading, writing, and arithmetic, and you're not done yet. Where are the story's pirates from? (Geography.) Why are they pirates? (Economics, history, ethics.) How were their ships built? (Anatomy of ship, science experiments on flotation, buoyancy, displacement.) Every pirate story involves a good storm—what happened? (Weather, measurement, graphing.) You might even enjoy learning a few practical skills right about now. (Map reading, knot tying, astronomy.)

Because of their popularity among home-schoolers, prepared unit studies are readily available. "Our curriculum, Five in a Row, uses a unit study approach and we cover all the subjects with one book a week," says Alysia. "It's been wonderful; I couldn't imagine using anything else. The only problem I've had is finding some of the out of print books."

A potential problem with prepared unit studies is that they may not be available on the subjects your child is interested in. Not to worry; lots of homeschoolers observe which topics "light their children's fires" and successfully create their own units.

A potential problem with prepared unit studies is they may not be available on the subjects your child is interested in. Not to worry; lots of home-schoolers observe which topics "light their children's fires" and successfully create their own units.

HOW WE DID IT

We do other subjects beyond reading, writing, and arithmetic, and always have. At times we relate subjects. Jacob was seven years old when we started homeschooling full time, and the first book we read aloud together was *The Secret Garden*. We looked up India, England, cholera. We searched old *National Geographics* for pictures of meadows. We looked up lots about plants and gardening, and the children made lists and plans for things they wanted to plant in a garden when spring came. We imitated a Yorkshire accent. We drew pictures based on the book, and made caricatures of characters we didn't like.

We try to broaden our learning from whatever single source we might be using. But we also set goals for ourselves in other areas. For instance, early on Jacob grew fascinated with ancient Egypt after seeing Abbott and Costello's *Meet the Mummy*. He read vast amounts on ancient Egypt, drew pictures of Egyptian gods, made a board game of ancient Egypt, and made clothespin dolls of ancient Egyptian gods. We also looked at maps of Egypt, learned about its geography, its animals, the contribution of ancient Egypt to math and science, the process of mummification, the kinds of food they ate, and so on. We found books

Pauline's family uses her homemade unit studies alone or with friends. "We've studied Ancient Egypt, China, King Arthur, and Canada (we're Canadians). It seems to work well," says Pauline, "especially if it's asked for by the children. I love it as much as they do, and am learning as much, too."

Oftentimes, real-life learning comes out just like a unit study, even though it's totally unplanned.

"I guess we use unit studies," Michaela figures. "We get interested in something then check out relevant books from the library, on ancient Egyptian mythology, compared those to other myths, and began expanding our ancient territories of study, moving on to Mesopotamia, Persia, Greece, Rome. When Jacob was eight we began studying Latin, using *Ecce Romani,* which has a continuing story and lovely illustrations.

We generally study science, history (both U.S. and world), geography, French, Latin, music, and art in addition to reading, writing (these including grammar, spelling, vocabulary), and arithmetic. We follow the children's interests in some areas. For instance, Marla does more science, Jacob more history. He recently became interested in military planes of various sorts; their design, and the features behind their design. Marla is taking up guitar; both study piano. We all listen to a lot of classical and folk music, and more recently are exploring musicals. Both children sew. Both use the computer, ride bikes, and run and climb. Marla plays basketball and roller-skates. John likes to use our treadmill. We always seem to have more we want to do than we have time.

—ANGIE

notice the thing in the world around us, visit Web sites, go to museums . . . we did this with earthworms last year.

"When we're interested in something and read voraciously about it and observe it if possible in nature or a museum," Michaela continues, "we often do something like write about it or just use the ideas when playing. When Amy got interested in the sunfish at the Monterey Bay Aquarium we did a Web search on sunfish, collected photos and articles and put them together in a book. When we were interested in origami we made lots of origami, but we also began noticing origami-type patterns in things around us, like right there in the folds of Amy's favorite blanket."

History-Based Possibilities

Yet another way to organize studies across the curriculum is to allow history to dictate their unfolding. A study approach based on history begins with the earliest civilizations and leads quickly into ancient Egypt, China, Greece, and Rome. Here's opportunity to learn about early uses of math and its development right along with the sum of 5 + 5. Your child can watch sciences develop through the ages, plac-

HOW WE DID IT

We love unit studies but haven't purchased any ready to go. So far the units we've done are *Learning About Idaho*, *Little House on the Prairie* about pioneers, *Medieval Times*, *Ancient Egypt*, and we're planning to start *American History* using the American Girls series. We do these units with other families, sometimes once a week, sometimes once a month. I love to do library research so I get tons of books that each family reads themselves at home during the week. When we get together we do some sort of written work like vocabulary, some art, cook lunch together, and maybe watch a video about the subject.

The units last about four to six months. We also write a play about each theme and then perform it at the end of the study for grandparents and friends. This has been very rewarding but difficult to get the children to agree on a story line, assigning parts, and so on. The three families currently meeting are now going to try a published play about one of the American Girls' instead of writing it ourselves. We perform the plays in the backyard, making all the scenes, costumes, and so on. It's a tremendous amount of fun and I think we all learn tons, too.

—BRENDA

ing famous scientists into the historic framework of their discoveries and theories.

If you don't necessarily want to move in time-line order with history, you and your child can just pick a time period to guide you, like Shannon's family. "We use it as a framework to explore various things that happened during that time frame," she explains. "Sometimes we work science into the unit, as when studying ancient Egypt we learned about pyramids and studied the use of levers. Usually it's just that someone will wonder about something, and we start studying to find the answer."

Interest-Initiated Possibilities

Alternatively called *child-led, learner-directed,* and *unschooling,* this is the most unstructured of typical study possibilities and requires the greatest amount of trust in a child as a "learning machine" who will learn what he needs to know when he needs to know it. This approach makes the most of the learning opportunity presented when the learner's interest is at its peak.

Much misunderstanding of this approach is expressed by critics and skeptics who have never trusted children to this degree (so they have no direct experience) and/or mistakenly believe it's akin to a *Lord of the Flies* existence for children. Nothing could be further from the truth.

As a loving parent who takes seriously the responsibility of your child's education, you are ever-alert and observant, picking up all types of learning clues from him. High interest in a subject is quite evident to you, and you then nurture it. You seek out ever more materials, classes, and necessary teachers, leading to studies that are both deeper and broader.

> The combination of learning the basics with catching a learning child's interest at its peak leads to very effective lessons.

This in turn exposes him to the ever-greater world of related knowledge, allowing his interest to expand learning into areas he originally didn't even know existed. The combination of learning the basics with catching a learning child's interest at its peak leads to very effective lessons.

"My main goal is for my children to see the interconnectedness of everything," explains Laura. "It's taken me years to tune in to that concept, and I hope to understand it more with them. How is math related to art, or science related to music? It's all one big puzzle, not discrete parts. It's one of the big reasons we homeschool."

Laura continues, "We use unit studies very little, but we do use interests and jumping-off points. *Little House on the Prairie* books start us on cooking, botany, and overpopulation. We used to study one particular topic a lot, too. It's more like we have jumping-off points, then we just go with them.

"We don't use unit studies yet. That may change as they get older; I don't know yet."

Corinne outlines a similar learning philosophy. "Our children all chose to learn to play musical instruments from six to seven years of age. Science, social studies, and such are not studied as subjects separately or otherwise," she explains. "We just learn from our reading, TV, radio, and exploration of our world. We discuss things of interest as they arise, and sometimes take them further, sometimes not."

The ability of frequent reading to "open the door on knowledge" grows quite evident in the interest-initiated possibility of homeschooling.

Wendy explains, "By reading good fiction and nonfiction we're introduced to history, social studies, science, and so on. This is our starting point. From there we explore interests as they arise."

"Topics just come up," adds Abby, "perhaps from reading a story about a certain time period, or from something we see on TV or a movie. Science is part of everyday life—how do things work, and why? If my son gets a notion he'd like to explore a topic further, he does. We don't itemize 'subjects'."

Still other homeschooling parents use the interest-initiated possibility because they subscribe to the "better late than early" theory of children's education. This allows the child time for the physical and mental development required for more formal study. Interest-initiated learning lets these families use the early years to slowly build a strong educational foundation for the future.

"I don't do much outside of basic reading, writing, and arithmetic with this age group," says Marlene. "We read stories and watch movies with historical content, as well as some with science material, but at ages three to eight 'school' is still very informal."

Priscilla views homeschooling's lack of a timetable as its greatest asset. "There is a natural progression of interest and learning that seems to go hand in hand with home educating young children," she says. "We have time to go with the flow of whatever interests us or catches our imagination. I don't have to bore my children doing something they have no interest in that day or hour and they don't have to stop the subject which just caught their imagination because 'it's time to put the paints away'."

Combination Possibilities

The study of "other subjects" during homeschooling's early years lends itself to myriad combination possibilities. Moving beyond the school model, there exist so many roads to learning, and so many interesting stops along the way, families often mix and match their options, expanding on the successful ones and dropping the failures. This approach is workable because of homeschooling's flexibility and the parent's intimate knowledge of the child's interests and abilities.

You, too, will be able to observe if something is boring your child to tears or, conversely, if the approach is fun but ineffective at building the skills you'd hoped for. Remembering there are always other ways—and that you are free to use any of them—will help keep you from placing undue pressure on yourself or your child. This keeps learning both meaningful and fun.

> Combination possibilities are as endless as they are interesting.

HOW WE DID IT

We studied French, American history, world history, geography, and science. We read a lot, went on field trips, listened to tapes. I tried to make each subject multi-sensorial with cooking, music, art, science, literature, and maps about the subjects. We also used science, history, and geography unit studies. We hardly ever incorporate math in unit studies; not all that much writing, either.

—GRETCHEN

Combination possibilities are as endless as they are interesting.

"We study history and geography, art and art appreciation, music and music appreciation, Spanish and some other subjects as a group," says Anna. "Science, health, reading, grammar and English, and some others are done individually. We've never used unit studies."

Lenore describes her family's approach as integrated. "We cover subjects in their complexity, like math in measuring for cooking, learning about the origins of foods, growing techniques, and the countries they come from, all in a stream-of-thought exploration and study. Sometimes my daughter initiates the effort, and sometimes I do."

In Rachel's home, curriculum components and outside lessons combine. "I used *Voice of the Martyrs* material for missions and geography and A Beka for history," she says. "We used outside instruction for Spanish and science lab. We studied the science text at home, but participated in lab with other homeschooled students."

"My children have a separate curriculum piece for thinking, nutrition, Spanish, music, and science," explains Dee, who then adds unit study to the mix. "We're currently living in Phoenix so our topic right now is the desert. We immerse ourselves in it—we read as much as we can about the plants, animals, and people. We look for all the science experiments we can do in this regard, and visit all the museums we can find."

In Upland, California, Denise uses unit studies only if her early years boys are interested in them. "Other subjects are easily incorporated into real life," she says. "We can learn them just as well in educational movies and TV programs and computer games. The important thing is to expose them to many different things so they can discover what they're really interested in," Denise explains. She's also discovered that, for her family, it's more useful to learn one or two subjects in depth than to skim over many different subjects the children aren't interested in.

"We hit other subjects through reading, writing, and math," says Daphne, whose three children have learned in their rural Maine home since 1996. "Everything is integrated."

Ruth concedes it's hard to put her family's approach into words. "We do it another way," she says. "We naturally combine practice and learning new skills, but it isn't exactly planned. Sometimes we discover some concept just hasn't been learned. That's when I'll give a direct explanation, and give them some practice."

Valerie is looking back on homeschooling in the early years, remembering her children learning geography from maps and TV, history from fiction books, adults talking, TV, and movies, and discovering science and math "everywhere."

"I found no reason for formal academic study before the age of eight or even ten. It took very little time to fill in any gaps for skills missed by not doing dozens of workbooks!" she says.

SCOPE AND SEQUENCE OF "OTHER SUBJECTS" IN THE EARLY YEARS

YOUR FAMILY may choose to investigate other subjects through a curriculum and textbooks, unit studies, or as part of reading, writing, and arithmetic, as they naturally spring up in daily life and through your child's expressed interest, or yet another way.

You may remain concerned about what other children the same age as your child are studying, or about your state's possible requirement to participate in annual standardized testing.

Many school districts will provide homeschooling families with a set of the grade-level textbooks they use. Here subjects are laid out, step by step, and a quick study of the materials gives you a good overview. (Additionally, it might make your local school personnel feel all warm and fuzzy to *think* you'll be using their materials.) If you don't want to take or can't get the school's materials, your local school should have its curriculum laid out and shouldn't have any qualms about sharing it. This curriculum will tell you what teachers hope to cover during the year.

Several large encyclopedia publishers, including World Book, create their own interpretations of grade-level courses of study. The commercially available Core Knowledge series, authored by E. D. Hirsch and consisting of the *What Your [1st Grader, 2nd Grader, and so on] Needs to Know* books, lays out a challenging curriculum by grade level. Peruse your library or local bookstore's shelves and you're sure to find at least one other interpretation readily available.

A basic curriculum outline is a map showing you where to go. Your freedom of choice still remains in deciding how you'll get there. You may choose a car (a school-type curriculum), but you're free to consider a boat, jet, train, bus, RV, bicycle, or cross-country hike, too. In other words, concerns about addressing materials on a standardized test are valid, but they don't have to limit you to the traditional *method* of study if other methods better serve your child's needs and healthy love of learning for a lifetime.

Homeschooling endows you with a great amount of time for cooperative and independent reading; time for your child to reveal and for you to observe interests, strengths, and weaknesses; time to experiment with varied materials and change course if necessary; time for your child's brain, eye-hand coordination, and desire for formal study to mature; and time for your child to enjoy the fleeting moments of childhood play. Given this learning environment, so antithetical to a government school learning environment, it makes sense to take full advantage of it, most especially during the early years. Now is the time your child's natural learning assets help him gather foundational knowledge.

As homeschoolers have noted, science is all around you, as close as your backyard, windowsills, and kitchen table. Exposure to early years social studies typically consists of understanding family and builds toward the greater community. A homeschooling child lives this every day. U.S. and state history come to life through good children's literature, movies, museums, and field trips. Health education, in the form of safety, nutrition, and even the workings of the human body can become mealtime conversation. Art and music, both their creation and appreciation, may weave their way into just about any current study topic. Physical education? Opportunities abound in the backyard, on "aerobic" walks, at support group playground days, and

HOW WE DID IT

I don't worry about school subjects. The children live and learn in a loving and supportive environment. There's lots of books and resource materials in the house and we get books from the library regularly, the children choosing their own. They participate in community learning activities, take piano lessons, study Spanish, and cook. They excel in areas that suit their talents and goals. They love to learn history especially by reading historical novels. And they love classic and contemporary great literature. We don't really use unit studies as they're not formally prepared, but rather real-life lessons. My oldest is so excited about her learning, and I'm thrilled I never forced any of it on the children.

—RITA

in organized community activities. Just try keeping a healthy child from attending to his internal drive for physical exercise!

From this perspective, you can see study of "other subjects" may flow naturally from living life as a family making a child's education top priority. At the same time your child discovers the reality of all subjects' interconnectedness. This greatly decreases the possibility you'll ever hear your child say, "I hate arithmetic" or "I'm no good at science."

> You know where you want to go; have fun choosing and using the vehicles that get you there.

Curricula from the sources listed in chapter 5 generally cover all subjects as a matter of course. Because of the vast array of study possibilities and the relative ease of obtaining a typical course of study and following it, if desired, the remainder of this chapter is devoted to a small sampling of the enormous selection of resources available to you whether or not you use a curriculum.

You know where you want to go; have fun choosing and using the vehicles that get you there.

RESOURCES

(Some resources in this section courtesy of *The Complete Home Learning Source Book* by Rebecca Rupp, Three Rivers Press, 1998.)

Art

Carlson, Laurie. *Kids Create! Art and Craft Experiences for 3- to 9-Year-Olds.* Williamson Publishing, 1990.

KidsArt (catalog): P.O. Box 274, Mt. Shasta, CA 96067; 916-926-5076; www.kidsart.com.

Lakeshore Learning Materials (catalog): 2695 E. Dominguez Street, Carson, CA 90749; 800-421-5354.

le Tord, Bijou. *A Blue Butterfly: A Story about Claude Monet.* Doubleday, 1995.

Micklethwait, Lucy. *The Child's Book of Play in Art.* Dorling Kindersley, 1996.

———. *I Spy* series. Greenwillow, various publication dates.

Provensen, Alice and Martin. *Leonardo da Vinci: The Artist, Inventor, Scientist in Three-Dimensional Movable Pictures.* Viking, 1984.

Sax Arts & Crafts (catalog): P.O. Box 510710, New Berlin, WI 53151; 800-558-6696. Contains some fun art games for early years children, as well as materials.

Terzian, Alexandra M. *The Kids' Multicultural Art Book: Art and Craft Experiences from Around the World.* Williamson, 1993.

Warner, Sally. *Encouraging the Artist in Your Child.* St. Martin's Press, 1989.

Wolf, Aline D. *How to Use Child-Size Masterpieces for Art Appreciation.* Parent Child Press, 1996.

Foreign Languages

Early Advantage: 25 Ford Road, Westport, CT 06880; 888-248-0480; www.early-advantage.com.

The First Thousand Words (series): EDC Publishing; 800-331-4418. More wonderful Usborne books for a head start in several languages.

The Learnables: 800-237-1830; www.learnables.com.

Storybridges: Audio-Forum, 96 Broad Street, Guilford, CT 06437; 800-243-1234; agoralang.com/audioforum.html.

Twin Sisters: Listen and Learn a Language: 1340 Home Avenue, Suite D, Akron, OH 44310; 800-248-TWIN; www.twinsisters .com.

Geography

Anno, Mitsumasa. *Anno's U.S.A.* Paper Star, 1998.

Cassidy, John. *Earthsearch: A Kids' Geography Museum in a Book.* Klutz Press, 1994. For the older early years child, or a younger child with your help.

Fowler, Allan. *North, South, East and West.* Children's Press, 1993.

Internet Homeschool Trucker Buddy Program: Send e-mail with subject line: Trucker Buddy to Mamaturtl1@aol.com. In return, child will receive daily e-mail from a homeschooling dad as he trucks across the U.S. Get a map and push pins!

Jeunesse, Gallimard, and Jean-Pierre Verdet, eds. *Atlas of the Earth.* Scholastic, 1997.

Lasky, Kathryn. *The Librarian Who Measured the Earth.* Little, Brown, 1994.

National Geographic videos: Box 5073, Clifton, NJ 07015; 800-627-5162. Videos that live up to their maker's quality reputation.

Uncle Happy's Train Game: Mayfair Games, Inc., 5211 W. 65th Street, Bedford Park, IL 60638; 800-432-4376; www.cool games.com. Learn state names, shapes, and more for ages six and older.

Wolfman, Ira. *My World and Globe: An Interactive First Book of Geography.* Workman, 1991. Comes with inflatable globe and lots of stickers.

History

American Girls Collection (software): The Learning Company, 6160 Summit Drive N., Minneapolis, MN 55430; 800-622-3390. CD-ROM for Windows and Mac.

Bluestocking Press (catalog): P.O. Box 2030, Shingle Springs, CA 95682; 800-959-8586.

Caney, Steven. *Kids' America.* Workman, 1978. Lots of history-related projects for the older early years child; some workable with younger child with help.

Chatham Hill Games, Inc. (catalog): P.O. Box 253, Chatham, NY 12037; 800-554-3039. Great games for the older early years child.

Childhood of Famous Americans (series): Aladdin Publishing. Biographies of famous folks' early years; can be read aloud to younger children.

Fritz, Jean: Lots of good read-aloud history from this author published by a variety of publishers.

HearthSong (catalog): 6519 N. Galena Road, Peoria, IL 61656; 800-325-2502. Early American craft kits.

Macaulay, David. *Castle, Cathedral, or Pyramid* are great books about how these buildings were made, and *Underground* shows what's happening under your city streets.

New True Books: Social Studies (series): Children's Press, P.O. Box 1331, Danbury, CT 06813; 800-621-1115. Part of the series contains stories on American government suitable to read aloud to young children!

This is America, Charlie Brown (video series): Movies Unlimited, 3015 Darnell Road, Philadelphia, PA 19154; 800-4-MOVIES; www.moviesunlimited.com.

Music

4 Fish Fly Free (videos): 877-346-2582; curriculum guides and lesson plans available upon request.

Anyone Can Whistle (catalog): P.O. Box 4407, Kingston, NY 12401; 800-435-8863. Interesting and child-size instruments.

Classical Kids Series (audiotapes or CDs): West Music, P.O. Box 5521, Coralville, IA 52241; 800-397-9378. For the older early years child.

Davidson's Music (Christian piano course): 6727 Metcalf, Shawnee Mission, KS 66204.

Fuller, Cheri. *How to Grow a Young Music Lover.* Harold Shaw Publishing, 1994.

Hart, Avery, and Paul Mantell. *Kids Make Music: Clapping and Tapping to Bach and Rock.* Williamson Publishing, 1993. Music activities for ages three to nine.

Hotchkiss, Gwen. *Music Smart! Ready-to-Use Listening Tapes and Activities for Teaching Music Appreciation.* Parker, 1990. Music appreciation curriculum from kindergarten through eighth grade.

Rhythm Band Instruments (catalog): P.O. Box 126, Fort Worth, TX 76101; 800-424-4724.

Venezia, Mike. *Getting to Know the World's Greatest Composers* (series). Children's Press, various publication dates.

Wee Sing (series): Published by Price Stern Sloan, a cassette tape accompanies a sing-along book for ages three to nine.

Physical Education

Elmocize (video): Music for Little People, P.O. Box 1720, Lawndale, CA 90260; 800-727-2233.

Footloose (game): Exercise game available in toy stores.

Marzollo, Jean. *Pretend You're a Cat*. Dial Books for Young Readers, 1990.

The Training Camp (catalog): P.O. Box 1602, Secaucus, NJ 07096; 800-284-5383. Sports equipment.

Waller, Stella. *Yoga for Children*. HarperCollins, 1996.

Whitney, Bruce C. *Home School Family Fitness: A Practical Curriculum Guide*. Home School Family Fitness Institute, 1995; 612-636-7738.

Workout with Mommy & Me (video): Movies Unlimited; 800-4-MOVIES. For toddlers to approximately six-year-olds; and Mom, too.

Potpourri

Bellerophon Books (catalog): 36 Ancapa Street, Santa Barbara, CA 93101; 800-253-9943. Inexpensive coloring and craft books for a wide variety of subjects and ages.

Carlson, Laurie, and Judith Dammel. *Kids Camp! Activities for the Backyard or Wilderness*. Chicago Review Press, 1995.

Charlip, Remy, and Mary Beth Miller. Handtalk: *An ABC of Finger Spelling and Sign Language*. Simon & Schuster, 1984. Good beginner's book for children as young as four.

Curiosity Kits (catalog): Box 811, Cockeysville, MD 21030; 800-584-KITS. Kits for a variety of subjects complete with all necessary materials; several appropriate for early years children.

Dover Publications, Inc.: 31 E. Second Street, Mineola, NY 11501. Many low-priced books, coloring books, masks, and more.

The Drinking Gourd: Box 2557, Redmond, WA 98073; 206-836-0336. Multicultural resources.

Eatonlya (game): Performance Education Technologies, Inc., 514 N. Third Street, Suite 107, Minneapolis, MN 55401. Nutrition lessons for ages five and up.

Evert, Jodi, ed. American Girls *Cookbooks*. Pleasant Company, 1994.

Fredericks, Anthony D. *Social Studies through Children's Literature: An Integrated Approach*. Teacher Ideas Press, 1991. Activities across the curriculum based on picture books, some of which are fun for children as young as five.

Gryphon Bricks (software): Davidson, 19840 Pioneer Avenue, Torrance, CA 90503; 800-545-7677. Lego-like blocks in a 3-D building kit.

Katzen, Mollie, and Ann Henderson. *Pretend Soup and Other Real Recipes*. Tricycle Press, 1994. Cooking for preschoolers and older.

Kohl, MaryAnn F., and Jean Porter. *Cooking Art: Easy Edible Art for Young Children*. Gryphon House, 1997.

Northrop Publishing Company (catalog): 352 Main Street, Bristol, CT 06010; 888-576-8532; www.javanet.com/~northrop.

Priceman, Marjorie. *How to Make an Apple Pie and See the World*. Dragonfly, 1996.

Real Power Toolshop (catalog): Natural Science Industries; 888-425-9113. Miniature jigsaw, drill press, sander and wood lathe, instructions, balsa wood; for children seven and older.

Scholastic Books Warehouse Sales: http://place.scholastic.com/bookfairs/us.htm. Check Web site for a sale location near you.

Science

A Question of Science (book series): published by Carolrhoda, available at bookstores, for ages five through eight.

Carolina Biological Supply Co. (catalog): 2700 York Road, Burlington, NC 27215; 800-334-5551. Source for The Bug Game and *Build Your Own Bugs Book* and Rubber Stamp Kit, among other wonderful resources.

Center for Marine Conservation. *The Ocean Book: Aquarium and Seaside Activities and Ideas for All Ages.* John Wiley & Sons, 1989.

Cole, Joanna. *Magic School Bu*s (series). Scholastic, various publication dates. Videos and software also available.

Edmund Scientific Company (catalog): 101 E. Gloucester Pike, Barrington, NJ 08007; 800-728-6999; www.edsci.com.

GeoSafari, Jr.: Educational Insights, 16941 Keegan Avenue, Carson, CA 90746; 800-933-3277. Electronic game for preschool: grade 2; reading/science/puzzles.

Let's Read-and-Find-Out (science series): Over fifty HarperTrophy books in two levels; one for preschoolers, two for ages six through nine, available at bookstores.

Margulies, Robert and Roger Culbertson. *3-D Kid.* W.H. Freeman & Company, 1995. Includes fold-out body wall chart.

Muse: Box 7468, Red Oak, IA 51591; 800-827-0227; www.muse mag.com. magazine; bimonthly; $24/year.

New True Books (science and math series): Children's Press; nicely illustrated books covering many topics for ages six through nine.

Parker, Nancy Winslow, and Joan Richards Wright. *Bugs.* William Morrow, 1988.

Science Kit Rentals: Museum of Science, Science Park, Boston, MA 02114; 800-722-5487.

Teachers' Laboratory (catalog): Box 6480, Brattleboro, VT 05302; 800-769-6199.

The Ultimate Visual Dictionary: Dorling Kindersley; look for other wonderful titles from the same publisher.

Water Wonders: Alex; 800-666-ALEX (water experiments and projects kit; ages five through eight.

Web Sites

Audio and Text Greetings in Many Languages: vraptor.jpl.nasa.gov/voyager/lang.html

Castles on the Web: www.fox.nstn.ca/~tmonk/castle/castle.html (virtual tours, photos, drawing contests, links, and more)

Children's International Summer Village Songbook: antenna.nl/~www cisv/songs.html

Emma's Dramatic Homepage: www.cream.une.edu.au/StudentFiles/HomePages/372_96/Emma.html (help for teaching drama to early years children)

Learning Kids Interactive: http://www.learningkids.com (games, contests, free stuff, "today in history," more)

Lullabies and Other Songs for Children: www.stairway.org/kidsongs

Mapmaker, Mapmaker, Make Me a Map: loki.ur/utk.edu/ut2kids/maps/map.html (mapmaking for youngsters)

Michael's Kids Club: michaels.com/kids/kid-main.html (puppets, arts and crafts)

New (as of late '98) *U.S. Quarters:* http://www.usmint.gov/50states/index.cfm

Sesame Street Lyrics Archive: globalserve.net/~rhonda/sesame1.html

Tales to Tell: www.thekids.com (children's multicultural stories)

Walking Tour of Plimoth Plantation: spirit.lib.uconn.edu/ArchNet/Topical/Historic/Plimoth/Plimoth.html

9

TAILORING
HOMESCHOOLING TO YOUR
FAMILY'S UNIQUE NEEDS

In This Chapter

✦ Too many bills and not enough money

✦ Single parents

✦ The gifted child

✦ The special needs and physically disabled child

✦ The academically labeled child

✦ Stay-at-home dads

✦ The only child

✦ Large families

✦ Simple starting points

✦ Resources

*N*OWHERE IS homeschooling's flexibility more evident than in the lifestyles of those who practice it. Sometimes homeschooling families hold nothing more in common than their belief that home is the best place for their children to learn and grow. While this would make it difficult to rally your homeschooling friends around your favorite political candidate, it's a testament to the families' dedication to embracing responsibility for their children's education.

TOO MANY BILLS AND NOT ENOUGH MONEY

YOU DON'T have to be a homeschooling family to feel the pinch of too many bills. As a homeschooler, though, you may feel pinched harder than others. Homeschooling, particularly in the early years, could require one spouse to at least temporarily give up a job—a challenging venture in our two-income society. But it's a feat daily accomplished as families examine life priorities, make adjustments, and find they receive much more than they give up.

Simplify, Simplify, Simplify

Henry David Thoreau's advice may seem too simple, but it's hard to argue with success. Truth is, keeping a job requires *x* amount of money earned that goes right back into keeping the job. There's transportation, special clothes, meals away from home, ceaseless fellow employee birthdays, and most likely day care and/or after-school care for your young children. There's that boost into the next tax bracket, which gives the government a larger chunk of your family's combined income. When she examined the actual results of her second income, one homeschooling mom found her $25/hour job only benefited her family's bottom line by $7/hour. She concluded time at home was worth much more than that.

> When she examined the actual results of her second income, one homeschooler found her $25/hour job only benefited her family's bottom line by $7/hour.

Take a look at your family's current budget. Deduct from your "must have" list all those expenses which would disappear if you kiss the second income good-bye. Examine your list for other possible deductions. Don't worry if you can only eliminate a few at this point. Remember, once you begin homeschooling it's going to affect your lifestyle.

"Living on an income that hovers right around the poverty line means we must always put food and medical care as priorities over educational supplies," says Sarah. "We can't participate in all the cool activities that our friends can, like Space Camp or attending plays or even taking music or swimming lessons.

"Believe it or not, this has all been beneficial," Sarah explains. "My children don't compare themselves unfavorably with others because of the labels on their clothes. We don't have to spend all the piddly chunks of cash we would if our children were in school, such as gifts for a Christmas party, or new shoes each year used only in the school gym. The children are learning lots of survival skills; bread making, hair cutting, gardening, and mending. A big public library full of books, audiotapes, and videos is a much richer resource than any one family's money could buy for themselves."

> Simplifying doesn't mean doing without; it's doing more with less.

Darby finds exercising increased care and judgment before a major purchase helps her family save. "Money is always tight on one salary but we prioritize and think carefully about purchases," she explains. "If it's a big ticket item we try to borrow one first to see if it's forgotten after the 'new' wears off."

Simplifying doesn't mean doing without; it's doing more with less. And once you become a part of the homeschooling community, you'll be amazed at the number of folks doing the same, helping each other along the way.

"We're on a tight budget, but not as tight as many others in our community," says Erica. "I share materials with as many as I can, especially cheap or low-cost items and items good for multiple uses. The library, buying used books and games, and sharing resources are the best ways to stretch a tight budget."

You may still conclude you need—or want—to work. Have you considered working at home?

Creating Work at Home

Work at home complements homeschooling and a family-first lifestyle. It allows you greater control of your schedule, eliminates most of those special clothes, transportation, and child-care costs associated with employment, and lets you make money doing what you love. Homeschooling sparks the entrepreneurial spirit in many people—a spark, according to trend analysts, ready to ignite all across our culture.

Paula works as a counselor and teacher from home. Rural Idahoan Meredith has homeschooled two children for three years, working at home through tax season. During this busy time the family "just does the basics," catching up when the season is over. Patty *and* her husband work from home, taking advantage of their flexible work hours to share responsibility for their children's education and activities. Hope started a medical consulting business "to pay for the student loans I incurred before I wanted to be a stay-at-home mom."

Homeschooling itself, coupled with a love of and a need for books, makes "what to do" regarding home work an easy choice for some. Jacqueline takes Scholastic, Carnival, and Trumpet book club

HOW WE DID IT

I manage the fifty-six-unit apartment complex in which our family lives. Most of the time I consider this a part-time job, although there are rare days where it's full-time work. I worked out a deal with our property owner so that from 10 A.M. until noon each weekday I can ignore the apartment phone and put a closed sign outside my door. This way I can focus on two hours of homeschooling without interruptions. I also ignore my home phone during that time.

Our homeschooling time usually extends beyond noon, sometimes until two or three in the afternoon, depending on my son's interest level, in which case I do answer the business phone and handle interruptions.

—LESLIE

orders for her children's Scout den in exchange for the free books her work earns her.

In England, Priscilla started a home-based mail-order book business. Now the children "see me involved in something I started myself, giving them the idea it's possible. The way the world is changing I think our children will have to think very differently about how they will earn a living."

Maureen, in Canada, combined her love of books and a problem she perceived, and took book selling to another level.

> Homeschooling sparks the entre-preneurial spirit in many people, a spark, according to trend analysts, ready to ignite all across our modern culture.

"I was disappointed we couldn't purchase homeschooling supplies locally. It's hard to tell from a little blurb in a catalog if you'll really use an item enough to buy it, so I approached one of the catalogs about becoming a distributor and having stock on hand. We worked out the details and as finances allow I set up accounts with other companies," says Maureen of her endeavor.

Maureen now combines working at home with an on-call food services job at the local hospital, working from 4 P.M. to 8 P.M. when needed. On days she's called to work, a homeschooling friend cares for her two children from 4 P.M. until their father gets them at 6 P.M. He credits Maureen's ability to "multi-task" for the family's success in juggling an oftentimes hectic schedule.

Full-Time Work Is Still Possible, Too

Okay. You've whittled down your "must have" list to the bare minimum. You've racked your brain for a work-at-home idea but come up blank. And that pile of unpaid bills isn't shrinking. Full-time work may be your destiny, but it doesn't have to mean the end of a homeschooling dream. You may just have to be a bit more creative than some families, and join the ranks of those remarkable souls who combine full-time work with learning at home.

Although she's still the primary homeschooling parent, Renee's husband increased his contribution as her work responsibilities grew. Part-time classes at community college led Renee to part-time work at her local library while classes continued. With her family's move she's taken a temporary job processing books at a new library, working 6 A.M. to 9 A.M. Another part-time job as reference librarian at another library brings total work hours close to full time.

With two of her three children over eight years old, Renee feels, "It's helped the boys learn self-responsibility. I have less time but use it more wisely. My attitude toward learning in college has made a good impression on the children. Plus—I love my job, another positive example for them. And," she adds, "you can't have a better job as a homeschooling parent than working in the library! All those resources at your fingertips. And no overdue fines on your books!"

When Melanie's husband was laid off right before Thanksgiving last year, she found work as a swing-shift telemarketer. When her husband gets another job she'll continue working part time in the evenings until the family catches up financially. The experience brought some happy surprises to this family.

Melanie points out, "It has worked well for us in many ways as my husband is very good with the children. It's been great to see him bond with our youngest as he worked a lot of overtime since she was born and never really spent much time with her before. Things will never be the same around here again.

> Full-time work may be your destiny, but it doesn't have to mean the end of a homeschooling dream.

"We've grown as a family and as a couple through this 'adversity.' My husband has grown spiritually and is a better father than I ever thought possible. If I was able to make the kind of money he does we'd probably stay in the roles we're now in. He's more relaxed. I tend to focus on what needs to be done housework-wise; he's more in tune to the children."

In Ariana's Texas household, bustling with three early years children, combining homeschooling and mom's job gives another dad more time with the children than he'd otherwise have.

Ariana's husband tends to 95 percent of the academic part of homeschooling while she works in the morning. In the afternoons, she takes the children to various lessons while he works the 3 P.M. to 11 P.M. shift at the hospital. "This schedule wouldn't work if the children were in public schools," Ariana notes. "With homeschooling, he gets to spend a great deal of time teaching them and playing a huge part in their everyday lives."

SINGLE PARENTS

CREATIVITY, FLEXIBILITY, and resourcefulness—the cultivated hallmarks of a successful homeschooling parent—appear in double doses in those parents who choose this journey as single parents. Not willing to let this opportunity slip away from their children simply because they don't have a partner, single parents often accomplish logistical feats that would impress an army general.

Initial considerations should include your former partner's stance on homeschooling. It's one thing to have a spouse not with you, but quite another to have a former spouse against you; homeschooling has been played as a trump card in divorce-related issues such as custody and child support payments.

How do your ex-spouse's parents feel? Will you get support, including moral support, from your own parents? How will you fill any gaps you perceive in your ability to keep your child in loving instructors' hands should you need to be absent at times?

Kailyn, homeschooling in California since 1991, found arranging child care during her work hours her biggest hurdle. Each week brought a new plan, and "each day was a different setting, from friends' houses to homeschool classes to relatives' homes. I considered it 'positive stress,'" Kailyn says, "compared to the 'negative' stress when we tried school briefly for the sake of its convenience."

Even though it's challenging and requires outside help, homeschooling gave Kailyn and her son "time to be together. In other words," Kailyn summarizes, "we could have a life!"

Callie decided to homeschool when her son was two years old. "I choose an alternative lifestyle requiring very little cash income so I have maximum time available for my son," she explains. "I initially received AFDC grant money, but now I have a job where he can come with me."

Callie credits her local homeschool support group for her family's success. "They're second family to us: the dads my boy otherwise didn't have; the siblings he's learned to love and with whom he has experienced the fuller range of emotions; the moms he knows are there for him; where he feels safe should I need to be away and as the care plan for him should anything happen to me."

THE GIFTED CHILD

GIFTED CHILDREN PRESENT a special challenge wherever they learn. Most public schools provide special classes for these children, but a parent must carefully consider what they are special in relation to. If better than regular classes in some way, are they better enough? More important, are they the best you might offer your child with special talents?

Rita's eight-year-old daughter was in day care, Montessori school, expensive private school, public school, then public school with a day in a gifted classroom and four days in a multi-age classroom. "Her school memories are like mine," says Rita, "doodling in a notebook, bored because she understood the concept in the first five minutes.

"Now at home, she asks lots of questions, follows her interests (animals, mummies, art, crafts, reading, playing the recorder), and I'm confident she's learning at her own pace."

Dee took a more direct route to homeschooling for her gifted five-year-old son. "At two he was speaking in full, clear, coherent sentences," she explains. "From this he skyrocketed forward. I oftentimes felt I was holding him back by not giving him everything he wanted to learn because his peers weren't doing that particular thing."

At this point the family researched homeschooling and decided it fit. "We still try hard to challenge him and yet give him time to do fun, kindergartner things," says Dee. "This is a hard balance to

HOW WE DID IT

There's need for patience, for clarity of directions, for repeating directions, for letting 'the wiggles' out, for finding appropriate methods for my child's learning style, and for following his interests instead of my own plan.

It has helped a lot to read about unschooling and to refuse to compare him with other children. I also make sure he gets enough time with his Brio and Legos. I remember that what is often called a learning "disability" is often just a learning *difference* that is not particularly acceptable in a school setting.

I've watched other boys like my son go to school. My son—without a doubt— would have been labeled "at risk" and would have been put in a special education class. With homeschooling, instead I have a son who is full of confidence, who is intelligent and interested in learning. His life would have been completely different in a negative way had he been trying to accommodate a teacher's plan for his life and learning instead of his own.

—SARAH

strike." Balance is important to the well-being of the gifted child and won't be overlooked by a loving, observing parent.

The gifted label is still a label, with implications which can last a lifetime. "At home, our daughter hasn't learned she is somehow 'superior' to other people simply because she is adept at playing the School Game," explains Sarah. "Here she just studies to her heart's content the things that interest her."

Parents find gifted children thrive in the home environment, even if it means more exercise. "When you let the child lead," Laura says, "you simply follow and guide. I just may need to jog instead of walk to keep up."

Whether you're walking or jogging through your homeschool learning journey, you may discover, as Rhonda did, "There's not a gifted program on earth that can compete with a homeschooling experience. If children aren't 'gifted' when they start, they'll find their gifts soon after."

THE SPECIAL NEEDS AND PHYSICALLY DISABLED CHILD

EQUALLY AS CHALLENGING as the gifted child, and a serious concern as many families consider the homeschooling option, is the special needs or physically disabled child. Parents realize public schools offer these children government-funded programs that pump extra money per student into the system to aid in their education. It's logical for a parent to question whether the home environment can compete. Those who decided to put home to the test, however, found it serves their children's needs well.

All three of Shannon's children have Tourette syndrome. When her two oldest were in school, "most people we dealt with had no idea what it was and no way to deal with it when we informed them." School was misery for the children, Shannon explains. "They were often persecuted by other children, sometimes teachers. They've been thrilled to be home where they have the freedom to be accepted and loved as individuals."

In St. Louis, Gwenn knew her second child was suffering from attention problems, so she took him to the doctor for a hearing check. He turned out to have mild to moderate hearing loss in both ears, and hearing aids have now increased his language use abilities. "As hearing and language development tests proceeded it was gratifying to note he pronounced all sounds well, unusual for a child with a hearing loss," Gwenn says. "The tester, his dad and I all feel this was due to the one-on-one attention he received when learning reading and phonics."

Parents find physical disabilities need not stop a family from homeschooling, whether those disabilities are temporary or permanent.

Renee's family just experienced what she calls "an unusual year." Her middle son had foot surgery, requiring crutches and extended physical therapy. "To top that off," she adds, "our youngest just had a seizure—his first ever. We're still working to figure out what it is, and the preliminary diagnosis is a type of epilepsy he'll grow out of.

"Homeschooling through all of this has helped. I don't know what I would do if they were in a traditional school setting. It would have been—and still would be—a great deal more stressful."

Sarah's daughter's physical disability isn't going away: she's missing her right hand and half her arm. "But," Sarah explains, "I don't think this makes our situation different from other homeschoolers, with the possible exception there are some chores for which we need to allow her a little more time. In fact, I often forget she is 'disabled', and only thought of it now because her situation has been questioned several times in the last few weeks.

"I think homeschooling has been good for her because she's not being teased by children at school all day," says Sarah. "We've also discovered that even the most well-meaning adults don't expect as much of her as they expect of a child who has two hands. I don't think any teacher could have expectations for her as high as they should be."

Whether to help a child fulfill potential, reduce stress, or pursue education with a "be all that you can be" attitude, homeschooling can be tailored to meet your child's special needs, too.

THE ACADEMICALLY LABELED CHILD

THE 1990S BROUGHT an explosion in the number of academic labels and the number of children receiving them. Parents are tailoring homeschooling to what they view as "learning differences," seeking help as necessary, and forging on, agreeing home is a very good place for children who would receive academic labels in a school setting.

Wanda homeschools three children in Lancaster, Pennsylvania, and is concerned about her middle child, who has little impulse control and is easily distracted. "As I learn about his differences I see how little agreement there is among 'experts,' but it's not imaginary. Sometimes parents need help to deal with this behavior," Wanda concludes.

Meredith's son Dan attended a special preschool for the learning disabled. When it came time for public school kindergarten no school personnel held much hope for success but Dan attended, anyway. In the meantime Meredith began homeschooling Dan's older sister.

Two months into Dan's kindergarten experience, Meredith and her husband attended a teacher conference only to learn Dan would receive a "needs improvement" in conduct.

"I asked why, thinking he was acting up," Meredith remembers. "The teacher said it was because he didn't like to play with the other children; he wanted to play by himself."

> Whether to help a child fulfill potential, reduce stress, or find lasting benefits of one-on-one attention, homeschooling can be tailored to meet your child's special needs, too.

Neither Meredith nor her husband thought this behavior particularly "bad," so Dan came home, too. "He's doing great and is very intelligent," says Mom. "His learning style is different than many children's. Extra attention helped him immensely."

Paula's two children never attended school, but she's convinced they both would have been labeled learning disabled if they had. "Instead," she says, "they've been labeled smart."

STAY-AT-HOME DADS

DADS AREN'T COMING HOME in droves yet, but if this lifestyle choice could make it possible for your family to homeschool, it's definitely worth considering.

Father of three early years children, *Home Education Magazine* columnist Jeff Kelety works from home in a software industry–related job. Jeff's work gets done in between apple pie baking, father and son volunteering at the local science center, and adventure-filled walks to the post office.

"In some ways, homeschooling for us was a logical evolution," says Ben, who in 1995 officially became a homeschooling dad in a Massachusetts college town. "When Kay went back to work after her first maternity leave I was already a stay-at-home writer, so it wasn't a great leap to stay-at-home dad.

"We're often asked 'who does the teaching' or people assume I do it since I'm home. But neither of us does more or less teaching—the children pretty much teach themselves, and both parents facilitate their learning, in different but equal ways. Both my wife and I juggle time with our children, along with our other duties and responsibilities, such as work, housework, and personal lives."

A disability keeps Marty home with five children while Monique goes to work. "I'm still the supervisor and organizer of our homeschool program. I find it difficult to share the responsibility and my husband feels left out much of the time," Monique admits. "We try to talk things out as much as possible. When things begin to fall apart we sit down together and regroup. He'll try to take over more responsibility and I attempt to relinquish control . . . not always easy.

"I'd like to say we have all the time in the world to be together but that's just not the case. I think we have more time together than the average public school family, though. We have meals together, read together, do chores together, and much more."

THE ONLY CHILD

IF YOU'RE CONSIDERING homeschooling an only child, you'll probably navigate more concerns about socialization than other families do. Folks will worry about everything from loneliness to learning how to share, from having someone to play with to discovering cooperation with peers. Parents of only children find all these worries can be overcome.

"I have to create situations for my son to interact with other children so he can have play time that doesn't involve me," says Jacqueline. "I also want him involved with other adults, seeing them as authority figures and role models. So we 'go' a lot—park day, Scouts, homeschool soccer days, and chess club. The local support group has been a great asset."

Michaela makes sure her only child gets together at least once a week with same-age cousins living nearby. Additionally, "She has an important relationship with the three older children who live in the home where I teach music," Michaela explains. "Our local homeschool group has been great for meeting a few children and getting together a few times each month." (More on support groups in chapter 12.)

> Dads aren't coming home in droves yet, but if this lifestyle choice could make it possible for your family to homeschool, it's definitely worth considering.

Having an only child homeschooling sometimes frustrated Louise, who saw both the bad and the good. "People say their children learned this or that just from playing a game. Their children played those games with one another, not just with Mom. Our options were limited in that way; there are only so many hours of games a mom can bring herself to play," Louise confesses.

"With one child, though, the freedom we've had to spend time doing whatever meets our needs or impulses has been terrific. Homeschooling with one child has given us the opportunity to follow those interests to lengths larger families can't go.

"I've made sure we stay in touch with special friends and I've initiated play days more often than other families need to. It took effort, but it was always possible to provide my son with enough of a social life to meet his needs."

LARGE FAMILIES

THE REVERSE OF THE only child coin is tailoring homeschooling to meet the needs of the large family. Here concerns wander to how in the world you could possibly keep track of—or keep up with—the activity occurring at several different levels of child comprehension?

Walk into Sarah's home amid the hubbub of six active children and you'll find a mom doing her best to shuffle attention between them. "I spend a lot of time helping the children rather than following my own interests," Sarah admits. "The older children help with the younger, and we do a lot of reading and activities together."

As always, the passage of time brings change. "Now that my oldest has her driver's license, the younger ones get to go more places than they used to. They've all learned character traits through living in a large family that are necessary in all of life."

Put Marlene in Sarah's home, and she might enjoy the relative peace and quiet—as a break from her activity level with nine children. "Time constraints and deciding who needs my attention most at any given moment are part and parcel of this," Marlene says pragmatically. "It's important the older children do more independent, self-guided work, and help teach the younger siblings, too. Friends have been a great help in our large family, but so has homeschooling. I can't imagine getting everyone up and out of the house to catch a school bus."

Homeschooling families are real people experiencing as great a variety of life circumstances as every other family. They've *made* homeschooling fit into their lives because family time sits high on their life priorities lists. You, too, can enjoy homeschooling's freedom and tailor it to fit your family's needs.

Once you've created a good fit, you'll need the materials to make it happen. We'll check out some of the many resources homeschoolers use to keep the learning journey fun and successful.

SIMPLE STARTING POINTS

✦ *Read up on simple living; it could spark ideas that help make homeschooling financially viable for your family.*

Try the following book list:
> Dacyczyn, Amy. *Tightwad Gazette I, II, and III: Promoting Thrift as a Viable Alternative Lifestyle.* Villard Books, 1993, 1995, 1997.
> Luhrs, Janet. *The Simple Living Guide: A Sourcebook for Less Stressful, More Joyful Living.* Broadway Books, 1997.
> St. James, Elaine. *Simplify Your Life with Kids: 100 Ways to Make Family Life Easier and More Fun.* Andrews & McMeel, 1997.

✦ *Work-at-home opportunities are increasing; research what others are doing to earn money while staying home.*

Here are some sources of ideas:

> Bayse, Jennifer. *101 Best Extra-Income Opportunities for Women.* Prima Publishing, 1997.
>
> Folger, Liz. *The Stay-at-Home Mom's Guide to Making Money.* Prima Publishing, 1997.
>
> Huff, Pricilla Y. *101 Best Home-Based Businesses for Women, revised 2nd edition.* Prima Publishing, 1998.

✦ *Plan a "family financial review week" with your spouse.*

Discuss and list all your expenses, no matter how minor. Discuss which ones you *could* live without and deduct them. Discuss which ones you can lower and deduct them. Discuss which ones you can eliminate when one parent stays home and deduct them. Discuss which ones you can eliminate with homeschooling and deduct them. Compute the federal and state tax savings of a lower income; don't forget the higher earned income credit you might receive. You may even find that second job is costing you money!

✦ *If your child is gifted, physically disabled, special needs, or labeled learning disabled, learn all you can about the specific condition.*

As you uncover the challenges of the situation, think about them in terms of applying a tailored homeschooling approach to education instead of a traditional approach. Note the differences.

RESOURCES

Books

Diller, Dr. Lawrence. *Running on Ritalin: A Physician Reflects on Children, Society, and Performance in a Pill.* Bantam Books, 1998.

Dominguez, Joe, and Vicki Robin. *Your Money or Your Life: Transforming Your Relationship with Money and Achieving Financial Independence.* Penguin USA, 1993.

Kenyon, Mary Potter. *Home Schooling from Scratch: Simple Living, Super Learning.* Gazelle Publications, 1996.

Morgan, Melissa, and Judith Waite Allee. *Homeschooling on a Shoestring.* Harold Shaw Publishing, 1999.

Periodicals

Back Home Magazine: P.O. Box 70, Hendersonville, NC 28793; 800-992-2546; backhome@ioa.com; http://www.ioa.com/home backhome.

HomeSchool Dad Magazine: 609 Starlight Drive, Grand Junction, CO 81504; hsd@acsol.net; http://www.acsol.net/hsd.

Natural Life Magazine: RR 1, St. George, Ontario N0E 1N0 Canada; altpress@netroute.net; http://wwww.life.ca.

Stay at Home Dad: Promoting the Home-Based Father: 61 Brightwood Avenue, North Andover, MA 01845-1702; 508-685-7931; athomedad@aol.com; quarterly, $12/year.

Web Sites

Blind Kids: http://www.az.com/~dday/blindkids.html

Dad-to-Dad: http://www.comet.net/clubs/dad-to-dad

Deaf Homeschool Network: http://www.cris.com/"Tlshell/deaf/html

Father's Resource Center: http://www.parentsplace.com/readroom/frc/index.html

Free Stuff for Kids and Teachers: http://www105.pair.com/free4kid/

Homeschooling Kids with Disabilities: http://members.tripod.com/~Maaja/

Homeschooling on a Shoestring: http://www.geocities.comm/Athens/4663/

Resources for Homeschooling Gifted Students: http://www.teleport
.com/~rkaltwas/tag/articles/hsing.html
Simple Living Network: http://slnet.com/hot.htm
Single Fathers: http://www.pitt.edu/~jsims/singlefa.html

E-Mail Loops

ADD/ADHD Homeschool List: Send e-mail to deborahbowman
@xc.org; use *ADHD HS* list as the subject line.
Aut-2b-Home: Send e-mail to Tamglsr@sgi.net; send bio along with
request to be added.
Homeschooling Gifted Children: Send e-mail to majordomo@
telepport.com; use *HGC-1* as the body of the message.
Newsgroup: alt.education.home-school.disabilities.
One Child: Send e-mail to hub@xc.org; use *subscribe one-child* as the
body of the message.

Organizations

Hewitt Homeschooling Resources: Box 9, Washougal, WA 98671-
0009; 360-835-8708.
National Handicapped Homeschoolers Association: 5383 Alpine
Road SE, Olalla, WA 98359; 206-857-4257; http://www.geoci-
ties.com/Heartland/Ranch/6544/nathhan.html.
Utgnet—Uniqueness, Twice-Gifted, Gifted Network: 10831 W.
Broad Street, #231, Glen Allen, VA 23060; 804-883-6757;
UniGift@aol.com.

Part Three

KEEPING THE LEARNING JOURNEY FUN AND SUCCESSFUL

10

RESOURCES FOR YOUR

LEARNING JOURNEY

In This Chapter

✦ You already have great resources

✦ More resources you may find helpful

✦ The early years emergency resource starter kit

✦ Simple starting points

✦ Resources

I SHOULD HAVE STARTED homeschooling my first son in first grade but I didn't know about resources," Rhonda recalls. "I didn't know about all the catalogs and learning supplies available so I didn't start.

"When I found the homeschooling support group and an online homeschooling community, I learned about the richness of resources and felt totally competent at that point."

Knowing you can get the tools to get a job done is as important to a homeschooler as it is to a carpenter. But rather than facing a lack of tools, a new homeschooler today may actually find the choice

> Knowing you can get the tools to get a job done is as important to a homeschooler as it is to a carpenter.

in resources overwhelming. Educational product companies have discovered the homeschooling market, and they're not shy about letting us know what's available. Many homeschooling families, to create meaningful, family-centered work from home, have also started businesses that cater to the homeschooling community.

Your challenge won't be *finding* resources but rather narrowing down the choices to those materials that best suit your family's needs, learning styles, and budget. A good starting point is your local library. Borrow one or two of the many books devoted to homeschool resources. If your library doesn't have any, check the interlibrary loan system, and ask your librarian to consider purchasing a couple of resource books so they're available to the parents of your community. Innovative educational materials aren't just for homeschoolers, after all.

When you review resource books, think of it as stepping up to a buffet table, perusing everything available before you decide what to take. Ask your children what they would like to learn more about, add their interests to the topics you know you want to cover, and search the books for relevant materials, perhaps with their help. If you see the opportunity here for real-life reading, discussion of budgets, practice with addition, and increasing excitement about learning, you're starting to think like a homeschooler!

There's no shortage of traditional curriculum materials in these guides. They review textbooks, workbooks, study guides, language tapes, and complete curricula that, for one price, include everything you need for a school year's worth of work.

The guides also include single traditional items from which you can pick and choose. But there's more beyond the bounds of tradition, too: good literature, audio and video story tapes, games, puzzles, organizations offering free or low-cost educational material, Web sites, activity books—the list goes on and on. Let this information help you start thinking "outside the box" and gently expand the definition of learning materials for you.

The ads in homeschooling magazines and newsletters can get you started if you can't buy or otherwise get a resource book. Some of the companies you contact do sell their mailing lists, so your mailbox may overflow with additional offerings you didn't request, but it's all apt to be interesting to glance through, even if you don't decide to buy.

Discovering the variety of resources, many of which will impress you as a marked improvement over the textbooks you used in school, you might feel like a kid with a sweet tooth let loose in a candy store. But just as I'd advise the child, beware: If you're not careful, you and your spouse could suffer a bellyache when your credit card bill arrives.

Before you go on a resource spending spree, note how many learning resources already surround you. Exercise your creativity, and think outside of textbooks, workbooks, tests and software. You'll be surprised at what you find.

YOU ALREADY HAVE GREAT RESOURCES . . .

> Before you go on a resource spending spree, note how many learning resources already surround you.

WHEN LEARNING AND life comingle as they do in homeschooling, you begin to look at the world differently. You realize every moment holds the potential to be a learning moment, every experience is a deposit in a knowledge bank, and every "thing" can contribute to the education of your early years child.

To help you see resources through the eyes of a homeschooler—and to save you money—the questionnaire asked respondents, "What items do you have in your home which you consider invaluable for homeschooling?" I expected an array of answers and did I get them! Here, for maybe the first time in homeschooling history,

homeschoolers reveal to the world their most highly regarded resources. Now you, too, possess knowledge of the heretofore secret
educational resources for early years children.

Household Items Already on Hand

- Library card
- Newspaper subscription
- Craft magazines
- Ruler
- Car
- Money and Coins
- Piano or other musical instruments
- VCR and videos
- CD player or tape player with CDs or tapes
- TV
- Glue
- Magnifying glass
- Needle and thread, fabric
- Radio
- Chess set
- Scissors
- Cookbooks
- Box of "useful things"—string, paper clips, rubber bands . . .
- Lots of assorted paper, for writing and creating
- Calendar
- Camera
- Clock
- Gardening tools
- Masking tape
- Toolbox
- Tape measure
- Scotch tape
- Binoculars
- Atlas
- Museum memberships
- First aid kit

People Already on Hand

- Parents
- Grandparents
- Friends
- Children's best friends

+ Interesting, creative people in the neighborhood
+ Pets, including dogs, cats, and horses
  (Give me some leeway here; our puppy is treated like people.)

Places Already on Hand

+ Entire kitchen
+ Greater community
+ Backyard plants and dirt
+ Workshop
+ Garage

Things You Thought Were Just Toys Already on Hand

+ Tinker toys
+ Yahtzee, Monopoly, Clue, Scrabble, Mancala, Life
+ Labyrinth
+ Blocks
+ Deck of cards
+ Dice
+ Dress-up trunk
+ Legos
+ Shovels and pails
+ Colored chalk
+ Assorted balls
+ Bicycles
+ K'nex set
+ Map puzzles
+ Stuffed animal collection
+ Playmobil toys
+ Wooden train set
+ Matchbox or Hot Wheels cars and toy construction vehicles
+ Children's magazines

Additional Items You Can Easily Make

+ History timeline
+ Alphabet posters
+ Journal
+ Hundred chart

HELPFUL RESOURCES FOR HOMESCHOOLING ON A TIGHT BUDGET

✦　The public library!!

✦　The Internet.

✦　Barter for skills from basket weaving to piano lessons with friends and family.

✦　Learn from a book instead of private lessons or classes.

✦　Attend homeschool park days for exercise with friends.

Surprise—your home is *already* an educational supply warehouse! Everyday household items sit waiting to be used in fun and creative ways. "Our finances aren't tight, but I choose to not spend much money on homeschooling," says Leslie. "We use real money, real clocks, and a real thermometer to learn about money, time, and temperature. For math manipulatives we pull out checkers, poker chips, Matchbox cars, Legos, M&Ms, or whatever else my son wants to use."

Looking for ways to expand the idea of "real" materials, Rachel thought a backyard garden would be a great resource. "It's amazing what you can end up investigating after even only a fifteen-minute session out there," she marvels. "We've learned how seeds germinate, figured out what's eating the plants, performed experiments with light and water, and we get to eat fresh veggies, to boot!"

While Rachel and her son knew what their harvest results would be, other backyards yield surprises. Holly and her son were visiting her cousin's farm, where they read that Civil War soldiers used pokeberry ink and feather quills to write letters from the battlefield. Holly says, "We brought home a handful of goose feathers from the farm into which we carved nibs. Then we picked pokeberries from our own backyard, crushed them, added a little water to make ink, and wrote with the results. It really worked!"

Many times the children themselves spot a great homeschool resource that adults fail to notice. Her children are now teens, but Valerie still treasures the pots made from clay dug out of the local creek bank where her little boys spent long hours playing.

Celia's six-year-old daughter has a knack for finding human resources. "She finds the ones I overlook. She's the one who remembered her Grandpa speaks French and could help out," Celia says. "And she doesn't mind questioning the lady in the grocery line behind us."

> Many times the children themselves spot a great homeschool resource that adults fail to notice.

Get rid of the notion that you need to consider spending anywhere near the amount of money your local school district spends on each child each year. Consider the items you already have, and then supplement these with others to fill in gaps you discover. Your pocketbook will thank you.

MORE RESOURCES YOU MAY FIND HELPFUL

QUESTIONNAIRE RESPONDENTS CONSIDERED a few more items invaluable, items that you don't necessarily already have. A savvy shopper, particularly one who frequents garage sales, could have fun seeking out bargains on the following:

+   Fishing gear
+   Globe

- ✦ Microscope
- ✦ Telescope
- ✦ Stopwatch
- ✦ Easel with whiteboard or chalkboard
- ✦ Maps
- ✦ Craft supplies
- ✦ Build-it-yourself shortwave radio

What About Books?

By now you're probably asking, "But where are the books?" The number and type of books is your choice. Remember, you've got your library card, and librarians are often sympathetic to a home-schooler's need to check out books for longer than the library's usual policy. It's worth checking into.

Then there are books just so beloved by your children it would break your heart *not* to make them part of their personal library. You'll know which ones they are by the number of requests to read them—again and again. Keep a list of favorite titles and watch for them at library book sales and garage sales. Share your list with family when birthdays and gift-giving holidays roll around. If your children receive an allowance, plant the seeds early that they can save to purchase books. It's a habit that could last a lifetime.

> If your children receive an allowance, plant the seeds early that they can save to purchase books. It's a habit that could last a lifetime.

You *will* become a book-gatherer, perhaps not even realizing it until one day you say, "Honey, we really need another bookshelf" (or three). You won't be able to help yourself. You'll notice books everywhere. You'll replace your current favorite saying with "so many books, so little time."

Gwenn likes to share the story of the time she found a perfect book in the bookstore of the St. Louis Gateway Arch. Written at the third- to fourth-grade level, it was a biography about the man who helped build her family's hometown. Trouble was, it was $22 and she sadly left it behind on the bookstore shelf.

The next day Gwenn attended her library's book fair. There on a table waiting for her was the same book, now part of her family's library for fifty cents.

Books for a Desert Island

Just for fun, questionnaire respondents were also asked, "If you had to homeschool on a desert island and could take only ten things for this with you, what would they be?" (See the top ten list in the sidebar on p. 217.)

Depending on how many other resources they wanted, respondents listed varying numbers of books, mentioning some by name and repeatedly. For your consideration and enjoyment, here are the ones mentioned most often:

For Parents

+ *You CAN Teach Your Child Successfully,*
  Ruth Beechick
+ *Teach Your Child to Read in 100 Easy Lessons,*
  Engleman, Siegfried, and others
+ *Teach Your Own,* John Holt
+ *The Homeschooling Book of Answers,*
  Linda Dobson
+ *How to Teach Your Child,* V. B. Bautista
+ *What Every _____ [fill in the blank with
  Kindergartener, First Grader, etc.] Needs to Know,*
  E. D. Hirsch
+ *Teaching Children,*
  Diane Lopez

Curriculum Related

+ Saxon math books
+ *A History of United States,*
  Joy Hakim
+ Five in a Row curriculum
+ Schaum basic math outline
+ *Learning Language Arts
  Through Literature*

Books for Children

+ *Swiss Family Robinson*
+ *Usborne History of the World*
+ *Tintin* books
+ *Chronicles of Narnia* boxed set,
  C. S. Lewis
+ Complete works of Dr. Seuss
+ A Beka readers
+ *Considering God's Creation,*
  Mortimer and Smith
+ Poetry books
+ *20th Century Treasury of
  Children's Literature*

Consider homeschooling purchases as carefully as you consider the many others you make. Solicit input from your child whenever feasible as she's the one who will be using the material—or not. Keep in mind that a book or game that another homeschooling family raves about might not fit your child's interests or learning style, and proceed accordingly. Mistakes in purchasing homeschool resources aren't life-threatening, but I'm sure I'm not the only homeschooler who looks at a book collecting dust on the shelf and daydreams about what useful resource we were doing without because of it.

IF YOU HAD TO HOMESCHOOL ON A DESERT ISLAND AND COULD ONLY TAKE TEN THINGS WITH YOU, WHAT WOULD THEY BE?

10. A book on local flora and fauna

9. Dictionary

8. Encyclopedia set

7. Musical instruments

6. Box of colored pencils, markers, and/or crayons and "one very large paper source"

5. Bible, hymnal, and/or catechism

4. Art supplies

3. Pencils and paper

2. Computer, software and Internet access

1. Lots of books (or as one person who got down to her tenth item said, "As many books as I could convince you are one!")

Of course, several of these ten "things" could get surprisingly bulky and varied—but that's how homeschoolers see the world: Where others set limits, they look for opportunities!

THE EARLY YEARS EMERGENCY RESOURCE STARTER KIT

Somewhere there's a local homeschool support group person excusing herself from the hot game of Scrabble she and her children are playing. She answers her phone to find a stranger on the other end.

The caller says, "We couldn't take it anymore and I just told the school, 'I'm going to homeschool my son'." She begins to cry as she relays one of a series of horror stories the support person has heard before. "What do I do now?" she asks, frantic and frightened.

As public school problems escalate, more families turn to homeschooling under emergency circumstances. The fears new homeschoolers typically harbor are compounded in these circumstances by lack of preparation or understanding. Like heart attack victims awaiting an ambulance, families in a homeschooling emergency situation need help *now.*

Realize first, the early years child is resilient and can usually bounce back unscathed when removed from the harm typically suffered as a result of public school problems. Large doses of hugs and kisses, positive reinforcement, and (most especially) homemade chocolate chip cookies enjoyed together work wonders to restore the young soul, and have been known to return a child to his normal self within a matter of weeks.

If your child is in this situation, consider providing what is commonly referred to as "decompression time," a time-out from worries about subtraction problems, penmanship lessons, and those nasty Roman numerals. This gives him a much-needed mental, physical and emotional vacation, and delivers time for the renewed bonding you and your child may need. Yes, this means he'll probably "fall behind" on the work you know his former classmates are proceeding with, but your mentally, physically, and emotionally refreshed child will quickly catch up if, in fact, you decide to continue providing a similar education at home.

Use this time for observation and conversation. Watch how he fills his vacation time: Does he want to read or be read to? Watch TV? Run and jump outside? Use the computer? Build castles with Legos or cardboard boxes? Pretend he's Superman? As mentioned before, these are all clues as to his interests and his preferred learning style; take note.

Ask what he'd like to learn, but remember that at this age—and under these circumstances—he may not know or be able to answer such a direct question. In this case, hints may come from questions he asks you in everyday conversation. "Mommy, what does it say on the cereal box?" (Early signs of desire to read?) "How does the mailman know which mail is ours?" (Mmm, post office field trip?) "How do they make chocolate chips?" (Let's check and see if Hershey's has a Web site. Or, why don't we write a letter to the company and ask?)

In an emergency, new homeschoolers additionally worry they don't have age-appropriate textbooks sitting around the house and can't proceed until they're in hand. You can get the textbooks you need or want soon enough. In the meantime, use the invaluable resources lists in this chapter to check what you already have. For starters, here's a low-cost, bare-bones emergency resource kit that, coupled with your ingenuity, will keep you and your child busy as you figure out where you're going to travel on this homeschooling journey built just for you.

If you're starting to homeschool under emergency conditions, consider providing what is commonly referred to as "decompression time," a time-out from worries about subtraction problems, penmanship lessons, and those nasty Roman numerals.

+ Library cards for both of you—good for books, magazines, videos, computer software, and audio stories on tape
+ Crayons, markers, and/or colored pencils
+ Paper—plain or lined, loose or bound for writing and drawing (check your local newspaper office for end rolls of newsprint), construction paper, tracing paper
+ Pencils

- ✦ Old magazines and catalogs from which to cut out pictures and letters; glue
- ✦ Scissors
- ✦ Scraps—wood, fabric, wrapping paper, yarn, tissue paper, and so on
- ✦ A couple of age-appropriate workbooks (from your local department store) if they make you feel better!

That's it! Now get to the library, load up a bag or box with interesting materials, include a couple of books and magazines on homeschooling for your evening reading, and have some fun! The road you need to take will soon reveal itself to you. If you find it leads you onto the Information Superhighway, we're about to visit that next!

SIMPLE STARTING POINTS

- ✦ *Settle down with a cup of tea, a pad and pen, and a home-school resource guide.*

Note sources of products that sound interesting.

- ✦ *Start requesting catalogs.*

There are so many resources available today it's a good idea to get an overview first. This way you won't settle for the first resource you find.

- ✦ *Check your home for the many useful resources you already have.*

Clip a sheet of paper to the refrigerator on which you can write down the little things you'd like to pick up on your next trip to the discount store to fill in gaps.

✦ *Gather resources slowly.*

You can always supplement your family's resources as you experience homeschooling and get a better idea of what you *really* need. Errant book purchases are usually only returnable for a brief time, and opened software, unless damaged, never is. Keep your budget in mind so homeschooling doesn't become an unnecessary source of financial stress.

> The road you need to take will soon reveal itself to you.

- *If you're turning to homeschooling under emergency circumstances, don't panic.*

Help is only a phone call, an e-mail note, or Internet search away. If the school is pressuring you for a curriculum, ask if you can borrow a set of their books. This will make them happy, give your child time for decompression, and give you time to gather more appropriate materials.

RESOURCES

Books

Pride, Mary. *Big Book of Home Learning, Volume 1.* Crossway, 1990. Christian perspective.

Reed, Donn. *The Home School Source Book.* Brook Farm Books, 1994.

Rupp, Rebecca. *The Complete Home Learning Source Book.* Three Rivers Press, 1998.

Favorite Early Years Magazines

Chickadee Magazine: 179 John Street, Suite 500, Toronto, Ontario M5T 3G5 Canada; 416-971-5275; ten issues per year.

The Dolphin Log: 870 Greenbrier Circle, Suite 402, Chesapeake, VA 23320.

Highlights for Children: 803 Church Street, Honesdale, PA 18431-1824; monthly.

KidsArt News: P.O. Box 274, Mt. Shasta, CA 96067; 916-926-5076.

Ladybug, the Magazine for Young Children and *Spider:* P.O. Box 300, Peru, IL 61354-0300; 815-224-6643; monthly.

National Geographic World: 800-638-4077.

Ranger Rick/Your Big Backyard: 8925 Leesburg Pike, Vienna, VA 22184; 800-588-1650.

Turtle Magazine for Preschool Kids and *Children's Playmate:* P.O. Box 567, Indianapolis, IN 46206-0567; 317-636-8881; bimonthly.

Periodicals

The Link: 587 N. Ventu Park Road, Newbury Park, CA 91320; 805-493-9216; hompaper@gte.net; free tabloid loaded with ads.

General Resources Catalogs

Homeschool Discount Store: P.O. Box 2794, Stockbridge, GA 30281; 770-474-8573; http://www.homeschooldiscount.com.

Homeschooling Information and Resource Guide: P.O. Box 1083, Tonasket, WA 98855; 800-236-3278; send e-mail request with postal address to HEM-Info@home-ed-magazine.com.

John Holt Book and Music Store: 2380 Massachusetts Avenue, Suite 104, Cambridge, MA 02140; 617-864-3100; http://www.holt-gws.com.

Rainbow Re-Source Center: 8227 Ulah Road, Cambridge, IL 61238; 888-841-3456; voicemail 800-705-8809.

Web Sites

The Education Source: www.edusource.com (don't forget to follow
the link to the new homeschool site, too)

Homeschoolers Curriculum Swap: http://theswap.com

Jon's Homeschool Resource Page: http://www.scruz.net/~jds.hs/

11

THE LEARNING JOURNEY
MERGES ONTO THE
INFORMATION SUPERHIGHWAY

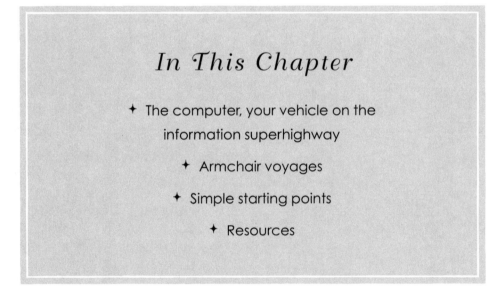

In This Chapter

✦ The computer, your vehicle on the
information superhighway

✦ Armchair voyages

✦ Simple starting points

✦ Resources

"W HEN I WAS young my parents used to tell me, 'Go look it up in the encyclopedia,'" Karla remembers. "But just one generation later, now I say to my son, 'Let's look it up on the Internet!'"

We've seen the information contained in a bulky set of encyclopedias shrink to fit on a disk smaller than a 45 rpm record. (Okay, now you know how old I am!) The cost of possessing that information has shrunk at the same time; today you can buy an encyclopedia-on-disk for less than the cost of a nice dinner for two.

It's no surprise the homeschooling community embraces the computer and its accompanying technology. It presents cheap, easy, rapid access to the information learning families need. Computers and on-line access, however, aren't the only technology families learning at home use. With access to a world of curriculum choice, homeschoolers take advantage of it all.

THE COMPUTER, YOUR VEHICLE ON THE INFORMATION SUPERHIGHWAY

IN 1997, David and David Enterprises, organizers of California's annual Home=Education Conference, surveyed its attendees, mostly homeschoolers. They found:

    89 percent own a computer.
    41 percent own a Mac, 50 percent an IBM or clone,
        and 9 percent have one of each.
    81 percent have CD-ROM drives.
    73 percent are online.
    58 percent spend $100 to $200 a year on software.
    32 percent spend $300 to $500 a year on software.
    10 percent spend $700 to $2,000 a year on software.

Homeschooled youngsters seem to take to computers like ducks to water. In their rural Nevada town, Ruth watched in amazement as each of her children came of age and "just started operating the computer, deftly pulling CDs in and out. They learned to use the peripherals," says Ruth, "before I even knew they existed!"

If you don't know how to operate your computer, just ask your child to get you started. Parents learn a lot during the homeschooling journey, too.

Soaring into Cyberspace with the Internet

The Internet is loaded with vast information potential—and potential danger. For this reason, questionnaire respondents who tap into the Internet with the three-to-eight crowd do so only with parental supervision. Once online, they find the Internet is as flexible as homeschooling itself.

Information Source

When our family went online a few years ago I spent (too much) time exploring, following links that got me lost, and testing search engines to see just how limitless our new tool was. Discoveries left me wishing it had been available when our children were younger, as it felt like a homeschooling miracle—information and help on virtually any topic only a few buttons and a brief search away.

Connection to the Internet means having a most extensive collection of information at your beck and call. Home Internet access makes it easy to follow up on a child's expressed interest quickly, while interest is at its peak. Responding to her son's question about ladybugs, Karla went online "to find hundreds of sites with pictures, stories, sound clips, even places we could mail-order ladybugs."

> If you don't know how to operate your computer, just ask your child to help. Parents learn a lot during the homeschooling journey, too.

The entire text of books awaits your inspection. If you're having trouble locating a book on which copyright may have run out, search the Internet for it. If you find one you'd like to read, download and print it. Your children can make a nice, sturdy book cover to help protect it.

Reference books await you, too. Whether you need a dictionary, encyclopedia, thesaurus, atlas, language translator, song lyric, or world atlas, Internet access places it at your fingertips.

Many educational product companies take advantage of the Internet as a marketplace and offer online classes, tutorials, and whole curricula for a fee. Offerings range from a complete year of learning to short-runs focused on a specific topic or skill. There's more selection for an older child, but if you run a search you may find just what you're looking for.

If you can't or don't want to pay a fee, don't worry. The amount of free curriculum material is overwhelming and guaranteed to keep you busy as long as you'd like. As with freebie curriculum materials offered to schools, some are little more than glorified commercials for the sponsors' products or point of view. If you know the sponsor of the Web site tends toward commercialism, you may want to check the material carefully for this before using it, just as you would check appropriate content in many areas.

> Filtering software allows you to restrict from your child's view anything you deem offensive or inappropriate.

On both educational sites in general and homeschooling sites specifically, you'll find unit studies, lesson plans, skill-specific worksheets, science experiments, art and music activities. Some of the material you print out. Other offerings require your child to stay on the computer and take part in an interactive program.

A Word About Filters

As home to information about *everything,* there's much on the Internet you don't want an early years child to view. While nothing beats your presence and supervision while your child is online, filtering software acts as a parental censor should your attention be momentarily diverted.

Filtering software allows you to restrict from your child's view anything you deem offensive or inappropriate. The programs contain various settings allowing you to choose those sites you wish blocked from use. Three of the many filter programs available are:

- ✦ Cyber Patrol 4.0: Windows 3.1/95/98, Macintosh versions
- ✦ Surf Watch 3.0: Windows 3.1/95/98, Macintosh versions
- ✦ Net Nanny 3.1: Windows 3.x/95/98 only

Additionally, several major Internet service providers include parental controls within their online service. For instance, users of

America Online can type in the keyword "parental controls," receive instructions and options, then set limits for each screen name. AT&T Worldnet, CompuServe, and Microsoft Network offer similar capabilities.

Support Source

Your children aren't the only ones who can find information on the Internet. It's home to a vast network of homeschool support and information, a place to meet and exchange ideas with other homeschoolers around the world. Hundreds of bulletin boards exist, many specializing in specific aspects of homeschooling, from Christian to unschooling to homeschooling disabled children and more. Many parents new to homeschooling turn to bulletin boards to ask questions of veteran homeschoolers, whom I've always seen as generous with their knowledge and support.

Once online you'll find companies that offer free e-mail service, giving you and your child additional opportunity to keep in touch with other homeschoolers. Homeschooled children enjoy communication with "e-mail pals" from down the street or across the globe. The speed and ease of e-mail make this a lot more fun than the

---

FAVORITE EARLY YEARS WEB SITES

American Girl: americangirl.com

Barbie: barbie.com

Beanie Baby: beaniebaby.com

Children's Television Workshop:
    ctw.org

Discovery: discovery.com

Disney: disney.com

Legos: lego.com

Nick Jr.: nickjr.com

PBS: pbs.com

Save the Manatee Club:
    savethemanatee.org

Sea World: SeaWorld.com

old-fashioned pen pal communication—which, to a child, always seems to take *forever*. Many questionnaire respondents see e-mail as a boon for young children as it gives them a real—that is, immediately rewarding—reason to practice writing skills.

Many free subscription newsletters produced by individuals or support groups can be delivered through your e-mail service. E-mail service also gives you access to the growing number of homeschooling e-mail *loops*, or networks of homeschoolers who all receive the same messages and exchange information and support much as they do on the Internet bulletin boards. You can ask anything, as these recent messages show: "I'm looking for a homeschool e-mail contact in South Dakota for a geography project with my son." (Answer: "Try http://www.valentinene.com/pw/homelee/homeschool.html.") "Does anyone know how to find the area of a kite?" (Answer: "Take a look at http://www.nrich.maths.org.uk/.")

You'll also find heartwarming messages like this: "To all the kind souls who offered advice, reassurance and points of contact, thank you. . . . Today we withdrew Todd from school. . . . He'd yet again come home early, refusing food at lunchtime. Just telling Todd seemed to lift his spirits higher than I've seen them for a very long time; he was actually singing and dancing which brought tears to our eyes. I have to confess to being a bit terrified now the deed is done, but as many of you suggested he'll get some time to recover. P.S. For those offering to be pen pals to Todd, when he's ready, I'm sure he'll jump at the chance—thanks."

Staying Closer to Home with Software

It's called *edutainment*—and the industry is booming. Edutainment's combination of brilliant graphics, interactive fun, and painless learning captures the attention of the early years child quicker than a mud puddle.

With the click of a button, children's software turns your computer into an art studio, a science lab, a word wizard's castle or, commonly, a word processor. A word processor allows your child to transfer his focus from writing mechanics to its creative aspect. Marlene remembers when her son, Jack, hated to write. After a field trip to the airport, she decided to let him use the computer instead of handwriting a summary of their trip. "The quality of the imaginative poem he created convinced me it was the physical part of writing that hindered him," she says.

> With the click of a button, children's software turns your computer into an art studio, a science lab, a word wizard's castle, or a word processor.

How Homeschoolers Use Software

Questionnaire respondents turn to software much more frequently than the Internet for use with the early years child. Some of their children started using computers as young as eighteen months. Most often, use began at whatever age the child happened to be when the computer was purchased.

Today, entire curricula are available on software. You may choose to buy one of many programs that present curriculum material in game form. Useful reference books such as dictionaries and atlases can be purchased on disk for your child. You may choose to use software for a particular subject like math, learning to read, writing stories, or to review lessons the child learned otherwise. And yes, there's software just for fun, too, with any resulting learning considered a "bonus" of its use.

The amount of time respondents' children spend on the computer varied widely, from "infrequently" to two hours per day. While some parents said they limit the children's access time, or the number of users in the home imposes limits, most said their children limit themselves.

For the youngest children, attention span curbs the time. They simply don't want to use the computer more than fifteen to sixty minutes during daily or weekly sessions. As Gail has seen, "There are just so many other things to keep them busy 'doing.'" Maureen noticed that often a computer game will give her two boys a new idea, then "they're off and running to accomplish it."

> Looking at computers with a practical eye, homeschoolers see their use as inevitable, a tool children will use for the rest of their lives and in most future jobs.

Veronica, whose oldest child is four and a half, says self-limitation "gives him time to explore and figure out how to do the activities." She adds, "He also tends to use the computer often for a while and not use it at all for a while so it evens out."

Marla applies the same approach to computer use as she does to TV use. "We haven't had a problem because we don't place any more importance on either tool than on doing anything else. It's not off limits, so it's not forbidden fruit."

Looking at computers with a practical eye, homeschoolers see their use as inevitable, a tool their children will use for the rest of their lives and in most jobs. Under these circumstances, children's exposure to computers, as long as a parent can make sure use is age-appropriate, instills knowledge and comfort to serve them well into the future.

Computer Cautions

While some questionnaire respondents sang the glories of computers, others were cautious about use with the early years child. They spoke of young children getting that "glazed over" look in their eyes and complaints of lethargy after computer sessions.

Words of caution centered around health issues. Common complaints and worries include back strain, potential radiation exposure, lack of exercise, wrist problems, and strain on developing visual systems. Computers haven't been widely used long enough for us to totally understand the long-term effects of their use, but today optometrists are seeing more and more patients with "computer vision syndrome," which the American Optometric Association (AOA) defines as that "complex of eye and vision problems related to near

FAVORITE EARLY YEARS SOFTWARE

Anything by EdMark

Anything by Humongous Entertainment

Carmen Sandiego: World, U.S.A., Math
  Detective

Casper Brainy Book

Creative Artist

Freddie Fish

I Can Be an Animal Doctor

Incredible Machine

Jump Start Series

Kid Pix

Lego Loco

The Logical Journey of the Zoombinis

Magic School Bus: Ocean (and others
  in series)

Mavis Beacon Teaches Typing

Microsoft Ancient Lands

My First Encyclopedia

Oregon Trail (and other Trails in series)

Putt-Putt

Richard Scarry's How Things Work

Sammy's Science House

School House Rock: Math, Science,
  Grammar, America

Sesame Street (series)

Thinking Things

Tonka Construction

Windows Paintbrush

Winnie-the-Pooh

(See chapters 5, 6, and 7 for reading, writing, and math software)

work experienced during, or related to, computer use." The AOA estimates 90 percent of the 70 million U.S. workers now using computers on the job will experience eyestrain and vision problems.

Cornell University researchers concerned with repetitive stress injuries, according to a March 15, 1999, *New York Times* report, "observed third-, fourth-, and fifth-graders and found a striking misfit between children and the equipment they used. . . . As a result the children worked with craned necks, hunched shoulders and flexed wrists." Repetitive stress injury symptoms include sore wrists, tingling fingers, and aching backs.

If your child will be using a computer, there are a few precautions you can take.

- ✦ Modify your lighting to eliminate glare.
- ✦ Purchase a micro-mesh filter.
- ✦ Set monitor controls at maximum contrast and moderate brightness.
- ✦ Make sure your child stays at least twenty to twenty-six inches away from the screen.
- ✦ Place the computer screen slightly under eye level so the center of the screen is about four to nine inches below eye level.
- ✦ Add a wrist support to your computer keyboard and teach your child when to use it, and when not to.
- ✦ Provide appropriate furniture.
- ✦ Train your child in proper posture and keyboard technique.
- ✦ Encourage your child to get physical exercise and engage in robust activity when not using the computer.

ARMCHAIR VOYAGES

SOME HOMESCHOOLERS don't own a TV, and others take it out of a box in the garage on the rare occasions they use it. But many consider it another useful machine in their educational materials toolbox. These folks highly regard offerings in children's educational programming, like *Bill Nye, Magic School Bus, Wishbone, Discovery,* and *Kratt's Kreatures.*

Honey, Where Would You Like to Go Today?

Wouldn't it be nice if in the course of your studies you could say, "Let's go to Africa and study real lions!"? How about "I'd like to see an Egyptian pyramid, too; c'mon!"? If these trips loom impossible, the next best alternative is to hear and see these things through someone else's eyes, particularly if that someone knows what he's talking about.

Educational TV, documentaries, and videos produced by travel bureaus can whisk you and your early years child off to strange lands where you learn about daily life, geography, and cultures beyond your own. The same can happen with movies and television shows with (good) historical content. One way to verify the quality of the historical content is to create a homeschool activity of listing historical "facts" from a dramatic production and then checking other sources to see if they're real or not.

Priscilla believes "Videos feed my children's imagination and creativity. One is currently mad about *Anastasia*, which includes something of Russian history (albeit rather glossy and embellished) that we can talk about. How many four-year-olds do you know who discuss Rasputin?"

Let the Animals Do the Teaching

"Children love to learn about animals and other creatures at this age and they learn a lot from watching them on TV," says second-year homeschooler Denise, who rents about five educational videos each month for her three sons. "This is in addition to exploring the backyard for creepy crawlers, visiting the zoo, and raising our own animals."

QUICK & EASY

If you plan to study a particular historical time period or geographic region, check your library or local video store for a good movie set in that period or region. You're watching for the information that will help bring your studies to life: clothing, foods, ways of speaking and accents, attitudes toward children, women, minorities. This list could go on forever. Now, when you read about that period or region, your child can "see" it and bring preliminary understanding to bear on what could otherwise be dry facts.

> If you've got a visual learner, concepts that just don't click otherwise can suddenly become clear when he "sees" the information.

Public television and the Discovery Channel, among others, offer excellent science and nature programs. They present opportunity not only to grow in knowledge and affinity regarding the highlighted animal, but at the same time your child picks up information about the environment, geography, history, climate, and perhaps even an interest in nontraditional jobs for scientists.

If a particular animal piques your child's interest, don't forget to look for one of the books scientists publish about their studies. Many use story form, are highly engaging, and are easily understood by young children when read aloud.

Supplements

While educational TV programs and videos can get your studies off to a good start and spark new interests, they can also supplement your child's study. Early learning videos abound and provide your child with a slightly different take on the lessons currently going on at home. Programs make a nice wrap-up to studies, too, serving as review of information previously presented.

Educational TV or video viewing, as entertainment or just part of everyday life, serves a similar purpose in households. Where less structured study occurs, this exposure to educational information is all part of the same learning pot. Here, parents observe and converse, making sure the information is hitting its mark.

Videos are often used as literature supplements. In many homes, families first read a good book. This exercises the children's imagination regarding characters and settings. Upon completion, it's time to settle down with a bowl of popcorn, watch the movie production, and compare notes. Sometimes a couple of different versions exist, doubling the fun.

Curriculum on Video

Does your child want to study French? Learn how to make Sculpy jewelry? Watch the American Revolution unfold before him? It's all available on videos to study at your child's convenience and as intensely as he likes. If you've got a visual learner, concepts that just don't click otherwise can suddenly become clear when he "sees" the information.

As with computer software, curriculum on video is available covering typical school subjects in step-by-step fashion. It can specifically address one subject and take your child into deeper study, or it can veer off the typical course of study and offer lessons in sign language, exercise, and bread making. There are even some good, old-fashioned sing-alongs.

Homeschool resource books and catalogs offer descriptions of many educational videos. PBS publishes its own catalog, but price breaks here are rare. The big online booksellers are pumping up their video selections, and descriptions most often come in the form of purchasers' reviews. Videos on very specific topics are best found through the catalogs of organizations that work in the field.

> When you record TV programs on your own videos, your child doesn't have to sit down in front of the television at a particular time each day—and you avoid development of a habit you might not appreciate.

Keeping Videos Cheap and Convenient

Purchasing videos can become an expensive endeavor and cut sharply into any homeschool budget. That's where your VCR comes in handy.

Catch multi-packs of videotapes on sale at the discount store where the tapes cost less than $2 each. At these prices you can better afford to create your own video library. Record programs your child is currently interested in, but keep in mind he's growing rapidly and a program inappropriate today could nicely fit in with studies just a year or two from now.

When you record TV programs on your own videos, your child doesn't have to sit in front of the television at a particular time each day—and you avoid development of a habit you might not appreciate. Recorded and saved, the tape is just waiting for you to pop into the VCR when the programs are particularly relevant, while your child is under the weather, or (heaven forbid!) when you just need a bit of time to yourself for a task. This way, the content is new and interesting instead of a repeat performance.

When the video's content is important to you, make sure you break off that little tab on the back. I learned the hard way that a child

THE EARLY YEARS CHILD AND COMPUTER USE

Homeschoolers have strong feelings about both pros and cons of children aged three through eight using a computer:

+ *Benefits*

Makes repetitive and drill work fun.

Gives child access to the world.

Internet can be used as a virtual home library.

E-mailing pen pals anywhere in the world increases opportunity for real-life writing practice.

Lets children learn about a tool they will use throughout their lives.

Provides a creative outlet.

Increases creative writing among children who don't like or aren't yet adept in the physical act of writing.

Children's software, clip art, and font choices increase desire to read and write.

eager to capture *Alice in Wonderland* doesn't think twice about recording over a program on Arctic exploration saved for future reference.

Public libraries house video collections, and interlibrary loan extends your reach into other libraries in your region, giving you an even greater selection. If you have colleges or universities in your hometown, get a library card there, too, and gain access to even more.

Obviously, lots of learning can take place in front of the TV on the living room couch. But who wants to watch a video when the sun is shining? In the next chapter, let's go see where homeschoolers head when it's a beautiful day to visit the neighborhood.

Children's software allows the child to learn about and create visual art.

Children's software allows the child to manipulate science materials and experiments that may not be available otherwise.

Improves eye-hand and fine motor coordination.

✦ *Problems*

Unknown long-term effects, including concerns about radiation exposure.

It's yet another screen to which the early years child could become addicted.

Need to create a time balance between sitting in front of a computer and getting necessary exercise.

✦ *Health Issues*

Strain on developing visual systems

Back strain

Wrist problems

SIMPLE STARTING POINTS

✦ *If you're new to computers and/or the Internet, head to your library, or in larger towns, some bookstores and coffee houses offer online access.*

Thanks to grants and reduced phone rates, even many small libraries are online with computers available for public use. If you don't have a computer, use the library's to accomplish research with your child. Libraries also keep children's software for use on their computers, and some make it available for loan.

✦ *If you'd like a computer but your budget is tight, check out used computers from online auctions, newspapers, or used computer specialty stores.*

You won't get the latest technology, and it's a "buyer beware" market because you're usually dealing with individuals and no warranties whatsoever, but prices are much lower than retail, and you may be able to find "enough" computer in your price range. A directory of online auctions is available at http://guestservices.hyper mart.net/list_1.htm. The eBay auction (www.ebay.com) is one of the largest.

✦ *If your early years child uses the Internet at home, consider purchasing filter software.*

Did you know if you enter the address www.whitehouse.com instead of www.whitehouse.gov, you're at a pornographic material site? Do you know what sites will turn up in a search for "kitten"? Even if your child wouldn't intentionally surf to an inappropriate site, the chances of finding one by accident are high.

✦ *Plan ahead to videotape educational TV programs for future use to save time and strain on your memory.*

Go through your TV program guide once a week and mark dates and times of programs you want to catch on your calendar. Of course, you'll have to develop the habit of checking your calendar daily!

✦ *Make sure you really want videotapes and software before you purchase them.*

They're not returnable once opened, no matter how bad. Check with friends who may have used them, read catalog descriptions, and check publications and Web sites that specialize in reviews.

RESOURCES

Books

Healy, Jane M., Ph.D. *Failure to Connect: How Computers Affect Our Children's Minds—for Better or Worse.* Simon & Schuster, 1998.

Orr, Anne, and others. *Young Kids and Computers: A Parent's Survival Guide.* Children's Software Revue, 1998.

Papert, Seymour. *The Connected Family: Bridging the Digital Generation Gap.* Longstreet Press, 1996.

———. *The Children's Machine: Rethinking School in the Age of the Computer.* Basic Books, 1994.

Polley, Jean Armour. *The Internet Kids and Family Yellow Pages, 1999 Edition.* Osborne McGraw-Hill, 1998.

Prince, Dennis. *Online Auctions at eBay.* Prima Publishing, 1999.

Periodicals

Children's Software Revue: 44 Main Street, Flemington, NJ 08822; 800-993-9499; bimonthly; $24/year.

Family PC: P.O. Box 55411, Boulder, CO 80323; 800-825-6450; monthly; $14.95/year.

Home PC: P.O. Box 42021, Palm Coast, FL 32142; 800-829-0119; monthly; $16/year.

Web Sites

Coyle's Where in the Web and Other Homeschool and Educational Stuff: http://www.geocities.com/Athens/Aegean/3446/

Eclectic Homeschool Computer Department: www.eho.org/compdept.htm

Educate Online Home Education Pages: http://www.educate.co.uk/homeed1.htm (lots of links)

Educational software catalog and reviews: http://smartkidssoftware.com/

Eldorado Academy: http://www.eldoradoacademy.org (core knowledge K–12)

Google: http://www.google.com (good search engine)

Kindergarten Online Curriculum: http://www.howard.K12.md.us/connections/elementary/kindergarten.html

Laurel Springs Learn Online Program: http://www.learnonline.com (K–12)

LearningWare Reviews: http://www.learningwarereviews.com

Montessori for the Earth: http://userwww.sfsv.edu/"lisab (distance learning for Montessori homeschooling; pre-K to age nine)

Upattinas School and Resource Center: http://www.chesco.com/upattinas

Homeschool Message Boards

Home Education Magazine Discussion Boards: http://www.home-ed-magazine.com/wlcm_brds.html

Homeschool Central: http://www.homeschoolcentral.com/message.htm

Unschoolers: http://www.unschooling.com

Yahoo List: http://beta.yahoo.com/Education/Online_Forums/Message_Boards/

Homeschool E-Mail Loops

ONElist: www.onelist.com: This is a free loop service that supports many e-mail loops. Click on education and then on home-schooling, and you'll get a list of loops available from this site.

American Homeschool Association Discussion Loop: Go to www. onelist.com; go to education list; find AHA and follow subscription directions.

Moderated list for parents and students: Get information at www .egroups.com/list/homeschool-aid.

Check with your local support group for information on loops specific to your state.

12

HOMESCHOOLERS' TOP THREE DESTINATIONS

In This Chapter

✦ Your community: a microcosm of the great wide world

✦ Your local library

✦ Support groups

✦ Simple starting points

✦ Resources

CALL A HOMESCHOOLING "stay-at-home" mom and you'll likely talk to an answering machine. Liberated from the school calendar, she's out and busy with scheduled trips or taking advantage of opportunities too good to pass up. Hold on to your hat; you're about to discover her top three destinations.

A COMMUNITY: YOUR MICROCOSM OF THE GREAT WIDE WORLD

HOMESCHOOLING FREEDOM moves your child beyond the classroom into the real world of work and play, youngsters and elders, the daily activities of a functioning society, and learning activities that take advantage of the world around you.

Field Trips and Travel

Top destination? Your own community! Nothing better connects an early years child to her community and reveals the value of her education than trips that show her real people doing real activities. Community members are usually thrilled to discover children are interested in their work. Some of the best field trips for the three-to-eight crowd are brief, cheap, and right around the corner. (See "Community Hot Spots" sidebar.)

Field trips are great anytime, but take on special meaning when they directly relate to your current study. This isn't as limiting as it sounds. You can use homeschooling's flexibility to help the trip fit by changing your studies if necessary. (We read Laura Ingalls Wilder's *Farmer Boy* in record time to finish before a visit to the Wilder homestead!)

Even if your local support group organizes field trips, consider arranging a few just for your family, particularly to places that can't accommodate a group. Your host could be more inclined to allow your child to handle tools or "do" some of the work. When I took three early years children to tour the municipal airport, our pilot-guide concluded our visit with a surprise plane ride, letting my oldest "drive." This couldn't have happened with a larger group—we filled the plane ourselves!

> Some of the best field trips for the three-to-eight crowd are brief, cheap, and right around the corner.

Finding Out What's Available

Start tracking your options by thinking like a tourist. Collect visitor guides to your area. Oftentimes they'll contain coupons to the more expensive "tourist trap" activities should any prove

HOW WE DID IT

We went to King's Dominion this year on the first day of school in Virginia. We practically had the whole park to ourselves—it was great!

—RENEE

valuable to your needs. Check for group rates for the more interesting ones. Our support group field trip coordinator discovered that even though tourists pay $50 for an Olympic bobsled ride, the Olympic Authority gave our group a *greatly* reduced rate. Children had a ball as parents stood at the finish line holding our collective breath.

Moving beyond tourist attractions, get as close to the source of information you desire as possible. Here are a few starting places:

- *Local or regional arts council:* Craftspeople, artists, actors, musicians
- *Library or bookstore:* Writers, poets, craftspeople
- *State agricultural extension office:* Farmers, foresters, nursery and fishery workers
- *Chamber of Commerce:* Business, professional, or service people
- *Civic, municipal, and government bodies:* Legislators, judges, policemen, firefighters, town clerk

If your child shows interest in learning more about a career or activity left uncovered, there's always the Yellow Pages.

When Leslie's son asked, "What happens when a person gets his foot chopped off?" she explained prosthetic arms and legs—but four-year-old Sammy wanted more. She pulled out her phone book, called a prosthetician's office, and—voilà—Leslie and Sammy had an afternoon appointment.

"Sammy could hardly wait! With wide eyes he sat in the waiting room looking at pictures of people doing all sorts of things with prosthetic legs," says Leslie. "When appointment time came, a real prosthetician took us into a back room and showed us examples of prosthetic arms and legs. We saw how they were constructed, how they're designed to attach to the residual limb, and how they're jointed to allow natural movement."

Toward a Happy Field Trip

While making arrangements for your trip, ask if there's anything you can discuss with your children, including vocabulary, to prepare for the visit. Places that see a lot of school groups often provide information sheets beforehand. Exchange information on what your guide will explain and what you'd like your children to learn. Ask how many visitors can be accommodated; maybe you can invite another family or your support group.

If you'll have young ones in tow, schedule your trip for a time they're at their best, well fed and well rested, so you too can enjoy yourself. Join your children in asking questions, bring paper and pencils for notes, and don't forget the camera!

> While making arrangements for your trip, ask if there's anything you can discuss with your children, including vocabulary, to prepare them for their visit.

Talk about your trip on the ride home. Share your ideas about what you found most interesting, things you learned that you didn't know before, and what your visit inspired you to learn next. This encourages your child to examine the trip in the same way, increasing its educational value.

Don't forget to send your field trip host an envelope full of thank you notes. Encourage your child to include comments about what she liked best and what she learned. (Thank you notes are much more fun than "field trip reports.")

Farther from Home

Travel beyond your community is an educational experience in and of itself, so when opportunity presents itself, grab it! Consider skipping the touristy spots to turn your family vacation into an extended field trip. This will probably save money, too!

"My husband is in the Navy Reserves and does two weeks of active duty in different locales so we often accompany him," says Pat, a Seattle-based mother of two girls. "In the hotel room we do basic subjects in the morning with texts we've carted along. In the afternoon, we visit the museums, parks, and libraries—all new to us. The girls love doing 'school on the go,' with the bonus of staying close to Dad."

Wherever your travels lead, you'll see the benefits. "I'm convinced of the value of learning vacations," Maria declares, "real-life experiential learning, getting in there and seeing, feeling, handling. It's about making connections—connecting the past to the present and putting all the pieces together into a whole."

QUICK & EASY

Keep a notebook titled "Library Books" handy. Each time you read a review or see a reference to a title you'd like to check out, write it down. Take the notebook to the library with you, and you're ready to find everything you're looking for. Note the date of requests for interlibrary loan books in case you need to follow up.

Volunteering, Mentorships, and Apprenticeships

The world of volunteering, mentorships, and apprenticeships opens wider as your children get older, but homeschoolers have found ways to give similar learning experiences to early years children, too.

For two years Shannon has provided the wheels for her children's monthly volunteer work in a Meals on Wheels route, and the lessons her children learned are clear. "They've learned to care about people, be dependable and responsible," Shannon says, "and not to be afraid of elderly or incapacitated people."

Jacqueline and son Tom's local support group participates in the Adopt-a-Highway program, providing cleanup services three times each year. As a Cub Scout, Tom helped unload Christmas trees at the city recycling center. And as a seven-year-old he committed to a minimum five-hour shift each week for four months to be a goat farm volunteer. "We live in the city and aren't exposed to farm life so he was thrilled with the idea," remembers Jacqueline.

"Each day we went we were assigned to a worker who would 'train' Tom. I mostly stood back and watched, but gave Tom additional guidance if I thought it was needed. The workers kept assuming he was older than seven," Jacqueline explains. "On the first day he got to herd goats from the barn area to the back pasture—he was hooked.

"Tom learned to feed and water all the different animals at the farm, and to herd and milk goats (which he didn't like very much)." He conquered a previously instilled fear of bulls while there, too. "Overall," says Jacqueline looking back, "it was a wonderful experience for both of us."

If you don't have a farm nearby, humane societies appreciate families willing to spend an hour or two feeding the cats, walking the dogs, and cuddling kittens and puppies.

While seeking volunteer opportunities for your early years child, keep her abilities, both physical and emotional, in mind. Marla learned some situations can be overwhelming. When both of her boys were younger than seven, they volunteered at a homeless shelter. "They benefited by seeing some of the harsh realities of the real world," explains Marla, "but they were so young they were uncomfortable so we haven't done it again. We'll volunteer more in the next

> If you don't have a farm nearby, humane societies appreciate families willing to spend an hour or two feeding the cats, walking the dogs, and cuddling kittens and puppies.

couple of years, as I think they're more empathetic than they would have been without the experience."

Institutions

Local institutions, blessed with space that sometimes sits unused during the day, are getting into the homeschooling craze, offering more learning opportunities to children, and listening to parents' ideas for creating them. Churches, science centers, libraries, and art institutes may have just the program—or the space—you're looking for.

The church-affiliated Pioneer Club meets weekly for nine months each year offering Christian children time for crafts, group games, and following a curriculum that emphasizes Bible principles and character development.

> Tiger and Cub Scouts and Brownie and Daisy Scouts offer weekly opportunities for fun, learning, and socializing.

Renee's family lives just five minutes away from a church sponsoring enrichment classes. "My two younger children are involved in physical education and art classes for two hours each week," says Renee. "We also take field trips with a small homeschooling group at my own church. If these weren't available, we'd just stay home. These are sort of icing on the cake."

Seattle's Pacific Science Center offers half-day, hands-on family workshops on awesome early years interests: programs with titles like "Rubber Band Technology," "Kitchen Chemistry," and "Minerals, Volts and Jolts." "They cost $20 for each parent/child team and my child gets to take home most of the materials we experiment with," Leslie explains. Her family travels about an hour each way to get there, and plans to continue attending once a month.

Tiger and Cub Scouts and Brownie and Daisy Scouts offer weekly opportunities for fun, learning, and socializing. Celia, active in her local troop, volunteers "for carpooling and craft projects and writes the troop newsletter. If this wasn't available I'd start a girls club or some sort of playgroup to meet more regularly than our support group does," she says.

Library story hours are tops with the early years homeschooling set. If your library can let you know which books will be featured, you can plan tie-in activities at home.

Community Activities

Entrepreneurs, listen up. "If more programs become available we'll certainly consider using them," says Monique. Dee agrees and explains, "This type of program isn't available to us, but we would use it if it was."

Homeschoolers are looking for educational opportunities in the community—for good reasons. Their own unique reasons.

Gail figures her budget can handle one extracurricular class per child. "Right now the boys take gymnastics and my daughter has a dance class since mostly I worry about physical activity. Neither my husband nor I are into that."

Soccer and T-ball are the team sports of choice with the early years crowd, and most every community can offer these to your child. Generally, community opportunities for sports teams dry up as the children get older, so take advantage of them while they're available. Increasingly, states are opening up participation on school teams to older homeschoolers, but these are a different experience from community sports activities.

Jacqueline finds community activities give her son learning experiences she can't, "like putting on a play or using gymnastics equipment. They also give him a wider range of acquaintances from which to choose friends," she adds.

When her soon-to-be eight-year-old son grew interested in acting, Abby found a program for young children called Broadway Kids. Abby says, "He really loved that, so he began trying out for 'real plays,' as he calls them.

"He just finished a run at a regional theater as Tiny Tim in *A Christmas Carol,* a wonderful experience for him," she continues. "We immersed ourselves in Dickens, *Oliver Twist* for comparison, and all of Victorian England and the times that prompted Dickens to write these stories . . . pretty deep stuff for a little guy. But this was all his idea, brought on by his interest and involvement in the play.

"The point is," Abby concludes, "when you homeschool, everything is an educational experience because it's part of being alive and being human."

Homeschool Programs

Wherever ten or more homeschooling families are gathered these days, new classes pop up, most often created by and for the families who use them. Talk about variety—homeschool choirs, geography clubs, computer classes, carpentry, and everything in between. If your child is interested in group activities, contact your local support group and see what they've got cookin'.

Joni's daughter participates about ten hours each week in a program funded by participants. "She may take dance or arts and crafts or sign language, things we normally don't do or for which we want a different approach," Joni says.

Maria describes the increasingly popular learning co-op when talking about her children's one-hour-per-week classes. "They've taken everything from hands-on labs and math to arts and crafts, drama, and creative writing." Maria explains how the co-op works. "Classes only cost whatever the materials cost and the home where the classes are held is donated by a homeschooling family. There's a $5 per child per class fee if you don't volunteer in some capacity, but there's lots of volunteer opportunities. A family can teach a class, copy materials, check papers, clean at the home

> If your child is interested in group activities, contact your local support group and see what they've got cookin'.

where classes are held, or baby-sit. The class I teach is usually held at my home."

If you don't find anything that interests you locally, consider starting something yourself. All it takes is a homeschooling parent or two with a vision and the will to make it happen. Homeschooling parents across the country have found that, "if you build it, they will come." Homeschool programs offer yet another fulfillment of educational freedom, learning free of compulsion and government regulation.

Alternative Education Programs

Alaska has long offered alternative education programs, delivering school to many rural children beyond the reach of school buses. But as other states began noticing the exodus of families toward home-schooling, alternative education programs have blossomed else-where.

"Kaitlin goes to class one full day each week for socialization with other 'gifted' children her age," says Mona of her local public school–funded program in Missouri. "They address science, foreign language, and other challenging curriculum for gifted students I don't feel qualified to teach. If the program wasn't available we would homeschool for five days instead of four."

In Canada, Maureen's family registered with an electronic bus-sing program. "They allow us to construct our own educational program," Maureen explains. "They have computer curricula or you proceed with your own as long as you show you're meeting the prescribed learning outcomes. They provide a computer, online teacher, Internet access, lots of resources, access to a software lend-ing library, and some financial reimbursements for educational materials."

Public schools providing alternative education programs receive local, state, and federal educational funding based on attendance

HOW WE DID IT

Our homeschool support group took a trip to the small county airfield. Because we weren't constrained by a school bus schedule and had a flexible spirit generally we were able to take advantage of several impromptu happenings.

An air force pilot in a 'shark' training plane passing through on his way to visit family chatted with us about his plane and flight training. A mechanic rebuilding a pre–World War II biplane let us poke around his hangar and talked about the plane's history and the materials it was made from. We found a butterfly chrysalis hanging from a bench at the airfield's fire station. My grandparents tagged along (my seventy-five-year-old grandfather had a blast), as well as an assortment of toddlers and babes in arms. It was what a learning experience should be.

—HOLLY

numbers, just as they do in traditional school programs. This is how they afford to give away educational materials. Because they take these funds, alternative education programs become subject to many, sometimes all, of the local, state, and federal regulations that accompany the money. These regulations, to varying degrees, have a tendency to erode educational freedom.

Holly explains, "Although I understand why some parents choose these programs, I worry about the implications such programs have for the rights of independent homeschoolers."

While Tanya doesn't use alternative education programs because she'd have a hard time having someone tell her how to teach her children, some members of her homeschool choir do use them. She has to send invoices for her services to the California organizations they belong to. "One of the organizations I deal with is so disorganized

I get paid late, they send me the wrong student forms, and their accounts with me are still unsettled," she says. "They've given me a very bad impression."

Homeschool programs represent an innovative approach to group learning experiences, and alternative education programs often look as though the public school authorities are taking valuable steps in the same direction. Nonetheless, it's possible that alternative education programs, because of their funding sources and regulations, will eventually turn out looking more and more like the

COMMUNITY "HOT SPOTS" FOR EARLY YEARS FIELD TRIPS

✦ **Social Studies/Business**
  Post office
  Newspaper office and
    printing facility
  Airport
  Bank
  Architect's office
  Florist

✦ **Public Safety/Civics**
  Firehouse
  Police station
  City Hall/Courthouse

✦ **Science**
  Farm
  Factory
  Hospital
  Fish hatchery
  State forest
  Research center

✦ **History**
  Historical homes and
    homesteads
  Old cemeteries, forts,
    mines, battlefields
  Historical sites-turned-
    museums

traditional public school educational approach, the very approach you're leaving behind in order to homeschool.

"Emphasis should be put on finding ways to mentor our children into the community instead of trying to duplicate the public school system," cautions Erica. "Let's bridge the gap with community resources instead of asking for public school classes in Latin, physical education, and Spanish."

Homeschool programs grow and use their connection to the community. They may take a little more parent time to succeed, be a little more expensive, and definitely won't offer you a new computer. But they'll keep your family free of the regulations that increasingly strangle educational innovation.

Weigh choices between these programs carefully. And remember, you don't have to participate in everything at once . . . being overburdened with homeschooling is no more fun than being overburdened with anything else. Time together in home's relaxed atmosphere is medicine for the soul, so make a point of giving your family frequent doses.

YOUR LOCAL LIBRARY

HERE WE ARE at the public library, the second top homeschooling destination and another example of educational freedom. Your library gathers and makes accessible information and sources for self-education. No one compels you to partake; no one tells you what books you must read before you access others; no one says you can't learn about *that* because you're the wrong age. All choice belongs to you and your child.

Early years children often grow up thinking of the library as a second home when they homeschool. "My son's only three, and he asks the librarian where to find books on particular subjects without batting an eye," says Karla. "I love that he's not afraid to approach adults with questions and he knows what to ask for to get what he needs."

Take a trip to your library today just to see what it can offer your homeschooling family. (Plan to spend some time.) Books are still the library's backbone, but you can get magazines, catalogs, videotapes, books on audiotape, and software, too. The interlibrary loan system electronically connects your library to others in your area, making it just as easy to borrow books and tapes unavailable locally.

Many libraries loan still more: curricula, textbooks, games, microscopes, foreign language tapes, and puzzles. See if your library keeps artwork for loan. If so, you may be able to borrow paintings and sculpture along with your books.

Collections of old magazines and newspapers are available via microfiche. With an early years child, it's fun to look up publications from her birthday, then Mom's, then Grandpa's. Compare headline stories, types of jobs available in the classified ads, and even the price of eggs. Think of more ways to help her enjoy using the equipment that will help her conduct research in coming years.

Speaking of collections, many libraries house local history archives; books, documents, photographs. These usually aren't available for loan, so you'll have to plan on staying at the library to use them.

And then there are computers; for children's play, for Internet access, for tracking down interlibrary loan titles, for researching magazine articles by topic. Your library card serves as your key to the Information Age door. Don't forget to get a few more keys at college and university libraries near you, too.

Librarians know homeschoolers boost their circulation rates, and books written specifically for librarians help them meet homeschoolers' needs. Librarians are increasingly arranging meetings with homeschoolers to discover how to assist their efforts. A 1998 *Penfield Post-Republican* (NY) article by Brian Anglin listed the results of such a meeting, shared here as possible starting points for dialogue with your library:

- ✦ Space to display children's projects and artwork
- ✦ An information center for homeschooling resources and suggestions
- ✦ A reading list of books broken down by grade or reading level
- ✦ Programs for school-age children during the day
- ✦ Greater access to the library's local history room
- ✦ Ability to sign out books for six weeks instead of the current three-week limit
- ✦ More books about children that don't focus on the traditional school environment
- ✦ Programs to help teach homeschooled students how to get the most out of library resources

> Whether you volunteer or not, make friends with your librarians; you'll soon be seeing quite a bit of them!

Libraries often welcome parent/child volunteer teams, letting your child become ever more familiar with the library while providing community service. Whether you volunteer or not, make friends with your librarian; you'll soon be seeing her a lot!

SUPPORT GROUPS

NEED THE NAME of a good book about Egypt? A day in the park with friends? Someone to tell you "this, too, shall pass"? Head for our third destination, a homeschool support group.

Nothing has contributed more to the phenomenal growth of homeschooling than grassroots efforts at connection. (See chapter 11 for online support groups.) Nowhere else will you unearth a more valuable source of usable homeschooling-specific advice and information than a support group. Add to this the emotional encouragement and the friendship of others living family-centered lives, and you'll understand why an estimated 4,000-plus groups dot the American landscape.

Local Groups

At the local level, support groups spread homeschooling one family at a time. Here, homeschooling finds solid roots cultivated by one-on-one attention and a self-help approach to your community's personal and daily homeschooling needs. (See *The Homeschooling Book of Answers* for an in-depth discussion of finding or starting a homeschool support group.)

Here are some of the benefits of membership in and support of a local group:

✦   Experienced voices regarding your local homeschool climate
✦   A chance to give and receive support and information
✦   Social opportunities and friends for children *and* parents
✦   Potential for team or club experiences
✦   A low-cost group rate for field trips and activities
✦   A chance to borrow or recycle resources

Nowhere else will you unearth a more valuable source of useable homeschooling-specific advice and information than a support group.

If you can't find a group in your area, or if existing groups don't mesh with your needs or philosophy, think seriously about starting a new one. It doesn't take much; most groups thriving today began when a couple of families shared coffee, potluck suppers, or a sunny day at the park—and a desire to create a better education for their children.

State Groups

At the state level, support groups pool talents, energies, and the strength of numbers. Also built by volunteers, state groups help promote connection among homeschoolers through the interests they share, oftentimes the legal and political climate within the state.

Here are some of the benefits of membership in and support of a state group:

+ Experienced voices regarding your state education department, legislators, and laws or regulations
+ An additional means of connection to other homeschoolers
+ A newsletter
+ Local contacts
+ Alerts to legislation pertinent to homeschooling
+ Protection of good laws or work to improve oppressive laws
+ A potential source of lobbyists for homeschooling interests
+ An information source for the media

There's always room for another pair of hands to keep the work of a state support group going. From watching legislation to writing for the newsletter to stuffing envelopes for mass mailings to members and more, you'll find satisfying work and camaraderie by supporting the supporters.

SIMPLE STARTING POINTS

+ *Start thinking of your community as your classroom.*
"Homeschooling" doesn't limit you to educating at home. Break out of the thinking that learning can only occur sitting down with a book, and make your greater community your classroom. It's full of interesting work, real-life applications of knowledge, and friendly people who will help teach your child.

+ *Keep a list or file of places and activities that sound interesting.*
Oftentimes you'll learn of educational opportunities while they're not age-appropriate, don't fit in with your studies, or you just

don't have the money. Unless you've got a super memory, keep the information organized. Your children will get older, your studies will change—and so may your financial situation.

✦ *Volunteer in the community—with your child.*

Your child will understand the connection to the community that real work provides. He'll learn the value and rewards of "it is better to give than to receive." Contributing to the community puts him in touch with adults whom he will consider friends and perhaps future mentors.

✦ *Support your local library.*

As a homeschooler your use (and appreciation) of the local library will increase; you won't find a better source of materials to keep learning activities fun, interesting, and affordable. In return, think about donating money, time, unused books for book sales, or even just writing a letter to the editor giving your librarians a public pat on the back.

RESOURCES

Books

Bundren, Mary Rodgers. *Travel Wise with Children: 101 Educational Travel Tips for Families.* Inprint Publications, Inc., 1998.

Dobson, Linda. *The Homeschooling Book of Answers.* Prima Publishing, 1998. Appendix includes an extensive list of local and state support groups.

Spizman, Robyn Freedman. *Kids on Board: Fun Things to Do While Commuting or Road Tripping with Children.* Fairview Press, 1997.

Tristram, Claire. *Have Kid, Will Travel: 101 Survival Strategies for Vacationing with Babies and Young Children.* Andrews & McMeel Publishing, 1997.

For Your Librarian

Bostrom, David C. *A Guide to Homeschooling for Librarians.* Highsmith Co., 1995.

Scheps, Susan G. *The Homeschooling Resource Guide.* American Library Association Editions, 1998.

Web Sites

Home Education Magazine Support Group Listing: http://www.home-ed-magazine.com/HSRS/hsrsc_grps.html.

Homeschool Central: http://homeschoolcentral.com/hsorg.htm (list of national organizations).

Homeschool Weblinks Page: http://members.aol.com/hmscsteve/web.htm#state (links to some state organizations).

The Homeschooler: http://www.thehomeschooler.com/guest/organiza tionsearch.htm (list of organizations).

Eclectic Homeschool Online State Resources: http://www.mitec.net/~eclectic/states.htm.

Karen Gibson's List: www.pipeline.com/~wdkmg/Karen/Lists.htm.

National Homeschool Association: http://www.n-h-a.org/.

Support Groups by State: http://pages.prodigy.com/ct_homeschool/support.htm.

13

ACCOMMODATING
YOUNGER LEARNERS

In This Chapter

✦ Baby on board!

✦ Tactics of inclusion and diversion

✦ Same family, different experience:
observations on birth order

✦ Simple starting points

✦ Resources

*T*HE LONGER THEY practice, the better homeschooling parents get at juggling the simultaneous needs of several children, much as an experienced circus juggler adds more and more objects to his act the longer he stays in the business. Homeschooling an early years child while nurturing very young siblings requires dexterity as little sister still needs lots of attention, often demanding it when least convenient.

Acquiring this flexibility brings great rewards. Your homeschooled child is growing up with little sister, getting to know and love her, even learning to help care for her. Lifelong bonds are being formed. Enjoy it while it lasts; you'll be checking into colleges before you know it.

BABY ON BOARD!

HOMESCHOOLERS WHO worried about starting their learning journeys with babies needn't have. Between numerous naps, in-arms contentment during reading, and close proximity to family activity, Baby tends to slip easily into a family's homeschooling rhythm.

Homeschooling with a new baby was the only source of doubt when Janelle began homeschooling ten years ago. "I worried that I'd never have enough time," she says. "Fortunately, experience overcame that doubt quickly."

When Allison started kindergarten, baby sister Karen was only six weeks old. Celia questioned her ability to cope. "To be honest, I wasn't sure I could do it, so my husband and I spent much time in prayer," she says. "We started with a curriculum that had daily lesson plans to save time and keep us organized. We'd homeschooled the year before 'on the fly,' using whatever was handy or available. This took a lot of creative thought on my part, though, and I didn't think I was up to it with a newborn in tow.

Your homeschooled child is growing up with little sister, getting to know and love her, even learning to help care for her. Lifelong bonds are being formed. Enjoy it while it lasts; you'll be checking into colleges before you know it.

"The lesson plans helped a great deal," Celia remembers. "Also, because homeschooling is all one-on-one time, it really didn't take us long to go through all the material we wanted to cover each day. If the baby was especially cranky I'd put her in the sling and nurse her or we'd move into the living room where she could see us much better. That was usually all it took to get through the day."

While babies may be content simply being in the proximity of homeschooling, they soon become toddlers who aren't going to be left out of *anything*.

TACTICS OF INCLUSION AND DIVERSION

CELIA CONTINUES: "It's actually more challenging now that the baby is eighteen months old. It's gotten harder to entertain her long enough for Allison to finish her work. My husband and I take turns with her when he has the day off, otherwise we 'play school' with her."

Celia shares her tactics of inclusion: "She has books to read while her sister reads. She colors and scribbles when her sister is writing."

And diversion tactics: "She has special toys and, if I'm really desperate, I'll allow her to watch *Winnie-the-Pooh,* which usually keeps her occupied for the duration. I don't recommend TV as a babysitter, but it's helpful in a pinch!"

And back to inclusion: "There are still many days when she winds up on my hip; she's nursing and wants to be very close to me for the most part."

Like many other parents learning at home, Celia practices a commonsense approach to inclusion and diversion, employing each tactic as the situation warrants.

Inclusion

"Me, too!" exclaims the curious young toddler upon seeing that big sibling is doing something that looks mighty interesting. And when it comes to learning, why not? This casual exploration of educational lessons and activities can have big pay-offs.

"If I was reading aloud the younger one would listen to anything," says Valerie. "Maybe he didn't absorb everything five years above his age level (although I sometimes wonder) but he just enjoyed being involved."

Pauline's children are only two years apart in age. "When I start an activity with Darla, I set something out for Frederick on the sidelines that has to do with what Darla and I are doing. If we're writing or doing math," Pauline explains, "I'll take out paper and pencil or math manipulatives. This is usually enough to make Frederick feel a part of what we're doing, and he absorbs much more than I ever imagined possible."

Janelle chose to cater to her young learners' artistic sense, as "the younger siblings worked on an art project which was in some way related to the older siblings' studies."

Monique's approach is even simpler. "I just make extra copies for the younger one so she feels a part of our work. At age three she usually just colors the papers."

In Shannon's household, the inclusionary tables get turned a bit. "I read a range of stories, some for younger children. Many 'younger' stories contain valuable information which older children learn from, too."

> "Me, too!" exclaims the curious young toddler upon seeing that big sibling is doing something that looks mighty interesting. And when it comes to learning, why not?

Whatever you're reading, don't miss out on read-aloud time as an opportunity for the younger sibling to feel a part of the learning action. "Do some subjects on the sofa so all can hear a reading at once and be snuggled," adds Marcia.

I'm sure you'll discover many more ways to include your youngest children in the homeschooling adventure as the unique rhythms of your household require. To make life a bit easier during this period of intense toddler curiosity, Renee adds this practical advice: "When they're going through the toddler stages it's best not to be too structured and to grab opportunities as they arise." Sounds like a formula for success to me.

Diversion

Thank heaven for naps and early bedtimes! Lots of learning, especially that involving particularly messy or dangerous elements (such as chemicals), occurs while the youngest learning journey travelers are diverted by sweet dreams.

Marie's family gets lots of work done during naps, before the little ones get up, and after they're down for the night. "Not my favorites," says Marie, "but I've done it!" When the youngest family members are up and about, she uses audiotapes with books, educational videos, crepe puzzles, and Lego Technic sets—things "that only come out when I need time with older siblings."

In Wendy's Houston, Texas, household, she and her five-year-old daughter "tend to watch for the times when our toddler otherwise occupies herself, then we take advantage of that time." (Ah, I remember this well!)

Sarah's family looks forward to good weather so everybody can work in the fresh air. Little ones draw or play in the sandbox nearby, or the older children take turns amusing them.

QUICK & EASY

COLOR MIX

Place a few drops of two colors of paint in a Ziploc plastic bag. Let child "mush" the colors together.

Just as Janelle used art as an inclusionary tactic, Priscilla finds the same method works pretty well as a diversion. She instructs, "Sit the youngest as far away as possible from the other child, not to exclude but 'out of reach,' and give her something really messy to do!"

Families sometimes turn to educational computer games and TV or videos when the older sibling needs Mom's attention for an extended time. Useful, although not high on anyone's list of "druthers," they're usually employed as a "tactic of last resort." Well, maybe not quite the last resort.

If her two-year-old son has made life challenging that day, Lucy patiently waits in her rural Texas dwelling until her husband gets home! He then becomes the diversionary focal point. If he happens to take his son to the store, he just may run into Ariana's husband providing his own favorite diversionary service.

Whether you like to admit it or not, your toddler will ultimately control whether inclusionary or diversionary tactics are the best choice on any given day. A tired, cranky, nagging toddler isn't likely

> Your youngest travelers will give you a chance to glimpse the world through the eyes of lovely, fleeting innocence. There's nothing like discovering the joys of Play-Doh for the first time—again.

to be swayed from her desires when it's your time and attention she wants. If her older brother is trying to concentrate or create at the time of the commotion, attend to her needs first as this is going to save time and aggravation in the long run. (This is how big brothers soon come to realize that little sisters have a few effective diversionary tactics of their own.) Marcia's sound advice should help keep these instances to a minimum, though: "Go to the young ones before they're clamoring, saturate them with attention, then return to your teaching." Everyone will appreciate the relative peace.

Your youngest travelers will give you a chance to glimpse the world through the eyes of one who still possesses a lovely, fleeting innocence. While diversion is sometimes necessary, inclusion is a lot more fun and beneficial. Besides, there's nothing like discovering the joys of Play-Doh for the first time—again.

SAME FAMILY, DIFFERENT EXPERIENCE: OBSERVATIONS ON BIRTH ORDER

DO YOU REMEMBER the old *Smothers Brothers Show* when Dick, the older brother, would reveal some taunting fact about their family life heretofore unknown to Tommy, who would then cry, "Mom always liked you best!"

Of course Mrs. Smothers didn't like Dick best, but those funny comedy routines were rooted in the reality that even as the brothers grew up in the same household, life was very different for "baby" brother.

Is the homeschooling experience also different for big and baby brother? Many younger siblings have literally grown up into learning in a home already alive with curiosity and filled with learning materials. I'd come to some conclusions about this based on my own family's experience, but I was always curious as to whether other homeschooling parents observed similar effects.

Baby Gets a Head Start

As toddlers get included in and maintain daily proximity to older siblings' learning, the effects *are* noticeable. "I've observed the second is more inclined to pick up things that we're doing much before her older sister did," says Kate. "I believe it's because we didn't 'do' a whole lot with Reba and allowed her to learn more on her own. Beth is much more interested in what Reba is doing."

Of course Mrs. Smothers didn't like Dick best, but those funny comedy routines were rooted in the reality that even as the brothers grew up in the same household, life was very different for "baby" brother.

Renee's "baby," now eight, has two older homeschooling brothers. "He's a bit accelerated academically, but emotionally he's an eight-year-old," she says. "He gets to do a lot of things at eight that

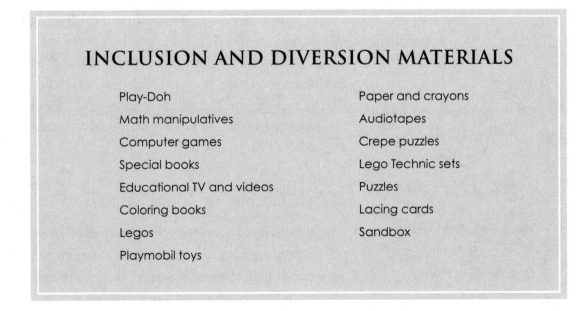

INCLUSION AND DIVERSION MATERIALS

Play-Doh

Math manipulatives

Computer games

Special books

Educational TV and videos

Coloring books

Legos

Playmobil toys

Paper and crayons

Audiotapes

Crepe puzzles

Lego Technic sets

Puzzles

Lacing cards

Sandbox

his brothers weren't allowed to do, partially because there are many things available to him at eight that weren't available to them.

"I think the younger children benefit from a trickle-down effect. They learn a lot while the older siblings are being taught."

But Renee also sees a two-way street. "The older children benefit tremendously from being around to observe Mom taking care of the younger one and being part of that. They help teach the younger ones, too, even if they don't realize that's what they're doing."

Baby Gets a Home Full of Role Models

For Sarah's youngest children, *big brother* and *big sister* mean teenagers. "They've got lots of positive role models to learn from right here at home," says Sarah. "The older children read to them when I'm busy, and the young ones now get carted around to the interesting activities of the teenagers."

With older siblings as role models, Brenda's seven-year-old daughter received a gift equally important to early learning. Brenda delights in observing her "baby's" ability to go off and do her own thing. "She is confident about gymnastics even though her older sisters didn't do this. This is a direct benefit of homeschooling," Brenda says confidently. "She has time to try out ballet, violin, soccer, softball, and then decide she really enjoys gymnastics. She also watched her older sisters work on projects and wanted to do the same thing. If the older two were in school she wouldn't have had those role models or been as confident on her own."

QUICK & EASY

HIGH CHAIR ART
Tape paper to tray; give child crayons.

Baby's Parents Are More Relaxed

The homeschool continuum showed that, overall, respondents moved toward a less structured homeschooling approach over time. This parallels a general tendency of parents to grow more relaxed in parenting in general as they move beyond the experimental first child and gain confidence in their abilities. The second, third, and later children generally get a more relaxed mom, and they may grow up into a more relaxed homeschool situation than the oldest sibling, too.

"The first was more dependent on me for learning experiences," explains Patty. "The second learns from the first and the third from the older two. Yes, I'm more relaxed as they come along. Because the first learned how to read, I know the second will and don't worry about it like I did before. By the third, I don't even think about it."

Marcia agrees. "The eldest got the most 'packaged' curricula while the middle child is getting a more 'distilled' education."

It helps when the oldest maintains a positive perspective on all of this. Gwenn's twelve-year-old, the oldest of six children, accepts her "learning parents" with a smile. "We've sometimes discussed such futuristic subjects as high school and college," says Gwenn, "and when I admit to not knowing what things might be like, she always grins and says, 'Ah, yes, I'm the *experimental* child.'"

> Later children generally get a more relaxed mom, and they may grow up into a more relaxed homeschool situation than the oldest sibling, too.

Older Siblings, Take Heart

I know my oldest will always tease me about his younger brother having it "made in the shade," and the number of responses describing benefits for the baby outnumbered those of benefits for the elder—but the older child scored some points, too.

When my children were young we took lots of field trips, some in the community and others farther from home. My oldest has fond memories of all of them, while the youngest has hardly any memories at all! "Oh, honey, you *must* remember when we put on big raincoats and got on the boat and went under Niagara Falls," I implore him. "You slipped on the wet deck and fell and got soaked," I add, confident this is the jog his memory needs.

> Older siblings, if your mother's time means anything, you get the prize here. What you may lose in an academic head start, on-site role models, or in having a "less than relaxed" mom, you gain by having her undivided attention focused on you.

"Nope, sorry," he replies. Remembered or not, most of our big family treks, unfortunately, are unlikely to be repeated.

Other trips won't be repeated in Corinne's family, either, but for different reasons. "The last suffers from burnout problems sometimes. I've gotten tired of some activities and trips by the fourth time around, so the youngest has missed out on some things."

And, older siblings, if your mother's time means anything, you get the prize here. What you may lose in an academic head start, on-site role models, or in having a "less-than-relaxed" mom, you gain by having her undivided attention focused on you.

"The oldest two children (of six) definitely got more attention to formal education," explains Sarah. "They had more of Mom's time to read aloud, two to three hours daily as compared to the younger children's half hour a day. They could also dictate the family's controlling interest, whether it was dinosaurs or the Civil War or Laura Ingalls."

There are good points and bad points to being the older or younger in a homeschooling family, just as there are in life in general. Remember as you take your homeschooling journey that birth order will always lend its unique contributions to your children's personalities and skills. Regardless of birth order, though, *all* siblings can contribute to the upkeep of the place they all call home.

SIMPLE STARTING POINTS

> ✦ *Let your homeschooling schedule twist around your baby's schedule instead of the other way around.*

Don't let expecting or caring for a new baby frighten or stop you from considering homeschooling your older child. The early years child requires very little by way of formal education. You also don't need to accomplish your daily learning goals in one sitting each day. (Let go of that school schedule!) Use homeschooling's flexibility to accommodate your baby's needs; there will still be plenty of moments plucked throughout the day for reading, games, and kitchen math lessons—and if not, there's always tomorrow.

✦ *Welcome your toddler's participation in learning activities.*

She'll eagerly emulate the older siblings she admires. There are a few activities best kept free of toddler hands, but she can join in the great majority *in her own way.* Satisfy her curiosity about the tools of learning by letting her experiment with them. Growing up in this way, learning will be a fun and natural part of day-to-day life.

✦ *Set aside a few toys, books, tapes, and other items that you can pull out when needed to divert your toddler's attention.*

When a toddler sees a "special" toy, it makes right now a special occasion! As he "celebrates," you and your school-aged child can accomplish what needs to get done in relative peace.

✦ *Take every opportunity to let each child know how special he is to you.*

"Mom always liked you best!" is funny when it comes from Tommy Smothers, but not so funny when it comes from a child whose feelings are bruised, even if unjustifiably so. Homeschooling gives you lots of time to spend with your children. Take just a few of those moments

MONEY SAVER

MAKE-IT-YOURSELF SEWING CARDS
Using wax-coated cardboard (the type frozen pizza cartons are made out of), cut out several different simple shapes—square, triangle, circle, and so on—about the same size. Using a hole punch, make holes around the edge of each shape. Cut a piece of yarn a bit longer than needed to go around the edge of card and through all the holes. Use a ball of Scotch tape on one end of the yarn to serve as the "knot," and a piece of Scotch tape to form a needle point on the other end.

each day to spend some time alone with each child, talking, telling jokes, hugging.

    ✦   *Remember to recharge* your *batteries.*

Early years children expend a lot of energy throughout their day, and it can be exhausting trying to keep up. Lots of homeschoolers incorporate a "quiet time" into their days, frequently after lunch. While babies and toddlers nap, older children read, write, rest, and otherwise occupy themselves for thirty to sixty minutes. This is a great time for your "power nap." Take advantage of it so you'll be ready for the fun and activity that will fill the rest of your day.

RESOURCES

Books

Cabellero, Jane A. *Handbook of Learning Activities for Young Children.* Humanics Publishing Group, 1987.

Gettman, David. *Basic Montessori: Learning Activities for Under-Fives.* St. Martin's Press, 1988.

Jasmine, Grace. *Quick and Fun Learning Activities for Four-Year-Olds.* Teacher Created Materials, 1997.

Kizer, Kathryn. *200+ Ideas for Teaching Preschoolers.* New Hope Publishers, 1997. Christian content.

Leidloff, Jean. *The Continuum Concept: In Search of Happiness Lost.* Addison-Wesley Publishing Co., 1986.

McGnee, Maria. *Quick and Fun Learning Activities for Three-Year-Olds.* Teacher Created Materials, 1997.

Web Sites

Idea Box: http://www.theideabox.com/

Crayola Family Play Activity Homepage: http://www.familyplay. com/ activities

Gryphon House Online: http://www.ghbooks.com/activity

Little Explorers: http://www.enchantedlearning.com/Dictionary.html

E-Mail Loop

Younglearners: Send e-mail to majordomo@familycom.org; use subscribe younglearners as text of message

14

KEEPING HOUSE (AND SANITY!)

AS YOU HOMESCHOOL

In This Chapter

+ Housework: a family affair

+ Finding time for you and your spouse

+ Simple starting points

+ Resources

*T*AKE BUSY YOUNG children at home. Add play time, a few art and science projects, and half a dozen sheets of papers they really don't want to put away just yet. Now think *"clean house."* Decide which is more important to you.

It's not really that cut and dried; the image just makes it easier for you to see that a redefinition of *clean* might be the only thing you need to keep your sanity regarding housework, homeschooling, and the early years child. As Jane says, "I'd have time to get so much more done if the children were gone all day, but what fun would *that* be?"

HOUSEWORK: A FAMILY AFFAIR

PAULINE SUMMARIZES THE problem: "When I get into a cleaning mode I just want to power clean and get it all done in a couple of hours. With the children around, I find myself doing a bit of cleaning here and there every other day and the result is that the house never looks really clean. I am by no means a clean freak, but it would be nice to have the house presentable when friends drop by."

> When the clutter gets too deep, home-schoolers know there's only one place to turn for help—the children. (Here's where your new, looser definition of clean comes in handy.)

When the clutter gets too deep, homeschoolers know there's only one place to turn for help— the children. (Here's where your new, looser definition of clean comes in handy.) Housework becomes a family affair, accomplished by the same team that created the mess. Turn on the music, get everybody singing, and before you know it, the house actually does look better. And everybody's had a good time working side by side.

"We set aside about thirty minutes in the afternoon before Dad comes home and straighten the house back up," says Jacqueline, adding, "I don't think our son would be as cooperative about helping if he'd been cooped up all day and just wanted to run and play."

Priscilla finds that if everyone does a little, no one has to do a lot. She keeps a big pine toy box in the living room, "and if it comes to it everything gets piled in and the lid shut. The house will always be here," she explains, "but my children will only be small for a short while. I prefer to enjoy them and try and ignore the dust. And I can always kick those Lego bricks and Barbie shoes under the sofa."

This might be what Sarah refers to as "working together to keep a nice medium." She notes, as do many homeschooling parents, "The house gets messiest when we're not there much. If we're out doing errands, visiting friends, and going to the park for baseball, home becomes a 'dumping spot.'"

Seize the cleaning fever moment while the children are still in their early years. "These are the days when interest is high, they *want* to help, so it's the perfect time to learn how. This changes over time," says Corinne. "As they get older and less enthusiastic about helping, at least it's not such a chore if they can work quickly because they know how to do things correctly."

The Piecemeal Approach

If large household tasks look overwhelming to you, imagine how they appear to your early years child. Think about breaking chores down into ten- or fifteen-minute sessions. Granted, you're not going to wind up with a home worthy of a *House Beautiful* cover shot, but every room will eventually get its share of attention. With this piecemeal approach, your early years children can keep their mind on what they're doing to the end and feel a sense of accomplishment when the task is completed.

Scatter three or four ten-minute sessions throughout the day, maybe after breakfast, before lunch, before Dad comes home, and one prior to bedtime. If your child likes to sweep the kitchen floor, that can be accomplished in session 1 and you can mop it during session 2. If you've dusted the living room during session 1, your child can then vacuum it in session 2. You can use one session to have everyone straighten up, putting away everything that isn't in its place.

Try "Beat the Clock" games that are cleaning sessions in disguise. Set the kitchen stove timer for ten minutes and see how much can be done before it goes off. The next time you tackle the same chore, tell your child you're going to see if the two of you can break your record.

You might prefer to do all the cleaning necessary in one room each day, so you can know at least one area is clean! Declare "Living Room

> Turn cleaning sessions into "Beat the Clock" games. Set the kitchen stove timer for ten minutes and see how much can be done before it goes off.

Day" or "Johnny's Room Day." (It really is a shame this doesn't work with teenagers.)

Multi-Tasking

Multi-tasking—alternatively known as the fine art of juggling chores—is for you, not your child. The best way to chop the amount

HOW WE DID IT

Our household is a bit different from most. My husband is disabled so he's home all day. I work part time—although with the travel to and from it seems like full time—as a school bus driver. My job allows me to be home for about four hours during the day.

My husband and the kids handle most of the housework, unfortunately not to my satisfaction; they never seem to find the dirt in the corners or under the furniture! I'm trying hard to adjust to keeping my mouth shut and not redoing what has already been done.

I do all the bills and correspondence. My husband keeps the cars running and fixes things around the house. With the help of the older boys, he also handles yard care.

Sometimes I wonder how we get everything done; it's definitely a challenge. My typical day goes something like this:

5:15 A.M.   Get up, take shower, get ready for work, feed baby.

6:15 A.M.   Leave for work.

9:45 A.M.   Return from work. Children are already at work, having started around 7:30 A.M. They do math, then language. If all goes well, they finish around 10:30 A.M. Those who are done first usually of time used on chores each day is to do two or more things at once. Accomplish relatively mindless tasks, like folding laundry or doing dishes, as your daughter reads aloud or works on math problems. As your child uses the computer, dust the room and clean the mirror. Pay bills while your son practices writing. Weed the garden and trim the hedges as your daughter enjoys the sandbox or swings. Get the washing machine going before you settle down to a game of Monopoly.

	read while waiting for the rest. While they're finishing up I'm feeding the baby and spending time with my four-year-old daughter. I also try to look at the newspaper.
11:30 A.M.	Lunch.
12:00 P.M.	Science. We're doing unit studies, presently the human body. I'll give them more to do while I go back to work, things like answer questions and look up information in the encyclopedia.
1:45 P.M.	Back to work.
2:00 P.M.	Children watch *Magic School Bus*.
2:30 P.M.	Children finish up assignments (if they don't "forget"). For the rest of the afternoon they'll read, play, and get chores done.
5:15 P.M.	I get home and we have dinner my husband prepared. Children and I clean up kitchen.
6:00 P.M.	Hubby and I watch news; kids are playing. The young children get in pajamas and I feed the baby—again—she eats all the time!
7:30–8:30 P.M.	With luck, the baby's in bed. We read Bible together; children get snacks.
9:00 P.M.	The remaining children go to bed.

—MONIQUE

Containers, sometimes a good buy at garage sales, provide a "place" that even very young children recognize as a resource's home.

Use one day a month to prepare and freeze meals ahead of time and gain an extra thirty minutes on other days to play a game or read a story while dinner heats up. The "once-a-month cooking" approach also means you can still have a nice dinner if a field trip or class keeps you out and about into the late afternoon.

Schedules and Organization Help

To ensure household tasks get accomplished, Darby creates a daily schedule. She explains, "For us, it's best to set goals for what we want to achieve

HOW WE DID IT

My husband gets ready for work and leaves by 7 A.M. I try to have the boys up by 8 A.M. For us, the early hours of the day are the hours when we get most of our "school" work done. The boys dress and eat quickly and one will walk the dogs. We try to start our studies by 8:30 or 9 A.M. I might read literature to them. They might do a math chapter from their books or a computer program. If I can run a load of dishes or laundry or straighten up the kitchen counter I'll try to fit it in. By 11 A.M. we're ready for lunch and we're usually done with our studies by 2 P.M.

The boys run off to play while I start on the house. I'll do a load or two of laundry and by midafternoon I'll ask the boys for help. They will normally help me for about a half hour—picking up and putting their things away, hauling clean laundry off to their rooms, emptying the dishwasher, and the like. Then they run off to play again and I go through the mail, read online mail, and start supper unless it's archery or guitar lesson days or support group park day. Then I take my mail with me or stash it until after supper, and we pick up some fast food on the way home.

but not set time constraints on those goals. It seems then every goal is met in a timely fashion but no one gets stressed about it."

Organization in Angie's house includes an art table, a crate for each child's homeschooling books, notebooks, and workbooks, and "lots and lots of bookshelves."

"We don't have the most spotless house in the world," says Angie, "but it's serviceable, even if no one has seen the surface of a coffee table since the movers carried them in. It looks relatively nice and works for us, although it drove my mother-in-law crazy when she lived with us for awhile."

"A place for everything" has saved many a homeschooling parent's sanity. Shelves for books and storage help make the most of space, and the lower shelves give easy access to the shortest family

After supper my husband, Michael, does another load of dishes and reads his mail while I do another load of laundry, vacuum, and mop the kitchen. We finish working about 9 P.M. and we're in bed by 10:30 P.M. at the latest.

Weekends are yard maintenance and bill paying time. Michael and I love yard work but we only have time for it several weekends each year. We have lots of natural landscaping, so it doesn't need constant manicuring and maintenance. Michael pays the bills and does paperwork several times a week, with much of it falling on weekends. He does all the home maintenance he can, as well.

We rarely watch TV, so we have a lot of extra hours each week that others spend unwinding in front of the television. We try to get outdoors and do something fun on weekends like hiking. Michael is a member of a soaring club and he spends about two Saturday mornings each month out at the air park. In the winter months, we often help a biologist band and weigh birds. We spend a fair amount of time running our boys to friends' houses, too.

—GRETCHEN

members. Large and small storage containers, sometimes a good buy at garage sales, provide a "place" that even very young children recognize as a resource's home. Check the sidebar, "Creative Organizers" for help to control the clutter as well.

Beyond Cleaning

Your child lends a welcome extra pair of hands keeping up with day-to-day cleaning, but "keeping house" encompasses much more than dusting and vacuuming. There are bills to be paid, groceries to be collected, cars to be maintained, and more. An extra pair of adult hands works wonders when you move beyond cleaning to other household demands on your time.

Wendy and Harry, parents of two early years children, maintain a simple plan: Whichever one is available gets the job done. "He does most of the cooking because he enjoys it," Wendy says. "I do most of the cleaning, home maintenance, and finances because I'm

TOP TEN REGULAR CHORES PERFORMED BY RESPONDENTS' EARLY YEARS CHILDREN

10.   Dust, cook, help with garbage (a three-way tie)

9.   Vacuum

8.   Clear plates from table

7.   Feed the animals

6.   Fold or put away laundry

5.   Empty the dishwasher

4.   Make beds

3.   Clean up toys

2.   Set table

1.   Clean room

more inclined to and, in general, enjoy it more. But we both do our share of all the work. And we enjoy it more when we are doing it together."

In Canada, Maureen and Dan created a system that works for them. "If it's important to you, do it," Maureen explains. "Fortunately different things are important to each of us so the work is fairly well divided."

Maureen has a low tolerance for mess so she does most of the housecleaning. "If I leave something long enough Dan will do it. It might just be a month or so before he gets around to it! He does most of the yard work because he enjoys it. I do some, but ever since I pulled up the wrong 'weeds,' Dan is reluctant to leave me alone in the yard. I enjoy planning the garden, so I figure out what to plant where, get the seeds started, and when it's time to plant, Dan takes over.

"We share meal preparation duties. Dan enjoys cooking and is very health conscious. When I work I'm not home for supper, so he either has to make something or pull something from the freezer.

"We've recently gone to computer banking and," Maureen explains, "it's a real time saver. I also call for all our library books on the Internet which saves time we used to spend searching shelves at the library. Someone who uses a curriculum which relies heavily on library books is paying me to call for her books, too.

"No matter what, Tuesday night is 'family night,'" says Maureen. If I have to work, we have it after I get home. We play games, do a craft, watch a video (we had cable disconnected—too much junk!), go for a walk, or do a fun lesson. The kids always look forward to this night because they know Mom and Dad will both be there."

FINDING TIME FOR YOU AND YOUR SPOUSE

IN TODAY'S BUSY world finding time for self and spouse isn't a problem unique to homeschooling, but this time takes on even greater significance when strong family ties are the backbone of your lifestyle. "For us to be the best parents we can be we must also be the best husband and wife we can be," explains Melanie. "We need to keep our marriage strong and not just focus on the children."

It's easy for a working parent focusing on making a living outside the home to lose touch with what's happening in homeschooling and feel left out of exciting learning experiences. Wendy says, "I share my thoughts about homeschooling with Harry so we are shaping our philosophy together. There are times we have both become so busy that I've taken off down some path and haven't found the time to bring him with me," she shares. "Then, we stop and catch up."

An informed spouse provides a reliable sounding board. "I spend my days immersed in the homeschool perspective. Harry can listen to my ideas with a fresh insight and add his own influence to what we're doing," adds Wendy.

Creating Time for Your Marriage

Mix together a large amount of desire, a helping of flexibility, and a pinch of ingenuity, and you've got a working formula for creating time to share with your spouse.

> Mix together a large amount of desire, a helping of flexibility, and a pinch of ingenuity, and you've got the formula for creating time to share with your spouse.

Melanie and Rob delight in simple pleasures. "We spend the evenings after the children are asleep talking, watching TV, or just gazing into each other's eyes. Whatever we do we try to do it together. At times we complete individual tasks we can't do while the children are up, but then we just end up staying up later so we can still have 'our' time."

Melanie explains, "A couple of times each month we have a family member care for the children so we can have a night out, especially important to the one of us who spends the most time at home! It doesn't have to be pricey evening, just visiting friends or going for a drive is enough."

CREATIVE ORGANIZERS

✦ A no-longer-needed lunch box stores stencils, protractor, and compass.

✦ A child-decorated soup can becomes a pencil holder (watch for sharp edges, though!)

✦ Garage sale spice rack, containing nine little drawers, holds paper clips, rubber bands, math manipulatives, coins, dice, and so on.

✦ Garage sale Rolodex file keeps changeable lists (perhaps chores), spelling or vocabulary words, reading book lists, multiplication facts, and so on. (I found a huge double-wheel metal Rolodex file for $2.)

✦ Large Kool-Whip container holds crayons.

✦ Milk crates are stackable and serve a variety of uses.

Creating time means getting up early for Wendy and Harry, and talks over coffee. Oh, and don't forget e-mail. "We can communicate privately without the girls listening and feel we're staying connected during the day," Wendy says. "This especially helps when we're really busy and keep forgetting to talk about something important."

The couple is also ready to try something new. "We're hiring a friend of mine to come over once a month to either clean the house or care for the girls—whichever we need more. I'm considering the cost an important homeschooling expense."

Weekends are part of the winning formula for Laura and Charles. "Friday and Sunday nights we both go into the office and work side by side on two computers and chat as we work—me on the Internet, him on his laptop. Sounds weird," Laura admits, "but it's nice. We get to talk about what's happened during the week, current events, and whatever pops into mind.

"Our son is finally willing to spend the night at his grandparents' house, which is only two miles away. So on some Saturday nights we take both children over there for dinner and we go out for dinner or eat in, relax all evening, and then sleep later the next day.

"It's been heaven," says Laura. "We get more talking done in that eighteen hours than in the entire previous week or two."

On other days of the week, Charles and Laura stay connected with phone calls and letters. "I send long heartfelt love letters, short love notes, risqué e-mails, quick Post-it notes," she says. "When Charles writes me a note, although seldom, I cherish it and read it over and over and keep it near my computer where I can see it often."

Creating Time for Yourself

Knowing how much you'd like to accomplish with your children, homeschooling, your spouse, and your house, it can feel "selfish" to steal a precious hour or two for personal interests or indulgences. Without opportunity to replenish your supply, though, your nurturing well—so vital to your children's well-being—will run dry. If you expect to provide a happy, healthy learning environment for your child, it's essential you provide yourself with the time necessary to be a happy, healthy person in your own right.

> If you expect to provide a happy, healthy learning environment for your child, it's essential you provide yourself with the time necessary to be a happy, healthy person in your own right.

Gretchen feels lucky she doesn't need a lot of private time. "Private time for me can be going out to coffee with a friend every two or three weeks," she explains. "It can be time online alone in the computer room, in the afternoon or at night after everyone else has gone to sleep, or a couple of hours in the afternoon running errands with my mom. Some nights I stay up late just to enjoy the unmitigated quiet and lack of interruptions!

"I'm happy with an hour or two of private time here and there," says Gretchen, "*and* a good night's sleep."

Holly knows for sanity's sake she needs a larger dose of private time and quiet, but with a

OFFICE SUPPLY STORE GOODIES

✦   In and out boxes stack different types of paper in one place.

✦   Framed bulletin-strips in various lengths allow you to tack up papers without taking up the space of a big bulletin board.

✦   Velcro dots or strips let you hang anything anywhere; help keep items in place inside drawers, too.

✦   Desk blotter calendar can be hung on wall; costs about $1.99; lots of space to jot "to do" list.

✦   Plastic paper sorters hold paper in upright position; a section for each workbook, papers on each subject, and so on.

✦   Magazine files help keep the stacks in order; plastic or corrugated cardboard are the cheapest.

✦   Look for sales on crayons, colored pencils, markers, glue sticks, and more while you're there!

six-year-old and a toddler she, too, winds up taking it in bits and pieces. "If I don't get enough quiet alone time, I'm not able to turn around and give time and attention to my husband." She elaborates: "Sometimes my husband will take one or both of the children on an errand or to play outdoors and that helps. I try to remember to rest and relax when I'm sitting nursing our toddler, especially if she dozes off afterward. But," Holly adds, "my ultimate refuge is a long, hot soak in the tub."

Besides serving to recharge your batteries, time for self allows space for reflection. Wendy explains, "I need time to consider our life as a family and my life as an individual. It's a time for my own thoughts and interests. The time I spend on my own is an important example that I set for my children and an important part of our learning philosophy. I want them to see that I have my own interests and take the time to pursue them. This is how we learn."

SIMPLE STARTING POINTS

✦   *Relax your definition of clean.*

If you're a clean fanatic I know I'm not going to sway you, so this is for everybody else. Thanks to mass media magazines, the cleaning products industry, and consumerism in general, our cleanliness expectations have been greatly exaggerated. There's a happy medium between sparkling and filthy, and during my family's early years homeschooling I called it, affectionately, "kid cleaned."

✦   *Teach home economics while the early years child is eager to learn.*

Your child is anxious to explore the world of adult work and activity. Allow him time to use the tools (dust rag, broom, vacuum, mop, and so on) in pretend help. Before you know it, that help won't be pretend anymore.

✦   *Perform a house clearing.*

Between additional books, games, and the projects your child creates, you'll find yourself looking for new places to put things. Rather than a cleaning, a house *clearing* is ridding your environment of unneeded and unfunctional "things" to make room for useful homeschooling items. A good rule of thumb is if you haven't needed it in the last six months, you probably won't need it in the next. Store these things in a box on which you record the date. If you haven't gone back to the box to get it within another six months, you don't need it.

✦   *Use the laundry dot system.*

To enable even the youngest child to help sort clean laundry, use a permanent marker to dot the children's clothes in an inconspicuous place; first child's clothes get one dot, second child's get two, and so on. Sorting becomes a matter of counting dots. If an article of clothing makes it to the next child, just add another dot.

✦ *Create a "things I'd do with an hour" list for yourself.*

On a busy day or during trying times, take a look at your list. It could help inspire you to actually take the hour and do what you want. You'll find you feel much better afterward.

RESOURCES

Books

Aslett, Don. *500 Terrific Ideas for Cleaning Everything.* Budget Book Service, 1997.

Bykofsky, Sheree. *500 Terrific Ideas for Organizing Everything.* Budget Book Service, 1997.

Halvorson, Christine and Sheldon, Ken. *Clean and Simple: A Back-to-Basics Approach to Cleaning Your Home.* Time-Life Books, 1999.

Taylor-Hough, Deborah. *Frozen Assets: How to Cook for a Day and Eat for a Month.* Champion Press Ltd., 1998.

Winston, Stephanie. *Stephanie Winston's Best Organizing Tips: Quick, Simple Ways to Get Organized and Get on With Your Life.* Fireside, 1996.

Catalog

Tooling Around: 385 Delmas Avenue, #A, San Jose, CA 95126-3626; 408-286-9770; real child-size tools.

15

PART-TIME HOMESCHOOLING: COMPLEMENTING PRIVATE AND PUBLIC SCHOOLING

In This Chapter

✦ You don't have much time—
where do you most want to go?

✦ Teachers turning home see the difference

✦ Simple starting points

✦ Resources

*P*ARENTS ARE DISCOVERING that public and even private schools aren't what they used to be when it comes to providing a solid academic foundation for children. Instead of focusing on the 3 R's, evidence reveals they now concentrate more on behavior modification with an emphasis on creating economic human resources. The big federal programs rapidly accomplishing this include Goals 2000: Educate America Act, the School-to-Work Investment Act of 1994 (STW), and the Workforce Improvement Act of 1997.

The diploma you think your child is working toward may not even exist ten years from now. In states at the forefront of putting federal programs in place, Certificates of Mastery, which certify that a child has acquired the necessary behavior and attitudes of a "good"

> The diploma you think your child is working toward may not even exist ten years from now.

worker, are replacing diplomas. Hoopla about new assessments disguises the basic fact that test content is changing because the curriculum has changed. States, too, are mandating their own programs, which use valuable student time in non-academic directions. And as the phonics and whole language sides of the "Reading Wars" battle for control of the curriculum, thousands upon thousands of children become part of the nation's statistics on functional illiteracy. Anyone with a child preparing for or already in public school would be wise to research the implementation of such programs in the local school. Unfortunately, these programs are given different names in different states (when met with resistance the names can even change within a state), so you'll have to look past the name to the meat of the programs.

Through homeschooling, you cut out the influences of non-academically motivated federal and state politicians on your child's learning life and refocus attention on providing a solid academic foundation.

If personal circumstances prevent you from full-time homeschooling, don't give up hope. Many families supplement their children's learning experiences with homeschooling in the evenings, on weekends, and during the summer months. They use the same methods and resources, and get results that have a lasting impact for their children.

YOU DON'T HAVE MUCH TIME— WHERE DO YOU MOST WANT TO GO?

EVENINGS, WEEKENDS, AND summer months don't give you a whole lot of time for homeschooling. Many children return home from school tired and stressed, presenting you with a different experience from learning with a child fresh from a good night's sleep. If your child is like most, weekends are as precious to him as they are to an adult nine-to-fiver who now wants to accomplish the things he *likes* to do—or recuperate on the couch.

For these reasons you may decide on a covert approach to additional educational activities at first. After all, who wants to see another workbook page when you've been doing them all day? Fortunately many of the educational resources you'll find through homeschooling circles give you a starting place that's fun, with games, crafts, kitchen science, and more. Fill weekends and vacations with exciting field trips to supplement or enhance school activities. Evenings can lend themselves to read-alouds of children's literature your child may not otherwise get to enjoy.

> Many families supplement their children's learning experiences with homeschooling in the evenings, on weekends, and during the summer months.

An important first step is deciding what you want to accomplish in your limited time. Do you want to supplement academic concepts and skills your child is having trouble with? Do you want to provide extra time for more advanced activity? Or time to pursue interests near and dear to your child's heart? Don't forget the possibility of complementary homeschooling as a chance to engage in learning activities just for the fun they offer, and to help you stay connected in a meaningful way with your busy and rapidly growing early years child.

Supplementing Academics

Parents participating in education e-mail loops from all around the country constantly repeat the story: The child receives good grades in reading and arithmetic, which leads the parent to believe the child is doing well. Parent takes opportunity to observe acquired skills. Parent is appalled by the child's inferior skill level, and wonders why he receives good grades.

These are some of the parents turning in record numbers to tutoring and extra help companies like Sylvan Learning Systems and Kumon. Sylvan reported record second-quarter revenues of $57.6 million in 1997, the result of $30/hour fees paid by worried parents. Kumon even calls its $75 to $90 per month service "a home education program where success depends on a parent's agreement that daily homework be completed."

Questionable school programs in early reading and arithmetic are leaving children academically ill-prepared. Why play catch-up at such high prices during your child's teen years when supplementary homeschooling in the early years can establish a solid academic foundation while your child is still naturally eager and curious about the world around him?

> Why play catch-up during your child's teen years when supplementary homeschooling in the early years can build a solid academic foundation while your child is still naturally eager and curious about the world around him?

Rhonda turned to supplementary homeschooling for math while her son attended private school. "I just looked over the teacher's shoulder and knew I could do better," she remembers. "They had science, but not *hands-on* science. They had writing, but my son wasn't doing it. They had math, but I had a better math program. I had more confidence after that year of part-time homeschooling, too."

Extra Time for Your Child's Interests

If your child excels in one or all areas of schoolwork, he may enjoy and benefit from extra activities that let him explore further. One caveat here, though. Even as complaints about lack of parental support reach a crescendo, public school personnel have been known to ask parents not to help out at home.

"We were told to stop teaching our children at home because they were too advanced and bored easily in class," says Eleanore, whose three children homeschooled and went back to "homeschool-supplemented" public school in Kentucky. "We decided to come back to full-time homeschooling because we saw no sane reason to stop the children from learning!"

Disappointed with her daughter's kindergarten experience, and convinced the school wasn't providing enough of what her children needed, Angie's family started "Mom's School" that summer.

"We used homeschooling as a complement to public school to explore the children's interests and keep their curiosity alive," Angie explains. "We picked projects the children thought would be interesting and we made things. We got library books on subjects they wanted to know more about. We did lots of artwork and went swimming. We read daily, too, school or no. Marla began music lessons at four years of age at her request, while Jacob wanted music appreciation and art classes in a community art school.

"This practice made it easier for us to move into homeschooling because we were already accustomed to lots of learning at home," says Angie. "Now we give our early reading son stimulating, interesting material, and tailor academics to the children's talents and interests."

Consider whether or not your child with special talents may be stifled by a limited school curriculum. The observation skills you're perfecting are a great aid in this area, and can help keep the spark of enthusiastic learning alive in your child.

Part Time Can Lead to Full Time

It's only fair to warn you that just this little taste of homeschooling—its freedom, its flexibility, its ease, its joy—can shatter so many of your misconceptions about children's education you could wake up one morning, aware somewhere deep inside you that compulsory school attendance is unnecessary, and perhaps even damaging, to your child.

Shawna's family used supplementary homeschooling during the children's early public school years, including on vacations. "It took awhile, but we realized we were dumbing down the children by staying in the school system," Shawna says. "Specifically I can remember a time when my first-grade son loved doing math problems. He wanted me to give him addition and subtraction problems to do everywhere; in church and in the car, too.

"It concerned me he was doing material that wasn't in the first grade curriculum. Should we stop so he wouldn't be bored in class? Should we continue because he's thriving on it?

"I'm terribly embarrassed looking back on it now," Shawna confesses. "We didn't understand until a couple of years later he was bored in school no matter what we did."

Like so many before her, Gretchen's commitment to her children's education brought her to the school weekly as a volunteer, even as she supplemented their learning at home. "I could see the school wasn't doing anything 'magical' I couldn't do. In fact," she says, "I was pretty sure I could do better. As it turns out, I had always been homeschooling but just didn't realize it and called it 'supplementing'.

"I'm sure supplementing led to full-time homeschooling," Gretchen declares. "I already had experience 'teaching' my children so I had the confidence to homeschool. I knew learning could be so much more than was offered at school because we had participated in some wonderful activities and I saw my children learn under more creative circumstances."

Observing her son's need for more advanced instruction led Rachel to part-time homeschooling, but both mother and son found it difficult, in part because it left Roy, an active little boy, with little play time. They chose home over school. "He was a depressed and angry child

> It's only fair to warn you that just this little taste of homeschooling—its freedom, its flexibility, its ease, its joy—can shatter so many of your misconceptions about children's education you could wake up one morning, aware somewhere deep inside you that compulsory school attendance is unnecessary, and perhaps even damaging, to your child.

when we took him out of public school," Rachel remembers, "and I thought we would be at odds the whole time. But within a few weeks his whole attitude changed. My son was fun to be with again. I felt like I got him back through homeschooling."

TEACHERS TURNING HOME SEE THE DIFFERENCE

TEACHERS, THOSE PARENTS with the most direct knowledge of school classrooms, are turning to home education in growing numbers. Former teachers with intimate knowledge of the way the system works offer important comparisons between public or private school and homeschooling for those considering both options.

> Former teachers with intimate knowledge of the way the system works offer important comparisons between public or private schools and home-schooling.

Through the Ages

It begins with preschool, according to Karla. "I was a preschool teacher for six years and felt so bad for some of the children in my classes. I taught full-time 'preschool.' For most parents it was day care," she explains. "Although we had great programs and activities, these were very long days for such young children."

Louise picks up the scenario in the elementary school years, recalling the year she was a substitute teacher after receiving her teaching credits. "The children weren't eager to learn in the way I'd expected. To the contrary," Louise says, "they seemed as if they were in what amounted to jail, and many of the teachers had the same attitude about the situation.

"I want to make it clear that I was never taught anything in all the elementary education classes that would qualify me to be a teacher of any kind," Louise continues. "I was one scared twenty-one-year-old when considering the prospect of taking on a classroom full of children to educate. While substituting I would run into old acquaintances from college who had once been very idealistic; they looked dull and bitter going down the halls with restless lines of children. Public education can be a noble ideal, but the reality is often sad."

Teaching music classes in middle school led to Tanya's disillusionment. "I saw how much time is wasted and how little learning occurs," she explains. "I now teach a homeschool choir and my teaching is identical. The only difference is, I don't have to use all those discipline tricks I had to use in public school."

HOW WE DID IT

I have a bachelor's degree in elementary education with a minor in early childhood education. I remember how hard it was for me to do my student teaching.

We had a team situation in the classroom; I got the lowest fourth-grade reading group and the highest second-grade reading group, all in the same room at the same time. I had twenty children in my fourth-grade reading group with twenty minutes to teach them about reading. I'd do the math and groan—one minute per child per day for those struggling with reading.

To make matters worse, the second-grade children were reading the fourth-grade books "for fun." I asked the teacher why we couldn't just let the second-grade children read the fourth-grade books. "They're not ready," she flatly stated, refusing to discuss it further.

I had many moments of frustration. I wondered why children couldn't just go at their own pace. Let them be free to go as fast or as slow as they need. Let them be free to find their own level.

—RHONDA

And, yes, differences were noted even at the college level, where Holly taught English when she decided to take the homeschool journey. "My reading—John Holt and David Guterson particularly—convinced me that homeschooling was the best way for our children to learn and grow. My affinity for unschooling was part of my decision to leave academe." Holly adds, "I found even in college the students are treated like feeble-minded clients."

Private School

Understanding the problems of public schools, some parents scrimp and save and stretch their budgets with high hopes that private school tuition will buy high academic results. After many years and the birth of her child, Louise, the former substitute teacher, believed things would be different.

"We tried a Waldorf school, and then a tiny, more scholastically oriented school," she recalls, "but it came down to the same old problem: It was a school, an institution that didn't, wouldn't, and couldn't accommodate my son's needs."

A former private school teacher in Missouri, Evelyn homeschooled her grandson last year, and is still pursuing it with him as a public school complement this year. When a few homeschooling parents asked her to tutor their children, Evelyn created yet another home-based homeschooling business.

"I've chosen to tutor homeschooled students mostly because of the lack of respect in the public and private schools," Evelyn explains. "In two different private schools my life was threatened and nothing was done about it. I'm under much less stress working directly with parents and children. If they don't like my rules they don't have to stay and I don't have to keep them. I haven't lost a single student because of disrespect.

"Now," she says, "I have time to work one-on-one with a child having difficulty or a child who needs to move faster. I can meet each child exactly where he is."

Emotionally Disturbed Children

A psychologist with a Ph.D. in education, Angie's pre-homeschooling work occurred in a residential school for severely emotionally disturbed children. For eight years Angie used her specialty of counseling psychology in the school. At various times she was a therapist, administered psychological tests, met with teachers and residence staff to plan programs for individual students, and served as clinical director for the girls in the program.

"My work experience influenced my decision to be an at-home mother," she attests. "I saw child after child whose history included frequent change of primary caretaker. I wanted to provide my children with the stability that having an at-home parent offers."

The Difference

Brenda's decision to homeschool was influenced by two main observations as a teacher. She felt the public school didn't spend enough time helping individual students, and found the quality of materials used inferior to those she could provide. "We would have spent as much time providing correct information and reteaching as we do homeschooling," Brenda points out.

> Brenda's decision to homeschool was influenced by two main observations as a teacher: teachers don't have enough time with individual students and learning materials in many classrooms are inferior.

"The schools are highly regimented without attention to the time needed to expand projects and thoughts. Very little attention is paid to unique interests. We wanted to give our children time to follow theirs. As parents and teachers, we enjoy participating in learning and consider ourselves lifelong learners and examples to our children."

When asked if she notices any traits in her children related to learning that she attributes to homeschooling, this former teacher's answer is a resounding yes. "They're not so influenced by peers. They have better social skills and relate well to people. They're also willing to question authority, which my husband and I value. However," cautions Brenda, "parenting them is very challenging."

The challenges of parenting "thinking" children are plentiful, but they must be weighed against the challenges presented by the possibility that the child you love will grow up without the academic skills necessary for a satisfying journey into adulthood, or without the attention necessary for a healthy sense of self. Homeschooling, even on a strictly complementary basis, can make the difference between a contented life and one filled with struggle.

SIMPLE STARTING POINTS

✦ *Research the public school system in general and your local school system in particular.*

Learn everything you can about the federal programs mentioned here and how they are funded and implemented in your community. Be attentive to references to schools and tests in newspapers and magazines, and on radio and TV news reports. Listen for the sums of money expended on schooling, and compare all information to what you're discovering in this book.

✦ *Set realistic goals for part-time homeschooling with your child.*

You don't have as much time available to you as a full-time homeschooler. In addition, your child spends hours each day learning in a different manner, which uses energy that won't be available to your own efforts. By homing in on a specific goal, you'll put remaining time and energy to a focused use.

✦ *Trust yourself and your child to accomplish your goals.*

A child with less than stellar report cards probably isn't filled with self-confidence, and the experience could leave you doubting his abilities, as well. Remember, there is nothing magical about the school's teaching method, and a bad report card could merely represent a mismatch with your child's learning style. Trust that the two of you working together can find the method that works. Be patient, observe, and allow small successes to build the confidence you both need.

✦   *Start slowly; keep it fun.*

A child who has learned to hate arithmetic or reading won't change his attitude overnight. Take it easy; use lots of real-life activities. Reading the daily comics is reading, and every opportunity to hear your child read out loud or along with you is an opportunity to provide gentle pointers. When you take your turn reading aloud, make sure your child can follow along in the book (let your finger guide his eyes), picking up clues as he connects your spoken words to the written words. For arithmetic activities, let him help you count and sort change, bake cookies, make a checkbook entry and calculation, and count how many socks are in six pairs. Offer up word problems related to whatever you happen to be doing, and encourage him to do the same. Let the fun and usefulness of learning rise to the surface; this will increase curiosity and enthusiasm for more.

✦   *Create a support system for your efforts.*

There's no need to feel alone as you supplement your child's education! Tap into your local homeschool support system for information, news on resources, and evening or weekend activities you can become part of. Local group members will be very understanding of your efforts, and have lots of advice and support to share.

RESOURCES

Books

Bloom, Allan. *The Closing of the American Mind.* Simon & Schuster, 1987.

Blumenfeld, Samuel L. *NEA: Trojan Horse in American Education.* Paradigm Co., 1993.

Gatto, John. *Dumbing Us Down: The Hidden Curriculum of Compulsory Schooling.* New Society Publishers, 1991.

Iserbyt, Charlotte. *The Deliberate Dumbing Down of America.* Conscience Press, 1999.

Kaseman, Larry and Susan. *Taking Charge Through Homeschooling: Personal and Political Empowerment.* Koshkonong Press, 1990.

Sheffer, Susannah. *A Sense of Self: Listening to Homeschooled Adolescent Girls.* Boynton/Cook Heinemann, 1995.

Organizations

Hillsdale College: 33 East College Street, Hillsdale, MI 49242; 800-437-2268 (free monthly magazine, *Imprimis*).

Separation of School and State Alliance: 4578 North First #310, Fresno, CA 93726; 209-292-1776; http://www.sepschool.org.

Web Sites

Diane Fessler's Homepage: http://www.fessler.com

Goals 2000/School-to-Careers Opposition Research: http://www2.inow.com/privacy.htm

Anita Hoge Save Our Schools (S.O.S.): http://www.3Dresearch. com/hoge/

National Center on Education and the Economy: http://www.ncee.org/ (watch the plans unfold!)

Bob and Barbara Tennison's Web page: http://www.rstennison.com

16

ENJOYING THE ROAD
LESS TRAVELED

In This Chapter

+ Not everyone will say bon voyage

+ Strategies that work to get them on your side

+ Overcoming homeschooling challenges

+ Aha! Who's teaching whom?

+ A look back at the early years

$\mathcal{E}$VERY DAY IN America and around the world another family begins a homeschooling journey filled with the same anxious anticipation anyone feels when embarking on a trip to a place they've never been before.

Every day in America and around the world another family takes stock of an ongoing homeschooling journey, and concludes it's a life-altering trip they wouldn't have missed for anything.

But even the most perfectly designed trips sometimes don't proceed according to plan. Sending children to school is an accepted norm, and when you announce you're rejecting that norm, not all friends and relatives will wish you bon voyage. Homeschooling parents, though, learn to look at challenges as learning experiences, and you will, too. Many marvel that they're discovering as much, if not more, than their children about life and learning. Now, these parents graciously offer the fruits of their "learning labor" as parting gifts to you. There are no greater gifts than these to help you enjoy this road less traveled.

NOT EVERYONE WILL SAY BON VOYAGE

YOUR DECISION TO homeschool is made. You've started gathering resources, hooked up with a local support group, and await your first field trip next week. Your parents are coming for dinner tonight, and you can't wait to break the news.

As you pass the peas to Dad, you make your announcement. He drops the bowl, sending peas tumbling to the floor, and you look up in time to see Mom chugging her drink, loosening the bite of roll she's choking on. What just happened here?

In Jane's case, "My mother tends to take things personally when I make different decisions as a parent than she did." Indeed, if anyone is most likely to be upset with your decision to homeschool it will be the children's grandparents.

> We were happily together during all those cozy, wonderful days and evenings. He didn't have to go to bed and get up early just so I could send him to a classroom where he didn't want to be, doing things he didn't want to do, with people he didn't want to be with.
>
> —LOUISE

Grandparents

Understand you *are* bucking the system, not only in terms of what everybody else's grandchildren are doing, but also regarding your parents' choices for you. This problem is compounded when the grandparents have a vested interest in public education.

"A lot of people were against the idea," remembers Devlin, who decided in 1985 to homeschool what would turn out to be six children in Grand Junction, Colorado. "My dad was very high up in the Los Angeles city school district so he thought school was wonderful. I explained homeschooling and fought with him about it. He finally said he would have to take this 'problem' to the grave. That was the end of it but we fought about it for five years."

Husbands

If there's a rift within the immediate family, oftentimes it's because one parent—usually the mother—caught the homeschool learning journey bug, and the other is hesitant to go along. If you look at homeschooling as a continuation of the nurturing process between parent and child (which it surely is), it's easy to see how women often grasp the concept intuitively; for us it's a matter of the heart. To many dads, however, education is a matter of the head. Practical concerns must be addressed, backed by sound reasoning, if you hope to persuade him to take the trip. "Honey, it just *feels* right" doesn't pack much punch.

"My husband was initially hesitant," says Kate, "so I researched homeschooling and read everything I could get my hands on, prepared to answer every question he could possibly have . . . it worked."

Rhonda used the logical approach. "I simply pointed out that everything I had taught our son he had learned superbly well. Everything the school taught was taught miserably. The kids and I eventually talked him into it."

Strategies That Work to Get Them on Your Side

In spite of your excitement and conviction, your parents, in-laws, or other relatives may be offended by your choice, or simply not understand. Rest assured it's not the first time and won't be the last. But there are ways to help them see the promise you recognize.

Make a Point of Sharing What You Know

There are lots of good homeschooling books, magazines, and mass media articles that reveal the positive effects of homeschooling on young children. Share these materials with the others who care deeply about your children's well-being.

"I gave both of my son's grandmothers a copy of *Homeschooling for Excellence* by David and Micki Colfax," says Louise. "After reading it, they both commented that it sounded interesting and rarely mentioned it again."

One evening Gretchen's father visited her home to express his concerns about homeschooling. Father and daughter settled down for a long discussion during which Gretchen explained to him her plans and showed him what his grandchildren had achieved over the past week. "He left declaring he was convinced I would do a great job," Gretchen says.

Gail's parents' concerns centered on their mistaken notion that all curriculum material available for homeschoolers was religion-based. Once Gail took some time to show them the enormous amounts of nonreligious resources available from a wide variety of sources, Gail says, "They subsided to being nonverbal, only slightly skeptical."

Let the Idea Grow on Them

Sometimes skeptical relatives just need a little time for "revolutionary" ideas to grow on them, the ease-'em-into-it method.

"*Both* sets of grandparents were uncertain," remembers Bernadette, "so we were careful to state that we were 'trying' homeschooling. That seemed to make it less of an issue."

> I won't miss hearing "Will you read this to me?" for hours on end. Actually, I do sometimes miss feeling that needed and important, but I also enjoy watching my children being more independent.
>
> —VALERIE

It appeared no one in Sarah's extended family was happy with their decision to homeschool. She and her husband patiently explained public school was out of the question, and parochial school would require a ridiculous two-hour daily commute. "You could say we worked the grandparents into the idea slowly." Sarah confesses, "We initially presented homeschooling as something we would do 'for awhile' even though we figured the children probably wouldn't go to school until high school or later."

Assert Your Parental Rights

It may sound like political jargon, but some newly homeschooling parents find they must assert their parental rights with relatives who would attempt to dissuade them from their journey.

"We tried to ease their concerns," Monique affirms, "but other than that, they're our children and we'll raise them as we see fit. The critics will have to adjust."

Marie's extended family was happy with homeschooling until her family began moving toward the unstructured end of the homeschool continuum. Painful "diatribes" about her and her husband's lack of qualifications ensued. "Finally," she says, "we had to tell them they had to trust us to do what was best for our children, assuring them we'd never do anything to harm them. Then we either changed the subject or left, whichever was most expedient at the time. The good news is with a child excelling in college we don't hear a lot of this sort of talk anymore."

> If all else fails at the beginning of your homeschooling journey, your children themselves could be the factor that turns critics' thinking around.

Hope and her husband take a quieter approach. "We intend to communicate our values, pray, and remember that it's not their decision or their children."

They Can't Argue with Success

I'll say it again: homeschooled children are its best advertisements! If all else fails at the beginning of your homeschooling journey, your children themselves could be the factor that turns critics' thinking around.

"One set of grandparents didn't react well at first," says Ben, "but we just did our thing and eventually they saw how our children were thriving." He adds, "Now they're vocal advocates of homeschooling."

Marcia jokes, "No one in our family gave us a parade or anything, but they can't argue with the outcome. Both older children read well at five years old, and like it!"

The grandparents in Valerie's family eventually came around, too. Valerie notes, "Homeschooling made the grandchildren more accessible as they live out of town." Now there's a benefit not too many grandparents will argue with!

Invite Participation

If willing, grandparents can add a rich dimension to any homeschooling experience. Invite them to participate, covertly, if necessary. "Could you please read this book while I make a phone call?" "If you bake your delicious cocoa cookies during his visit, would you double the recipe and ask him to help figure it out?" (This way you take home the extra cookies, too.) "We're going to the Civil War reenactment—want to join us?"

Give skeptical relatives a chance to *experience* homeschooling. Everybody wants to be part of a winning team and, as happened for Ben, the very same relatives could eventually become your most vocal supporters.

OVERCOMING HOMESCHOOLING CHALLENGES

THROUGHOUT *Homeschooling: The Early Years* you've gotten a good sense of the challenges parents face in their day-to-day lives, from those who know them best—homeschooling parents. We've explored in depth the most frequently cited challenges, but several respondents offered such rich food for parting thought that their comments are too important not to pass on. Let their triumphs shine a light on the path for you if you ever find yourself facing similar hurdles.

"When I'm having an off day," explains Pauline, "I have trouble dealing with the demands of a three-year-old and a five-year-old who are asking the thousandth question of the day, and demand another immediate answer." Pauline's solution? "I just take the day a minute at a time, and remind myself that these little ones are looking to me for guidance on how to behave. That usually keeps me in line."

Maureen finds her eight-year-old's questions daunting, too, but offers up a different resolution. "He's interested in all kinds of stuff that I've never even thought about," she says. "I send him to Dad with those questions!"

Valerie's greatest challenge appeared when she "tried to cope with those moments (days?) of worrying 'am I doing the right thing?' 'Why is he still not reading for pleasure?' 'Is he missing out on something important in public school?'" When these days occurred, "I

I've enjoyed facilitating my children's learning at all ages. I loved to see that "spark" that told me they'd become fascinated by something. I loved to hear them say something they'd come up with independently. I loved watching them become engrossed in something.

—ANNA

got to a support group park day or e-mail support group and found the encouragement to handle them all."

"Keeping a personal sense of self," topped Laura's short list of challenges, followed by "dealing with a truly horrible, messy house and too much junk and maintaining a relationship with my husband. These are probably the same things public school parents deal with," she admits, "only more of it." To get over the hump she simply reminds herself, "We don't have to deal with all the mess that comes home from public school!"

"Keeping up," Priscilla says when asked about her greatest hurdle. "It would be foolhardy to suggest that home educating is the easy option, but it's the right one for us. As the main person at home I can feel pulled in many directions. It's very important that home educators have a place where they can say, 'I had a lousy day' and not be told, 'Well, send them to school then' or even be given advice on what to do, but just have someone understand because they've been there." Priscilla finds it helps a lot to remember, "Tomorrow is always another day."

Finally, "My challenges are more related to parenting in general than homeschooling in particular," Jacqueline explains. "Overcoming my own bad days, being present when I'd rather be taking a hot bath or nap or talking to adults, really listening when I have fifteen other things on my mind.

As I look back on homeschooling my oldest son, the greatest benefit was that I saved his soul, and not in a religious sense. He was suffering at school and if I had left him there it would have crushed his spirit and destroyed him.

Homeschooling healed and saved him, and I nurtured him into the strong, vibrant thirteen-year-old lover of learning we have today.

—RHONDA

"It's also a challenge for me to value what *I* do," she adds. "I feel the culture I was raised in (average America) taught me the important things are outside the house—I should want a career and I'm giving something up to be a parent. It creates a paradox in my mind because I *know* I'm doing the most important job there is, but I'm 'socialized' to think what I'm doing isn't as important as making $30,000 a year and carrying a briefcase."

These parents and thousands like them accept, meet, and overcome daily challenges on the homeschool journey because they know the road less traveled gives them occasion to see sights they'd never otherwise view. These sights include life-altering lessons, and who would have thought some of the most important always come from the early years children themselves?

AHA! WHO'S TEACHING WHOM?

I'VE HEARD HOMESCHOOLERS from coast to coast try to explain what could be called the oft-repeated homeschooling phenomenon of teacher learning as much as student. For those who have never experienced this, it's hard to fathom. Perhaps it's because so many of us grew up under an educational system where the teacher has the answers and parcels them out to her pupils.

Homeschooling allows for—no, it requires—a lot more honesty between its participants. At home you can say, "I don't know"—then join your child in the joy of discovery. Instead of a hierarchy that serves to place the two of you at different levels, a partnership is born. You and your child take this journey together, in the true sense of together. In this context, the idea that parents are learning too isn't far-fetched at all.

Parental Lessons About Learning

Some parents receive lessons about education in general. "We spent two months doing nothing but studying the desert," says Dee. "I know more about the plants and animals, than I ever would have been exposed to otherwise. I believe my excitement will help keep my son's spark burning."

After researching education and choosing a "better late than early" homeschooling approach for her son, Jacqueline maintained "an underlying fear that I'm doing it all wrong—but this is my nature.

"He's reading above grade level, learning things we didn't actually work on, and asking questions about everything. I just have to keep practicing staying out of the way, and letting go of my own fears," she concludes.

Erin's interest in tidepooling and marine invertebrates led her to purchase a chart for field use that illustrated common shoreline creatures. It was lying on the dining room table one evening after dinner when her four-year-old daughter picked it up. She began pointing to things, asking what they were.

"I read their names back to her," Erin says. "It then became a game, with me taking turns pointing out creatures for her to name. At some point my eighteen-month-old son climbed up on to a chair to watch for a while. Then we all went to bed.

"The next morning, the eighteen-month-old sat up in his bed and said, 'gumboot?'

"Momentarily taken aback I thought, 'Is he talking about the Gumboot Chiton on the field guide from last night?' Puzzled, I asked him, 'Where's the Gumboot, Edward?'

"He climbed out of bed, went to the table, picked up the chart, pointed to the Gumboot Chiton picture and repeated, 'Gumboot.'

"This was a lesson in how much you don't realize what your younger child is learning while you're talking to the older child—or other people in the world, for that matter!"

Others learn lessons about homeschooling specifically. "The children make me happy so much of the time. People say to me, 'Oh, you homeschool. You're so selfless and patient. I could never do that.' But *I* really feel like the selfish one," Laura says. "I'm no slave to school schedules. I get to raise my own children. It's so easy this way. Why doesn't everyone do it?"

Four years ago when our youngest was seven years old we hosted the president of a Russian university in our home for a dinner party. While I was busy cooking and serving, both of our daughters entertained him. He spoke no English and they had learned only a few phrases in Russian. But we had a translator and lots of Russian-American dictionaries. While I worked I heard bits and pieces of serious and fun discussions, including his questioning of my homeschooling them.

At the end of the evening he took me aside and said: "Lenore, I have a university full of students between the ages of seventeen and twenty-two. They all can speak to me any time they want to, about anything they want. But they do not. They know nothing of the world, of the environment, of the importance of education. Your two daughters were able to look me in the eye, speak to me about things which are important to them; environmental issues, welfare of animals, and why it is good they are educated by their mother and are part of her business. They asked me intelligent questions about Russia and could answer me intelligently about their home, America. I have never been more impressed with two children."

And I have never had such a compliment or testament to the decision I made seven years ago. I have never regretted my decision.

—LENORE

Rachel's homeschooling experience was short-lived but powerful. "We homeschooled because our son was having problems in public school during first grade. We didn't approach homeschooling from the conviction that it was the only acceptable way to educate children, nor do we believe that still," she explains. "However, it was absolutely necessary that we had that option for our son. Even the wonderful private Christian school he's in now wouldn't have helped him at that particular time.

"As a result," says Rachel, "I'm an advocate for homeschooling. I'll work to ensure it continues as an available option. We need to be able to make choices for our children, and it should be the parents' choice, not the state's."

Parental Lessons About Self

Few lessons are as life-altering as the ones that allow us a momentary flash of ourselves as we truly are. By seeing ourselves during those "aha! moments," warts and all, we truly grow and become better individuals. It's a bonus when those lessons come courtesy of the children we love.

Helen's aha! moment came at a place and time she least expected it. "We were observing an anthill," she says, "and I was amazed at what my young son could see that I could not. I realized how in tune with his surroundings he is and, by comparison, I'm not. I saw my life as passing through to the next chore," Helen realized, "and it was a lesson I needed."

Not long after we made the decision to homeschool Amy we were running errands downtown. It was pouring rain and on a whim I stopped the car at a beautiful little church. We went inside to enjoy the peace of the place.

We just sat there together in that stained-glass quiet, and then someone started practicing the organ. We were the only people there, and for the longest time we sat enjoying the music and the rain pounding on the roof—a perfect moment. I thought to myself, "This doesn't have to be a rare once-in-a-year experience. If we homeschool we'll be able to have them any number of times. Perfect, full moments can be part of our lives."

Two and a half years have passed since then, and we have experienced many such moments. Homeschooling has been a real change in lifestyle and is, in my perspective, how life should be lived—transforming, really.

—MICHAELA

When her family began homeschooling, Paula's main focus was avoiding an abusive school system so she didn't have to spend time fighting institutional policies. "It was all about giving children freedom of choice," she explains. "My greatest realization came when I recognized how much I enjoy our emphasis on growing as a family. Realizing that I enjoy parenting was so much slower coming to me!"

Let your children brighten your life with lessons only they can provide, making you an even more valuable partner on your joint homeschool journey. We teach our children best as we allow them to teach us at the same time.

A LOOK BACK AT THE EARLY YEARS

IT WASN'T THAT long ago that important, first-hand knowledge of childbirth, nursing, and raising children crossed less rigid "generation gaps" than exist today. This provided young parents a connection to wiser, more experienced community members through word of mouth and the helping hands of nearby relatives, close friends and neighbors. Even as our culture loses this connection, the nature of the homeschooling community is such that grassroots connection has been vital to its success. Members of this community continue to weave the threads that bind. They have found happiness and success on their journeys, and know the same awaits other families if they but take their first steps on the educational road less traveled. They remember how difficult those first steps can be, and lend their hands to support others, just as they, too, may have received a hand when first steps were tentative and wobbly.

Many parents are now looking back at homeschooling in the early years. Those who have journeyed before you take the lessons born of their travels and incorporate them into all they do, into all they become—as people, as parents, as friends. Please accept their gifts in the spirit in which they are intended; a guiding hand, for the times you may stumble, from friends you've yet to meet.

Bon voyage.

INDEX

A

Academic labeling, 196–197
Activities file, 261–262
Addition, 147
ADHD, *see* Attention deficit-hyperactivity disorder
Adopt-a-Highway program, 250
Alexander the Great, 25
Alternative education programs, 254–257
American Optometric Association, 232–233
Anastasia, 235
AOA, *see* American Optometric Association
Apprenticeships, 249–251
Approaches, homeschooling, 10–11, 79–81
Arithmetic
  abilities, 138–140
  addition, 147
  counting, 143–144
  division, 152–153
  field trips, 156
  foundations, 137–138
  fractions, 147
  games, 141, 148, 156
  measurements
    graphs, 151–152
    money, 148–151
    tables, 151–152
    time, 148–151
  multiplication, 152–153
  numbers, 141, 144–145
  opportunities, 138–140
  osmosis method, 145
  patterns, 143–144
  posters, 156
  readiness, 140–142
  resources, 156–159
  sequencing, 146
  shapes, 140, 143–144
  signs, 146
  sizes, 143–144
  software, popular, 139
  starting points, 155–156
  subtraction, 147
  textbooks, 142–143
  word problems, 153
Armstrong, Thomas, 28
Arts, resources, 176–177
Arts and crafts, 253
Assessments homeschooling, 11
Assistance, outside, 14, 84–85
Attention deficit-hyperactivity disorder, 46–47
Attention spans, 24
Auditory skills, 132
A Winter Day, 131

B

Beat the clock games, 281
Bedtimes, 268–269
Bell, Alexander Graham, 82
Bible study, 55
Birth order
  advantages
    older, 273–274
    younger, 271–273
  differences, 270–271
Bonding, importance, 50–54
Books
  arithmetic, 156–157
  for children, 216
  community outreach, 262–263
  on computers, 241
  family needs, 201–202
  gathering, 214
  homeschooling, 86–87, 306–307
  on homeschooling, 18
  housekeeping, 293
  on Internet, 227
  on learning, 36
  learning styles, 62–63
  obtaining, 214–215
  for parents, 215
  on reading, 112–113
  reading favorites, 98
  on resources, 221
  reviews, keeping, 249
  text, *see* Textbooks
  toddler activities, 276
  values, 62–63
  writing, 134
Budgets, *see* Finances

Building block method, 108
Business skills, learning, 153

C

Caesar, Julius, 25
Calligraphy, 130
Capitalization, 126–128
Cassettes, stories on, 115
Catalogs
  arithmetic, 157–158
  housekeeping, 293
  reading, 114
  resource, 222
Certificates of Mastery,
  295–296
Challenges, overcoming,
  315–317
Children
  academically labeled,
    196–197
  attention spans, 24
  attitudes, changing, 306
  books for, 216
  chores, 280–281, 286
  curiosity, 22–26
  depression, 58
  disabled, 194–196
  emotionally disturbed, 304
  energy, 21–22, 33–35
  enthusiasm, 31–32
  fears about, 67–68
  gifted, 192–194
  imagination, 26–27
  interest, time for, 298–299
  needs, 265
  only, 198–199
  role models, 70–71
  time with, 275–276
Chores, see Housekeeping
Christian curriculum, 55

Christie, Agatha, 82
Clean, redefining,
  286–287, 292
Clocks, 150
Clustering, 130–131
Coins, 149
Communicable diseases, 57
Community
  activities, 252–253
  as classroom, 262
  exploration
    activities, 252
    alternative education,
      254–257
    apprenticeships, 249–251
    benefits, 245–246
    field trips, 246–248
    homeschool programs,
      253–254
    institutions, 251–252
    library, 257–259
    mentorships, 249–251
    resource, 262–262
    starting points, 261–262
    travel, 249
    volunteering, 249–251
  support, 207–208
Computers, see also Software
  benefits, 238–239
  health issues, 232–234, 239
  importance, 82
  library, 240
  popularity, 12, 226
  problems, 239
  resources, 241–243
  starting points, 240–241
  vision syndrome, 232–233
  writing on, 129
Conferences, attending, 86
Consonants, 101–102
Contractions, 126–128

Costs, see Finances
Counting, 143–144
Creativity, 29–30
Curiosity, 22–26
Curricula, see also specific
    subjects
  basic, 174
  books on, 216
  Christian, 55
  compartmentalizing, 162
  creating, 92–93
  greater context, 163
  guides, 208–209
  on Internet, 228
  nontraditional
    combination, 171–173
    general, 164–168
    history-based, 168–169
    interest-initiated,
      169–171
  popular topics, 162
  public school, changes, 296
  purchasing, 92–93
  reading, 113–114
  requirements, 161
  resources, 176–183
  scope, 173–176
  sequence, 173–176
  software, 231
  traditional, 163–168
  unit studies
    application, 163–168
  on video, 237

D

David and David
    Enterprises, 226
Decompression time, 218
Depression, 58
Deprivation, sleep, 57–58

Dickens, Charles, 253
Direction, changing, 15–17
Disabled children, 194–196
Discovery Channel, 236
Division, 152–153

E

Edison, Thomas, 82–83
Editing, 127
Educate America Act, 295
Edutainment, 230–231
Einstein, Albert, 137
Elkind, David, 28
E-mail loops
    homeschooling, 243
    newsletters via, 230
    special needs, 203
    toddler activities,
        276–277
Employment
    costs, 186
    full-time, 189–191
    home-based, 187–189
Energy, children's
    for learning, 31–32
    levels, 21–22
    manifestations, 33–35
Equivalency laws, 74
Extracurricular programs,
    253–254

F

Families, *see also* Grandparents;
    Parents
    chores, 280–281
    extended, 53–54
    large, 199–200
    needs, addressing
        bonding, 50–54

resources, 201–202
    starting points, 62
opposition, 311–314
single child, 198–199
two-income, 186
values, 54–56
Fathers, 197–198, 311
Fears
    inadequacy, 67–68
    overcoming, 69–70
    socialization, 67–68
Field trips
    arithmetic, 156
    arranging, 248
    bargains, 246–248
    benefits, 246
    popular, 256
    researching, 247–248
    tourist attractions, 246–248
Filters, Internet access,
    228–229, 240
Finances
    home-schooling cost
        assessing, 78–79
        survey, 10
    limited, 186–187, 212
    resources, 201–203, 212
    reviewing, 201
    sacrifices, 185–186
    starting points, 200–201
Flexibility, 265
Foreign languages, 177
Fractions, 147, 148, 150
Friends, missing, 60

G

Games
    arithmetic, 141, 148, 156
    housework, 281
    word, 129

Geography, 177–178
Gibran, Kahlil, 33
Gifted children, 192–194
Grades, fallacy, 297–298
Grammar
    incorrect fund, 105
    teaching, 124–126
Grandparents
    objections, 311
    participation, 314
    relationships, 53–54
Graphs, 151–152
Group meetings, attending, 17
Growing Without Schooling, 4
GWS, *see Growing Without
    Schooling*

H

Health
    care, long-term, 58–59
    computers and, 232–234
    fostering, 57–60
Hearing, 195
Hirsch, E. D., 174
History
    homeschooling, 3–4
    resources, 178–179
    studying, 168–169
Home Education Magazine, 4
Homeschooling
    accoutrements, 5–6
    challenges, 315–317
    complementary
        advantages, 296–301
        reasons, 303–305
        resources, 306–307
        starting points, 305–306
    continuum, questionnaire
        conclusions, 14–15
        respondents, 8–9

Homeschooling, *continued*
   variables
      approach, 10–11
      assessment, 11
      assistance, outside, 14
      cost, 10
      list, 7–8
      motivation, 8–9
      parental involvement,
         13–14
      physical space, 13
      technology used, 12
   emergency, starter kit,
      217–220
   extracurricular programs,
      253–254
   history, 3–4
   image, 3–4
   laws governing, 74
   opposition, family, 311–314
   part-time, 65–67
   praise for, 39–40
   preparing for
      resources, 18–19
      starting points, 17–18
   teacher's support, 301–305
   transitioning
      challenges, 60–61
      starting points, 85–86
House clearing, 292
Household items, 210
Housekeeping
   assignments, 286–287
   family's role, 280–281
   list, 293
   multi-tasking, 282–284
   organization, 284–286
   piecemeal approach,
      281–282
   resources, 293

   schedules, 284–286
   standards, 279
   starting points, 292–293
Humane society, 250
Hundred chart, 144
Husbands, 197–198, 311

I

Imagination
   children's, 26–27
   creativity and, 29–30
   playing and, 28–29
Inadequacy
   fears of, 67–68
   triggers, 74–75, 80
Individual Home Instruction
   Program, 76–77
Infants
   and homeschooling
      concerns, 266
      resources, 276–277
      starting points, 274–276
      strategies, 267–270
Innocence, 32–33
Institutions, opportunities at,
   251–252
Interest-initiated study, 169
Internet, *see also* E-mail loops;
   Web sites
   information sources,
      227–228
   newsletters, 230
   supervision
      importance, 226–227
      software for, 228–229,
      240
   support source, 229–230
Involvement
   survey, 13–14

J

Jobs, *see* Employment

K

Kelety, Jeff, 197

L

L'Amour, Louis, 99–100
Laundry dot system, 292–293
Laws, 74–76
Learner-directed study, 169
Learning
   age-appropriate, 43
   arithmetic
      addition, 147
      counting, 143–144
      division, 152–153
      field trips, 156
      fractions, 147
      games, 141, 156
      measurements
         graphs, 151–152
         money, 148–151
         tables, 151–152
         time, 148–151
      multiplication, 152–153
      number recognition, 141
      numbers, 144–145
      opportunities, 138–140
      osmosis method, 145
      posters, 156
      readiness, 140–142
      resources, 156–159
      sequencing, 146
      shapes, 140, 143–144
      signs, 146
      sizes, 143–144
      software, popular, 139

starting points, 155–156
subtraction, 147
textbooks, 142–143
word problems, 153
assessments, 81–82
disabled, 196–197
enthusiasm for, 31–32
lessons, parental, 317–320
letters, 99–100
money management,
    148–149
paths, public school, 6
reading
    consonants, 101–102
    curriculum, 100–101
    letters, 99–100, 105–106
    methods
        building block, 108
        determining, 94–95
        osmosis, 107–108
        traditional, 109–110
    readiness, 97–100
    resources, 112–113
    single words, 106–107
    snuggle factor, 96–97
    starting points, 111, 133
    traits, 95–96
    vowels, 102–105
resources, 36–37
rushed, impact, 59–60
starting points, 35–36
strengths, building on,
    45–48
styles, 40–43
weaknesses, shoring up,
    43–44
writing
    capitalization, 126–128
    contractions, 126–128
    grammar, 124–126

methods, 118–119
punctuation, 126–128
readiness, 110–121
resources, 134–135
spelling, 124–126
starting points, 133
Letters
    capital, 126–128
    learning, 99–100
    upper case, 105–106
    writing, 118
Libraries
    benefits, 259–261
    collections, 258
    computers at, 240
    importance, 111
    personal, 111
    as resource, 208, 214
    story hours, 252
    video collections, 239
Lifestyle, simplifying,
    186–187, 200
Long-term care, 58–59

M

Mad Libs, 125
Magnetic resonance
    imaging, 94
Marriage, time for, 288–290
Materials, *see* Supplies
Mathematics, *see*
    Arithmetic
Meals on Wheels, 249
Measurements
    graphs, 151–152
    money, 148–151
    tables, 151–152
    time, 148–151
Mentorships, 249–251

Message boards, 242–243
Money management, 148–149
Moore, Dr. Raymond, 4
Motivation
    knowledge of, 78
    self, children's, 31
    survey, 8–9
MRI, *see* Magnetic resonance
    imaging
Multiplication, 152–153
Multi-tasking, 282–284
Music, 179–180, 253

N

Naps, 268–269
Nature programs, 235–236
Newsletters, Internet, 230
Numbers, 141, 144–145

O

Objections, 311–314
Organizations, 19, 203, 307
Organizers, 289
Osmosis methods,
    107–108, 145

P

Parents
    books for, 215
    –children
        volunteering, 262
    fathers, 197–198, 311
    involvement
        determining, 83–84
        homeschooling
            survey, 13–14
    lessons learned, 317–321

Parents, *continued*
  rights, asserting,
    313–314
  as role models, 71–72
  single, 191–192
  time alone, 287–292
Part-time homeschooling
  advantages, 296–301
  reasons, 303–305
  resources, 306–307
  staring points, 305–306
PBS, *see* Public Broadcasting
  System
Penmanship, 121–124, 130
Periodicals
  arithmetic, 158
  on computers, 241
  family needs, 202
  homeschooling, 18–19
  on learning, 37
  on reading, 112–113
  resource, 221–222
  on writing, 134–135
Phonemic awareness,
  94, 108
Phonics, 94
Physical education, 180
Physical space, 13, 82–83
Piecemeal cleaning,
  281–282
Pioneer Club, 251
Playing, 28–29
Posters, arithmetic, 156
Private schools
  laws, 74
  problems, 303
Programs
  arithmetic, 157
  reading, 112–113
  writing, 135
Public Broadcasting System,
  236–237

Public schools
  alternative education pro-
    grams, 254–255
  attendance, normalcy,
    309–310
  curriculum model, 163–168
  problems with, 304–305
  researching, 305
  standards, decline, 295–296
  supplementing, 296–301
Punctuation, 126–128

Q

Quiet time, 276

R

Readiness
  arithmetic, 140–142
  reading, 97–100
  writing, 110–121
Reading
  book favorites, 98
  brain processes, 94
  consonants, 101–102
  curriculum, 100–101
  enjoyment, 111
  group, 109
  importance, 91–93
  letters, 99–100, 105–106
  methods
    building block, 108
    determining, 94–95
    osmosis, 107–108
    traditional, 109–110
  pre, skills, 97
  readiness, 97–100
  resources, 112–113
  single words, 106–107
  snuggle factor, 96–97
  starting points, 111, 133

  traits, 95–96
  vowels, 102–105
Record-keeping, 76–77
Reference books, Internet, 227
Repetitive stress injury, 233
Resources, *see also specific*
  subjects; Supplies
  basic, 18–19
  emergency homeschooling,
    217–220
  hand made, 211
  household, 210
  human, 210–211
  places, 211
  starting points, 220–221
  toys as, 211
  winnowing, 208
Respiratory diseases, 57
Role models
  baby's, 272
  choosing, 71
  importance, 70–71
  parents as, 71–72
Rulers, using, 150

S

Safety, fostering, 56–57
Scales, using, 151
Schedules
  babies and, 274–275
  chores, 284–286
  class work, 164
Schools, *see* Homeschooling;
  Private schools; Public
  schools
School-to-Work Investment
  Act of 1994, 295
Science, resources, 182–183
Scouting programs, 251
Self-motivation, 31
Sewing cards, 275

Shapes, 140, 143–144
Sibling relationships, 52–53
Sick building syndrome, 57–58
Simplification, 186–187
Single parents, 191–192
Sizes, 143–144
Skills, grades *vs.,* 297–298
Sleep deprivation, 57–58
Smothers, Dick, 270–271
Smothers, Tommy,
    270–271, 275
Smothers Brothers Show,
    270–271
Snuggle factor, 96–97
Socialization
    family, 50–54
    fears about, 67–68
    friends, 60
    opportunities, 48–50
Software, *see also* Computers
    educational, 230–231
    Internet, 228–229, 240
    popular, 233
    reading, 115
    uses, 231–232
    writing, 135
Spelling, 124–126
Sports, 252
Stories on cassette, 115
Strengths, building on, 45–48
Stress, 57–58
Subjects, *see* Curricula
Subtraction, 147
Supplemental material, 236
Supplies, *see also* Resources
    diversion, 271
    hand made, 211
    household, 210
    inclusion, 271
    invaluable, 213–214
    key, 217
    office, 291
    real, 212–213
    toys as, 211
Support groups
    benefits, 259–260
    local, 260
    seeking out, 86
    statewide, 260–261

T

Tables, reading, 151–152
Tape measures, using, 150–151
Tape recorders, 132
Teachers, 301–305
Teaching, *see* Learning
Technology, 12, 82
Television
    nature programs, 235–236
    as supplement, 236
    travel via, 234–235
    videotaping, 238, 240–241
Textbooks
    age-appropriate, 219
    arithmetic, 142–143,
        156–157
    availability, 174
    on Internet, 227
Theater programs, 252–253
Time
    for children, 275–276
    decompression, 218
    for marriage, 288–290
    personal, 287–288,
        290–292
    quiet, 276
    vacation, 218
Time, learning, 144, 148–151
Toddlers
    and homeschooling
        concerns, 266
        inclusion, 275
        resources, 276–277
    starting points, 274–276
    strategies
        diversion, 267–270
    special toys, 275
Tourette syndrome, 194–195
Tourist attractions, 246–248
Toys, 211, 275
Travel
    benefits, 246, 249
    via television, 234–235

U

Unit studies, 163–168
Unschooling, 169

V

Vacations, 218, 296–301
Videos
    benefits, 235
    cameras, 132
    curricula on, 237
    discount, 237–239
    library, 239
    making, 238, 240–241
    as supplements, 236
Vision problems, 232–233
Volunteering
    benefits, 249–251
    new families, 86
    parent/child, 262
Vowels, 102–105

W

Watches, 150
Weaknesses, shoring up, 43–44
Web sites, *see also* Internet
    arithmetic, 158–159
    community outreach, 263
    on computers, 242

Web sites, *continued*
  curriculum, 183
  family needs, 202–203
  favorite, 229
  homeschooling, 19, 307
  reading, 115
  resource, 223
  toddler activities, 276–277
  writing, 135
Wilder, Laura Ingalls, 25,
  246, 274
Wonder, sense of, 32–33

Word games, 129
Word problems, math, 153
Words, learning, 94, 106–107
Workforce Improvement
  Act of 1997, 295
World Book, Core
  Knowledge, 174
Writing
  capitalization, 126–128
  contractions, 126–128
  creative, 129–131
  cursive, 121–124

  grammar, 124–126
  inspiration, 117
  methods, 118–119
  motivation, 128–133
  numbers, 141, 144–145
  physical act, 118
  printing, 121–124
  punctuation, 126–128
  readiness, 110–121
  resources, 134–135
  spelling, 124–126
  starting points, 133

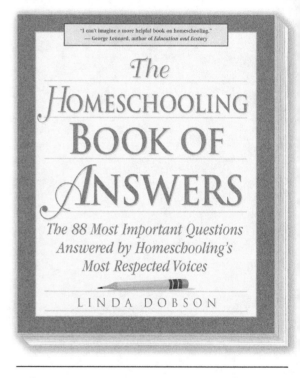

Don't Even Think About Teaching Your Child at Home—Until You Read This Book

Discover why millions of parents are homeschooling their children. In this revised edition of her groundbreaking book, Mary Griffith tells you everything you need to know about the fastest-growing educational movement in the country, including:

- **When, why, and how to homeschool**
- **Detailed learning ideas for the primary, middle, and teen years**
- **How to navigate the local regulators**
- **Strategies to avoid burnout and strengthen family relationships**
- **And more!**

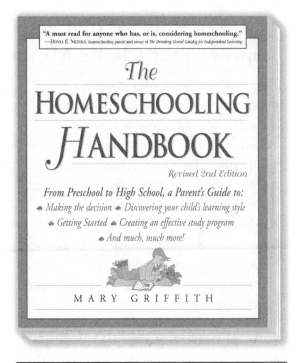

ISBN 0-7615-1727-8 / Paperback / 320 pages
U.S. $16.95 / Can. $25.95